Long Time Coming

RURAL STUDIES SERIES
of the
Rural Sociological Society

Rural Studies Series

Long Time Coming

Racial Inequality in the Nonmetropolitan South, 1940–1990

Mark A. Fossett and
M. Therese Seibert

WestviewPress

A Division of HarperCollins*Publishers*

To our children
Lane, Tyler, and Katherine Fossett
and
Marisa Stafford

Rural Studies Series, Sponsored by the Rural Sociological Society

Copyright © 1997 by Westview Press, A Division of HarperCollins Publishers, Inc.

Published in 1997 in the United States of America by Westview Press, 5500 Central Avenue, Boulder, Colorado 80301-2877, and in the United Kingdom by Westview Press, 12 Hid's Copse Road, Cumnor Hill, Oxford OX2 9JJ

A CIP catalog record for this book is available from the Library of Congress.
ISBN 0-8133-8932-1 (hc)

The paper used in this publication meets the requirements of the American National Standard for Permanence of Paper for Printed Library Materials Z39.48-1984.

10   9   8   7   6   5   4   3   2   1

Contents

Tables and Figures

Tables

Figures

Preface

This work has taken many years to complete and along the way we have become indebted to a great many organizations and people who have provided us assistance and support. First and foremost among these are the Aspen Institute and the Ford Foundation. Their initial funding of our research via the Rural Poverty Research program permitted us to assemble a longitudinal data set for investigating changes in inequality in southern, nonmetropolitan areas from 1940 to 1980 and led to the preparation of a lengthy report summarizing our findings on this subject. These earlier efforts provided the starting point for this monograph. We subsequently submitted our report to the Aspen Institute to Dr. Forest A. Deseran, editor of the Rural Studies Series for the Rural Sociological Society, for his consideration. He gave us encouragement to pursue the project and offered many valuable suggestions for improvement. More importantly, he endorsed our plan to extend our work to include data for 1990 and he helped us work out a contract with Westview Press to publish the monograph. Dr. Lionel J. Beaulieu succeeded Dr. Deseran as editor of the Rural Studies Series and helped see us through to the completion of the project. In conjunction with our agreement with Westview Press, the Rural Sociological Society provided modest funds which we helped defray costs incurred in preparing the manuscript. We are grateful to the Society and to the series editors Dr. Deseran and Dr. Beaulieu for their assistance and support.

We should also acknowledge many others who provided varying amounts of direct and indirect support which contributed to the completion of this project. We extend our thanks to the Population Research Center at the University of Texas at Austin for institutional support which helped us prepare our original proposal to the Aspen Institute and Ford Foundation Rural Poverty Program (at the time we submitted the original proposal we were both affiliated with the Center). Mark Fossett expresses his thanks to the Race and Ethnic Studies Institute and its director, Dr. Gail Thomas, for providing support for extension of the original data set through 1990 and to the Department of Sociology at Texas A&M University and its head, Dr.

Dudley L. Poston, Jr., for providing general institutional support and funding of graduate assistants and student workers who helped complete the longitudinal data set. Therese Seibert offers her thanks to the American Association of University Women and the Department of Sociology at the University of Virginia for support they have provided her that directly and indirectly benefited her participation in the project. We gratefully acknowledge the assistance of all of these individuals and organizations. Without it, it would have been very difficult for us to undertake the work reported here.

We would also be remiss if we did not note that the efforts of a great many people are reflected in our work. Conscientious data entry was provided by part-time student workers at Texas A&M University and the University of Texas at Austin. We especially wish to thank Lalitha Kasthuri-Rangan, Mark Probert, Sarmeesha Reddy, Kristie Mayhugh, Diana Collins, and Maureen Adams who worked on the original longitudinal data set and Kodali Sailaja and Stanley Hall who help prepare the additional files needed to extend the data set to include 1990. We also recognize the efforts of Cynthia Cready and Stanley Hall, graduate students at Texas A&M University, who helped supervise data entry and data management tasks. We were fortunate to work with students such as these whose concern for the success of the project led them to work with care and diligence on tasks that were often tedious. Gordon Wong, Starling Pullum, and Pat Short, all of the programming staff at the Population Research Center at the University of Texas at Austin, deserve our heartfelt thanks for assistance in some of our more difficult computing tasks especially in preparing files which were used in developing the socio-economic status scores for occupation categories from 1940-1990. We also thank Winnie Brower of the Department of Sociology at Texas A&M University and Cecilia Dean of the Population Research Center at the University of Texas at Austin for their capable administration of the Ford Foundation grant. Finally, we would also like to thank Cynthia Cready, Forest A. Deseran, and Dudley L. Poston, Jr., for their carefully reading and critique of preliminary versions of this manuscript.

We worked closely with a number of individuals at Westview who helped us get the manuscript into final form. In particular, we would like to thank Jill Rothenberg, Lynn Arts, Lisa Wigutoff, and Karen Johnson for their patience and repeated assistance.

We would also like to express our heartfelt appreciation to our families for their support and encouragement. Mark Fossett wishes to recognize his mother Carolyn Fossett for her unwavering love and encouragement over the years. In addition, he wishes to acknowledge with affection the steadfast support of his wife Betsy Fossett who has graciously endured the loss of many, many evenings and weekends "stolen away" by this project and whose healthy skepticism of academic pursuits has helped him keep things in perspective. Therese Seibert wishes to express appreciation to her colleagues Steven Finkel, Paul Kingston, and Steven Nock for their help and encouragement on this and other research projects. She also wishes to thank her mother Marie Seibert and sister Maureen Adams whose love and support have made it possible for her to meet the demands and challenges of academic life.

In closing, we reiterate our dedication of this work to our children Lane, Tyler, and Katherine Fossett and Marisa Stafford. We hope that the questions we now study will be less compelling in the world they inherit.

Mark A. Fossett
College Station, Texas

M. Therese Seibert
Charlottesville, Virginia

1

Introduction

Racial inequality is one of the most striking features of the American stratification system. That this remains so as the twentieth century draws to a close is surprising and sobering given the sweeping political and social changes that have taken place over the past three decades. It has now been more than thirty years since landmark Civil Rights and Voting Rights legislation was enacted into law in the mid-1960s. These acts and subsequent related legislation, executive orders, and court decisions ended state-supported segregation and formally prohibited discrimination in voting, public accommodations, housing, education, and employment. Also at this time the Equal Employment Opportunity Commission was established to promote equality of opportunity in education, employment, and housing and was later empowered to require remedial actions if employers were found guilty of discrimination (Burstein 1994; Rose 1989). In conjunction with executive orders and court decisions it fostered implementation of policies of "affirmative action" aimed at redressing inequalities of the past. As these changes in the legal sphere were taking place, remarkable changes in racial attitudes also were occurring. Levels of racial prejudice openly expressed by Whites fell dramatically and expressed support for equality of opportunity irrespective of race increased significantly (Schuman, Steeh, and Bobo 1985). Had sociologists and other social scientists of the 1950s been informed that these social changes were about to transpire, they could not have been faulted for predicting that racial inequality would be well on its way to being a thing of the past by the close of the century.

Of course this is not the case; racial inequality endures. To be sure, a few long-term trends suggesting movement toward equality can be noted for select groups (e.g., the young and highly educated) and for a few indicators (e.g., the representation of minorities among

1

elected officials). But, in general, broad population-level comparisons between Whites and Blacks in areas such as health, housing, education, employment, occupation, and income continue to reveal extensive inequality.[1] When the present and the readily foreseeable future are viewed through the lens of the hopes and expectations raised by social and political changes in the 1960s, one thing is abundantly clear — equality has been a long time coming.

In retrospect it is obvious that racial inequality is a much more intractable social problem than the lay public, policy makers, and social scientists generally perceived a generation ago. Despite this fact, the problem of racial inequality is not a priority issue in public opinion and national policy debate. Concern on the part of Whites has diminished in the past two decades. Indeed, many Whites perceive that racial inequality has been greatly reduced; and more than a few express the belief that racial inequality is a thing of the past and that racial minorities may even be advantaged in the labor market, the educational system, and other arenas of socioeconomic competition. Given this, White support for policies aimed at addressing racial discrimination and racial inequality has faltered. Previously implemented policies have been subject to reexamination, critique, revision, and occasional dismantling and no new policy initiatives have been offered in their place.

Many factors have shaped the trend of declining concern among Whites regarding issues of racial discrimination and racial inequality. The Civil Rights movement of the 1950s and 1960s was successful in garnering broad support among Whites for racial equality regarding civil and political rights. Once these rights were secured, however, White support for goals of promoting racial equality began to erode in the late 1960s.[2] This coincided with a shift in the rhetoric and emphasis of Black political leaders from a focus on goals of obtaining political and civil rights to a focus on goals of redressing long-standing social and economic inequalities. This shift ultimately had important consequences because it represented a change toward seeking equality in the distribution of goods that were perceived by Whites as being "zero-sum" in nature.

Many Whites, especially Whites in the South, viewed the extension of voting and other civil rights to Blacks as a threat to the existing social order. However, the achievement of equality in political and civil rights for African Americans did not in any *absolute* sense diminish the political and civil rights of Whites. Equality was attained by creating "more" of this good rather than by redistributing the existing stock. White "losses" associated with this were thus limited to changes in *relative* advantage; that is, Whites' advantages over

Blacks were substantially eliminated but Whites continued to enjoy the same legal rights and protections they had enjoyed previously.

In decided contrast, efforts to promote and secure greater racial equality in areas such as housing, higher education, employment, health care services, jobs, and income had potential consequences for socioeconomic outcomes which were fundamentally zero-sum in nature. That is, these outcomes involved goods which could not be quickly expanded in the short run as political rights had been. Not surprisingly, Whites, working-class Whites in particular but middle class Whites as well, perceived policies aimed at promoting rapid reductions in racial inequality as threatening to their socioeconomic position. These fears were not groundless; *movement toward equality on zero-sum goods requires redistribution of the existing stock and necessarily entails absolute as well as relative losses for advantaged groups.*

That Whites would initially be cautious and lukewarm in their enthusiasm for policies aimed at reducing racial inequalities and then later become increasingly resistant and opposed to such policies is hardly surprising. This is the expected reaction for an advantaged group. It also is not surprising that, over time, appeals by Black political leaders to values and moral principles became less effective in enlisting the support of Whites. It is always an open question as to whether moral arguments can carry the day when the distribution of zero-sum, material goods is at stake. In addition, however, the increasing ineffectiveness of Black leaders' appeals to higher values and moral principles can be traced not only to the fact that the appeals involved goals which contradicted Whites' material interests but also to the fact that Black political leaders were not successful in legitimating their post-Civil Rights goals as consistent with core values of American society embraced by Whites.

Earlier phases of the Civil Rights movement stressed principles of equality of opportunity and inclusion based on citizenship and individual merit. These ideals were broadly endorsed by Whites, in word at least if not always in deed. More significantly, they were codified into law. Equally importantly, the rhetoric of the movement emphasized reformist goals of assimilation and inclusion into the broader society and gained support among Whites by highlighting dramatic inconsistencies between stated principles and reality in American society. In a manner predicted by Myrdal (1944), White resistance to extending voting and other civil rights to Blacks was thus undercut by the fact that the Civil Rights movement was legitimated in terms of values and ideals which were generally accepted and held in high regard by Whites. This was not the case when the objectives of the movement shifted from equality of opportunity to equality of outcomes.

Whites have not accepted the goal of equal outcomes, especially group outcomes, as legitimate. To the contrary, studies of public opinion suggest that Whites view such goals as contradicting accepted principles of individualism and equal opportunity.[3] Thus, there has not been a moral dilemma in the minds of Whites regarding racial inequality in socioeconomic outcomes. One reason for this is that a clear majority of Whites attribute Black socioeconomic disadvantages in significant part to personal characteristics such as lack of ability and/or motivation (Kluegel 1990). Older Whites are more likely than younger Whites to emphasize lack of ability rather than lack of motivation, but persons who accept either of these "individualistic" explanations for Black disadvantage are less likely to support policies promoting racial economic equality (Kluegel 1990). Thus, declines in "traditional prejudice" among Whites which result as younger White cohorts with replace older White cohorts does not imply that Whites will be more supportive of policies to promote equality (Kluegel 1990). Indeed, younger Whites sometimes feel that discrimination, especially in its more virulent forms, is largely a thing of the past. They are also likely to believe that they did not participate in and have not personally benefited from discrimination in earlier eras and thus share no responsibility for either past discrimination or present day inequality.

Moral appeals proved to be relatively unsuccessful in persuading Whites to support goals of racial equality for another reason — namely, changes in the rhetoric of Black political activists. Rhetoric which had earlier stressed reform and inclusion of African Americans as full participants in American society began to increasingly emphasize explicitly pluralistic and nationalistic goals which many Whites categorically rejected. Equally significantly, rhetoric which had earlier emphasized philosophies of nonviolence and strategies of civil disobedience began to increasingly include more assertive slogans such as "Black Power" and phrases such as "by any means necessary" which were perceived by Whites as ominous and which added to their emerging concerns about the implications of racial equality for socioeconomic redistribution. Widespread civil disturbances in the urban ghettos of major cities across the country in the late 1960s crystallized these concerns on the part of Whites and heralded the emergence of White working-class backlash and status anxiety as a potent political force in American politics.

Changing macroeconomic fortunes further served to diminish White receptiveness to goals of promoting racial equality. Middle and working class White families experienced significant and relatively steady growth in real wages and material living conditions in the 1950s and 1960s. These gains were substantial from the vantage point of intra-generational comparisons and were even more dramatic when contrasted with material living conditions of previous generations. Under these conditions, issues of political inclusion and racial justice could be more easily advanced in public policy debates. If material standards of living are improving very rapidly, redistribution of material goods (e.g., good housing, quality health care, education, etc.) can occur even as everyone, Whites included, experiences significant absolute and relative improvements in comparisons within and across generations.

In contrast, the 1970s and 1980s were decades in which increases in real wages and incomes for working and middle class Whites were modest at best, stagnant and even declining at worst (Levy 1987; Levy 1995). Improvements in family income were realized primarily through the emergence of the two-earner family as a norm. This economic reality combined with other ongoing social and economic changes (e.g., economic restructuring, the rapid movement of women into the labor force, a resurgence in immigration, globalization of economic competition, etc.) to fuel concerns on the part of Whites that their social and economic position was precarious and uncertain if not actually eroding. It is not surprising that in this context working and middle class Whites became increasingly skeptical and resentful of redistributive policies such as affirmative action, racial preferences, set asides, and quotas.

In the 1980s and 1990s yet another factor was added to the mix and served to lessen the priority given to issues of racial equality in national policy. It is that increasing numbers of White workers and voters have little direct personal knowledge of an earlier time when racism was overt and when race discrimination and segregation were explicitly embodied in laws enforced by the state. Recent generations of Whites have come of age at a time when equality of opportunity, not segregation, was the formal law of the land and plainly spoken race prejudice and racist ideology had retreated from mainstream public debate. An increasingly large fraction of Whites in the labor force had not even reached first grade in the early 1960s when television brought nightly images of police dogs and firehoses being turned on lawful protesters calling for the end of state supported segregation. They have never heard prominent politicians and elected officials openly espouse racist, segregationist ideology for public consumption or seen them stand in front of institutions of publicly funded higher education to physically block desegregation efforts. As a result, it is more difficult for them to understand and acknowledge, much less accept, minority concerns about prejudice and racial discrimination.

Because recent generations of Whites have never directly participated in the *overt* and state-supported systems of racial segregation and exclusion that were largely dismantled in the 1950s and 1960s, they are likely to view widespread racial discrimination as a thing of the past. They take it for granted that systems of formal segregation and discrimination ended with civil rights and equal opportunity legislation and also tend to believe that *informal* discrimination flowing from individual prejudice and racism has largely disappeared as a result of dramatic cultural change in racial attitudes. Since they are inclined to see discrimination and involuntary segregation as historical in nature, younger generations of Whites are loath to accept the notion that they may have benefited even indirectly from racial discrimination. Indeed, a significant and increasing fraction express the belief that racial status today works to the *advantage* of, not the disadvantage of, Blacks and other racial minorities. Many Whites who believe this also see affirmative action and related policies as unfair and contrary to the spirit of equal opportunity. Many even argue that these policies may have perverse negative consequences for minorities.[4]

Recent generations of Whites are unlikely to understand enduring racial inequality as a reflection of discrimination and differential opportunities. They are more likely to instead attribute contemporary racial inequality to perceived "deficiencies" in African American families, communities, and culture. They are unlikely to identify structural factors as the primary explanations of enduring inequality and increasingly are likely to point to the unintended negative consequences of the welfare state and affirmative action policies as a factor. Consequently, to the extent that younger White cohorts see racial inequality as a policy concern at all, they tend to assign it a low priority and are likely to view government policies aimed at promoting equality as part of the problem itself not a potential tool to be adopted as part of a possible solution.

Social science research has also played a role in reducing the priority given to issues of racial inequality in national policy debates. Many influential studies conducted in the 1960s, 1970s, and early 1980s reported substantial, steady, and seemingly inexorable declines in racial inequality in education, occupation, and income (Fox and Faine 1973; Hare 1965; Johnson and Sell 1976; Palmore and Whittington 1970; Siegel 1965; Smith and Welch 1984). These and other studies suggested that social and economic opportunities for African Americans were slowly but surely expanding. Optimistic assessments of these trends raised the hypothesis that these trends represented the beginning of the end of racial stratification in America; that after centuries of exclusion African Americans were finally being drawn into a process of inclusion and assimilation similar to those observed previously for voluntary immigrant groups (Neidert and Farley 1985). The implications of such interpretations for policy are clear; further action and concern are largely unnecessary; inequality will gradually wither away without intervention. The only point of debate is whether the pace of change was acceptable or not.

Unfortunately, these hopeful notions proved to be premature and overly optimistic. Subsequent analyses have shown that movement toward racial inequality has not occurred across the board, but has instead been limited to only some socioeconomic outcomes. Thus, every encouraging trend that can be documented is matched with another that is less encouraging. For example, segregation of Whites and Blacks in primary and secondary schools remains exceptionally high with only minimal change, if any, suggested by trends in the recent past (Farley and Allen 1986; National Research Council 1989). White-Black differences in percentages enrolled in and graduating from colleges and professional programs began to widen in the 1980s after closing in the 1960s and 1970s (National Research Council 1989). White-Black differences in employment and labor force participation have expanded in recent decades (Farley and Allen 1986; National Research Council 1989). Black residential isolation and concentration in poverty neighborhoods increased in many major urban areas (Wilson 1987; Massey and Denton 1993). And, White-Black differences in incarceration have almost doubled in recent decades as incarceration rates for young Black males especially have skyrocketed.[5]

Subsequent analyses have also shown that many of the most encouraging trends in inequality were for select groups (i.e., the young and highly educated) whose experiences proved not to be indicative of experiences for broader populations. For example, Cotton (1989) has shown that, while White-Black income comparisons for men who are employed full time and year round have steadily become more equal over time, White-Black income comparisons for *all* men have scarcely changed. The first and more encouraging trend results because men who are not fully employed (i.e., employed only part-time or part-year, unemployed, or not in the labor force at all) and thus have lower incomes are excluded from the analysis. The second and more discouraging trend reflects the fact that White-Black disparities in access to stable employment have increased to such a degree that they largely if not entirely offset gains resulting from movement toward equality in income for similarly employed White and Black men.

Another factor which contributed to excessive optimism on the part of social scientists is that they observed certain encouraging trends and then optimistically but incorrectly projected that they would have greater salutary consequences than they ultimately did. Perhaps the most telling example concerns expectations generated by trends in racial educational inequality (Allen 1995). Movement toward equality on certain indicators of educational attainment has been dramatic over the past several decades. In particular, differences in median years of schooling completed and percentages completing high school have narrowed considerably (Mare 1995; Farley and Allen 1986; National Research Council 1989).[6] These encouraging trends are significant in their own right (although it could be noted that since 1970 group differences in percentages attending and completing college have by and large remained constant, or even increased, rather than declining). However, many social scientists anticipated that this seemingly strong convergence in education would subsequently lead to equally dramatic reductions in racial disparities in employment, occupation, and income.

Of course, this did not happen. In our view it was because the original expectation was based on a naive understanding of the link between racial disparities in education and racial disparities in economic attainments. We will argue later that there are strong theoretical reasons to discount expectations that broad improvements in minority education will lead quickly to dramatically improved economic outcomes.

A second and more technical reason to discount such expectations is that the kinds of indicators which have exhibited the greatest convergence (i.e., White and Black attainments for nominal years of schooling completed) are not the most important ones for indexing the economic implications of racial education differences. All years of schooling are not equal in terms of their consequences for employment, status, and income attainments. Years of college and professional school education are much more valuable in terms of employment, occupation, and earnings than years of primary and secondary schooling and credential-conferring years in high school and college are much more valuable than other years (Mare 1995). As a result, the smaller gap in *years* of schooling completed which today separates Whites with some college from Blacks with no college may be nearly as consequential, or maybe even more consequential, in its impact on economic attainments than the larger gap in years of schooling completed which in the 1950s separated Whites with some high school from Blacks with less than high school. Failure to better appreciate the complex and changing relationship between education and economic attainments has fostered unrealistic expectations regarding the consequences of trends toward equality in White-Black education comparisons.

The final point we make on this theme is that social scientists have contributed to an excessive optimism about trends in racial inequality by being too quick to conclude that trends toward racial equality on socioeconomic outcomes reflect expanding social and economic opportunities for African Americans. In fact, the explanation of trends toward equality when they are observed is often more complicated and less encouraging. For example, much of the movement toward equality in national-level comparisons between Whites and Blacks on income and occupation in the post-war era can be directly attributed to the consequences of demographic redistribution rather than expanding opportunities in a strict sense. One of these important demographic changes was the dramatic shift of the Black population away from the rural South to urban areas in the North, Midwest, and West. This geographic redistribution of the Black population accounts for a large portion of the reduction in occupation and income inequality at the national level in the post-war era (Fossett, Galle, and Burr 1989; Gwartney 1970; Reich 1981; Smith and Welch 1986; 1989).

This massive demographic change was a response to variation in the severity of racial stratification across regional and local labor markets; Blacks migrated from areas of higher inequality to areas of lower inequality (Burr, Potter, Galle, and Fossett 1992; Fligstein 1981; Stinner and DeJong 1969). Aggregate inequality at the national level declined as a result, but this decline did not reflect any fundamental change in the nature of racial stratification in regional and local labor markets. Indeed, inequality *within* regional and local labor markets often changed little from decade to decade (and occasionally even *increased*) as inequality at the national level was falling (Fossett, Galle, and Burr 1989; Burr, Galle, and Fossett 1991).

Reductions in inequality at the national level which resulted from Blacks migrating to areas where relative opportunities were more favorable are very "real" in one sense and should not be discounted. However, it is important to understand that, since inequality decline resulting from this process does not reflect fundamental change in the structure of opportunity in local areas, it has quite different implications for policy and expectations for future trends in inequality. Failure to recognize and appreciate this led observers to overestimate the pace of change in relative opportunities for Blacks and the impact that legal reforms and changes in racial attitudes were having on these opportunities. It also led observers to significantly underestimate the inertia behind racial inequality and White advantage in local areas.

Failure to appreciate the role of demographic redistribution in generating reductions in racial inequality at the national level led observers to have overly optimistic expectations for future trends in inequality because the effects of demographic redistribution eventually "played out." After generating substantial reductions in inequality at the national-level in the 1940s, 1950s, and 1960s, Black interregional migration began to lose its capacity to generate further reductions in inequality because interregional inequality patterns began to converge in the 1960s and 1970s (due to disproportionate declines in inequality in the South). Thus, after 1970 inequality reduction would have to come primarily from expanding opportunities for Blacks in local areas, a factor which had not been nearly as important in the past (Fossett, Galle, and Burr 1989).[7]

These several points can be summarized quite simply; sociologists, other social scientists, and interested observers have been prone to misinterpret the meaning of national-level trends in inequality in ways that promoted overly optimistic expectations for the future. Even seemingly straightforward trends can be difficult to interpret because they are shaped by many disparate factors. One obvious conclusion to be drawn here is that careful and detailed analyses of trends in racial inequality are needed so we can gain a better understanding of what factors have been shaping changes in racial inequality over time. Such studies are needed so public discussion and policy debate concerning racial inequality will be informed by a fuller and more accurate accounting of how it has changed over time and a better grasp of what factors have impeded and what factors have facilitated reductions in racial inequality.

This assessment motivates the present study. While there are many ways in which the study of trends in racial inequality might be extended, we are particularly concerned with addressing the lack of attention given to describing how racial stratification in local areas has been changing over time and investigating the role that structural factors have played in shaping these changes. In our view, much of the misunderstanding and misplaced optimism about trends in racial inequality might well have been tempered if more attention had been directed to these issues. For example, we expect that descriptive analysis in this area is likely to lead to greater appreciation of the fact that inequality in regions and local areas has been changing much more slowly than has been suggested by the more widely examined national-level trends in racial inequality. Likewise, we expect that analysis of determinants of change in inequality in local areas will suggest a more realistic and sobering perspective on why racial inequality has changed in the past and what changes should be expected in the future.

It was with these thoughts in mind that we undertook the comparative, community-level analyses of racial inequality in southern, nonmetropolitan areas reviewed in this monograph. Our decision to adopt a comparative approach is guided by our assumption that "place" has been and continues to be an important factor in racial stratification and racial inequality. Communities vary greatly both in the level of racial inequality observed at a given point in time (Blalock 1956; Frisbie and Neidert 1977) and in trends in racial inequality observed over time (Burr, Galle, and Fossett 1991; Fossett and Stafford 1990). Moreover, trends in inequality for local areas may differ from trends observed at higher levels of aggregation. Thus, we will report below that, while racial occupational inequality at the national level was steadily declining with each decade since 1940, inequality in southern nonmetropolitan areas was either stable or increasing between 1940 and 1970 and did not begin to decline significantly until after 1970. In this respect, they follow a pattern previously documented for southern metropolitan areas (Burr, Galle, and Fossett 1991).

These findings suggest that racial stratification in local areas is, at least in some degree, independent from national and regional stratification structures and that factors specific to local areas can affect the pace and even the direction of change in racial inequality. This means that analysis of trends in inequality in local areas is needed to provide a more complete description of trends in racial inequality in America. It also means that investigation of trends in inequality in local areas provides an important avenue for gaining a more complete understanding of the dynamics of change in racial inequality.

Community-level studies of racial inequality were once relatively common in the literature on racial and ethnic relations. In recent decades, however, the literature has been increasingly dominated by studies investigating race differences in the relevance and efficacy of various individual characteristics for socioeconomic outcomes (e.g., Duncan and Duncan 1968; Featherman and Hauser 1976; 1978). This research is guided by the status attainment tradition — a tradition which investigates *individual* attainment outcomes and only occasionally takes account of community-level predictors.[8]

We do not hesitate to acknowledge the many ways that studies of racial stratification conducted in the status attainment tradition have expanded our understanding of racial inequality. Studies in this tradition have documented that racial inequality flows in part from the fact that race is directly salient in stratification processes and has effects on socioeconomic outcomes net of controls for other determinants such as education, training, and experience, and family background. They have shown that the economic "payoff" associated with education, training, and experience and other personal and "human capital" investments is weaker for Blacks and that this contributes to inequality both directly and also indirectly by retarding incentives for Blacks to "invest" in these resources. They have shown that effects of socioeconomic origin (e.g., parental education, status, and income) are weaker for Blacks and thus it is more difficult for Blacks to maintain and consolidate socioeconomic attainments from generation to generation (Duncan and Duncan 1968).

Finally, studies in the status attainment tradition have documented that minority disadvantages in personal resources (e.g., education) and socioeconomic origin (e.g., parental education, status, and income) have important consequences for White-Black inequality in socioeconomic attainments, so much so that, even under optimistic (and highly implausible) scenarios where race per se is assumed to be irrelevant in stratification processes, this legacy of previous eras of racial stratification will perpetuate substantial racial inequality in socioeconomic attainments for many generations to come (Lieberson and Fuguit 1967; Daymont 1980).

Still, as valuable as the contributions of this research tradition are, it is important to recognize that investigation of racial inequality from the point of view of individual status attainments also has had some unfortunate consequences. The one that is most relevant in the present context is that research in this tradition has deflected attention away from questions about racial stratification systems and thus undercut analysis of trends in inequality in local areas. The reason for this is simple; the status attainment tradition has not been concerned with and is not well suited to investigating questions about how racial stratification systems vary over time and place.

On the whole, status attainment theory tends to be individualistic and social psychological in orientation. The data sets and methods of analysis used are optimized for investigating the effects of individual characteristics on socioeconomic outcomes. Status attainment theory rarely speaks to how stratification and inequality in general, and racial stratification and inequality in particular, are conditioned and shaped by local economic, political, social, and demographic structures and conditions. It should come as no surprise then that data sets constructed for the purpose of estimating status attainment models provide only limited opportunities to test effects of community structure on racial inequality; they rarely include relevant variables and their sample designs do not facilitate reliable analysis of inter-community variation in inequality.[9] As a consequence, no existing data sets commonly used in status attainment studies can sustain the analysis of trends in inequality over time in local areas.

We believe that the comparative, community-level analyses of trends in racial inequality we pursue in this study provide a welcome and needed complement to (not a substitute for) studies which investigate racial stratification from within the status attainment tradition. One justification for our view is that analysis of trends in inequality in local areas focuses attention on variation and change in stratification *systems* by examining stratification outcomes for *populations* residing in given communities and local labor markets.

Communities are arenas for individual and intergroup competition; that is, they are circumscribed environments within which individuals and groups compete to secure social and economic outcomes. The community is thus a logically relevant unit of analysis to adopt when investigating the effects of factors thought to affect the structure of opportunity within stratification systems. Analysis at this level provides an opportunity to test macro-level theories about racial stratification that, for reasons enumerated above, cannot easily be addressed within the status attainment framework which has been primarily geared to explaining individual status attainments rather than variation and change in stratification systems.

Communities are not the only logically relevant unit that might be used to investigate macro-level theories of racial stratification. We also considered longitudinal analysis of inequality at the regional and national level. It quickly became obvious, however, that a community-level design had significant practical advantages for our purposes. Community-level analysis allowed us to follow a sizable sample of cases over a significant time interval. Regional- and national-level designs also would have permitted the analysis of changes in inequality over long time intervals. However, they afforded only limited opportunities for testing hypotheses about variation and change in racial stratification *systems* since only a handful of cases are under observation; indeed, in national-level, time-series analysis, only a *single* stratification system is under observation.

In addition to this consideration, we found the the community-level design to be attractive because communities exhibit considerable cross-sectional and temporal variation on many structural characteristics which are hypothesized to affect racial stratification systems (e.g., relative group size, labor demand, industrial structure, etc.). This is obviously an important practical advantage for testing hypotheses about the effects of different structural variables using multivariate statistical models.[10]

It is with these several theoretical and practical considerations in mind that we attempt in this present study to reestablish community-level research on racial inequality by investigating changes in racial inequality in southern, nonmetropolitan counties between 1940 to 1990. We do not offer our study as a substitute for recent work on racial inequality conducted within the framework and methodology of the status attainment tradition. Rather our intent is to round out a literature which has recently tended to emphasize individualistic perspectives in stratification theory and neglect theoretical and empirical traditions which have a macro-level focus.

Our study draws on and extends a prior literature of comparative analysis of racial inequality (e.g., Blalock 1956; 1957; 1959; Bahr and Gibbs 1967; Burr, Galle, and Fossett 1991; Frisbie and Neidert 1977; Jiobu and Marshall 1971; Glenn 1963; 1964; Hill 1974; Roof 1972; Turner 1951; Wilcox and Roof 1978). Like most efforts in this literature, our study is guided by the ecological/structural perspective. (See Fossett and Cready [forthcoming] for a review of ecological theory pertaining to racial and ethnic inequality). This perspective is macro-level in orientation and work in this theoretical tradition adopts the general hypothesis that macro-level structural characteristics of local communities and local labor markets may influence racial inequality in a variety of ways. For example, structural variables such as rates of immigration and minority growth, ethnic diversity, and relative group size are thought to affect the salience of racial and ethnic characteristics in competition for social and economic rewards (i.e., race prejudice and discrimination). Structural variables such as population growth and labor demand are also thought to affect tendencies for competition for social and economic rewards to be organized along ethnic boundaries. And, structural variables such as urbanization and industrial structure are thought to affect inequality by constraining the expression of race prejudice and discrimination in stratification processes. We draw on and explore these and other ideas which are basic to the ecological tradition.

Methodologically, our study is distinguished from previous comparative research on racial inequality by the fact that we adopt a longitudinal design and follow changes in inequality in local areas over several decades. This is a welcome innovation because causal inference in previous ecological studies has been based solely on analysis of interarea variation in inequality at a single point in time. By directly observing change in inequality over time, we are better able to assess whether empirical associations previously established using cross-sectional data do in fact reflect dynamic processes.

Our study is also distinguished from the previous literature by the fact that we investigate trends in racial inequality in occupational attainments in southern, nonmetropolitan areas. In the past decade and a half, comparative studies of racial inequality in the ecological tradition have focused primarily on racial residential segregation in metropolitan areas.[11] Indeed, research on poverty and racial inequality generally has been overwhelmingly preoccupied with themes focusing on urban poverty and the urban underclass while research on poverty and racial inequality in nonmetropolitan settings has been broadly neglected (Tickameyer and Duncan 1990).

Our focus on nonmetropolitan areas is a welcome addition to the literature for several reasons. First, it can provide insight into whether findings from metropolitan-level studies generalize to non-metropolitan areas. Second, even after a century of sustained movement to metropolitan areas and away from the South, a large fraction of the African-American population nationally continues to live in southern nonmetropolitan areas. As recently as 1990, about 15 percent of the Black population nationally resided in nonmetropolitan areas of the South, and, of Blacks residing in the South, about 28 percent resided in nonmetropolitan areas. This sizable population has been largely ignored in recent decades; most research on racial inequality has focused on the growth of the "underclass" in large metropolitan areas.

Finally, focusing on nonmetropolitan areas presents advantages for theory testing because, compared to metropolitan areas, non-metropolitan areas exhibit more variation and change on industrial, occupational, demographic, and other structural characteristics hypothesized to affect racial inequality.[12] Furthermore, following Tickameyer and Duncan (1990) we argue that study of racial inequality in nonmetropolitan areas is critical to a *general* understanding of racial inequality. Tickameyer and Duncan argue,

> Sociological neglect of rural poverty has left us with an incomplete understanding of poverty in advanced, capitalistic, and *urbanized* society. ... [U]nderstanding the circumstances of [rural poverty] ...can deepen our understanding of the poor in both urban and rural areas. (1990:70).

Substitute the phrase racial inequality for rural poverty and this statement is no less compelling.

Plan of the Book

Our monograph is organized as follows. Chapter Two provides a review of ecological and structural theories which identify potential determinants of changes in racial inequality over time in local areas. Chapter Three reviews key methodological issues we had to come to terms with to complete our study. Chapter Four presents descriptive analyses which document the basic patterns of change in racial inequality in southern nonmetropolitan areas between 1940 and 1990. Chapter Five presents the results of regression analyses which investigate *cross-sectional variation* in racial inequality. Chapter Six presents the results of panel regression analyses and analyses of covariance structures which investigate *change over time* in racial inequality. Chapter Seven briefly summarizes the major findings from the analysis chapters and attempts to place trends in racial inequality in the nonmetropolitan South in perspective as we approach the beginning of a new millennium.

Notes

1. For comprehensive reviews which examine trends in racial inequality for many different aspects of socioeconomic attainment see Farley (1995), Farley and Allen (1986), National Research Council (1989).

2. White support for interventions to insure equality of opportunities, much less outcomes, has always been lukewarm compared to White support for ideals of equal opportunity (Schuman, Steeh, and Bobo 1985: Chapter 3). Similarly, the percentage of (primarily White) respondents who identified civil rights as the nation's most important problem peaked during the late 1960s and fell to near zero by the early 1970s (Schuman, Steeh, and Bobo 1985:27).

3. See National Research Council (1989: Chapter 3, Racial Attitudes and Behavior), Schuman, Steeh, and Bobo (1985), and Kluegel and Smith (1986) for analysis of Whites' attitudes toward affirmative action and other policies addressing racial inequality.

4. Thus, recent decades have seen the emergence of the curious combination of beliefs among many Whites that state sponsored initiatives to end discrimination and establish equality of opportunity have been so successful they are no longer needed and yet further efforts to expand opportunities for disadvantaged groups and redress inequalities should not be undertaken because past efforts have either failed or been counterproductive.

5. Nationally, the percentage of Black men ages 25-29 in correctional institutions increased from approximately 4.5 in 1980 to approximately 8.2 in 1990 (McGruder 1995). For Whites, the percentage was much lower ini-

tially and changed little over time (i.e., it was 0.6 in 1980 and 0.8 in 1990). Consequently, the White-Black differential expanded dramatically from 3.9 to 7.4 (McGruder 1995).

6. On the other hand, the White-Black difference in the percentage graduating from college has been stable or expanding over time.

7. Demographic redistribution became a less potent source of change in inequality because levels of inequality in different regions and local areas steadily converged after 1940. This made it more difficult for Blacks to improve their standing relative to Whites by migrating from one area to another (Fossett, Galle, and Burr 1989).

8. It is interesting to note that comparative studies of racial residential segregation have thrived in recent decades even as community-level studies of racial socioeconomic inequality have become less frequent. We speculate that the main reason for this is that existing individual-level data sets do not readily permit the investigation of "neighborhood" as a status attainment outcome.

9. For example, cost concerns dictate the use of cluster sample designs which typically result in only a small portion of local areas being represented as primary sampling units in the sampling frame. Similarly, few subsamples for local areas are large enough to permit reliable interarea comparisons on racial inequality (the small size of the Black subsamples is especially problematic here). Finally, individuals are disproportionately sampled from large urban areas which are relatively homogeneous in terms of structural characteristics. This satisfies the goal of obtaining a nationally representative sample, but it simultaneously stacks the deck against obtaining efficient and statistically significant local area effects.

10. By contrast, estimation of multivariate models in national-level, time-series analyses is complicated by the fact that independent variables are often changing in unison such that it is very difficult to estimate their separate effects.

11. In the past two decades, most ecological analyses of racial inequality have focused on intermetropolitan variation in racial residential segregation (e.g., numerous studies by Douglas Massey and co-authors). This reflects a concern with investigating macro-level theories of racial residential segregation and the growth of the underclass in large metropolitan areas.

12. For example, the hypothesis that urbanization undermines racial inequality is better tested with data for nonmetropolitan areas because metropolitan areas exhibit little meaningful variation on urbanization.

2

Determinants of Racial Inequality in Nonmetropolitan Areas

We have two primary goals in this chapter. The first is to briefly review the previous literature which has investigated racial inequality in nonmetropolitan areas of the South and indicate how our research builds on and extends this literature. Our second goal is to discuss in some detail hypotheses which link structural characteristics of communities to racial inequality. In so doing, we develop theoretical rationales for the various predictor variables we include in the models of inequality we report in Chapters 5 and 6. In addition, we also discuss selected theoretical concerns which are relevant to understanding racial inequality in nonmetropolitan areas but which for various reasons cannot be directly reflected in our modeling efforts.

Previous Research

Comparative analyses of racial inequality have always focused primarily on metropolitan areas and this has been especially true in recent decades. However, nonmetropolitan areas have not been totally neglected and thus a brief and selective review of prior studies is warranted. Two studies by Blalock (1957; 1959) were among the first ecological studies to investigate racial inequality in nonmetropolitan areas.[1] In the first of these studies Blalock investigated the impact of relative minority size and the rate of increase in the minority population on racial inequality.[2] He reported strong positive correlations between relative minority size and selected measures of racial inequality and weaker positive correlations between minority increase and racial inequality. The study firmly established the "relative minority size" or "competition" hypothesis (discussed in detail below) which has continued to be a central focus of research in later years.

Blalock's second study of inequality in nonmetropolitan areas attempted to investigate the conventional view that forces of urbanization and industrialization weaken ascriptive stratification structures and pave the way for reductions in racial inequality (Blalock 1959). Blalock argued that racial stratification structures are more resilient than conventional theory would suggest and thus predicted that urbanization might have no appreciable effect on inequality *in the short run*. His empirical analysis indicated that urbanization had positive effects on status levels for *both* Whites and Blacks as predicted by conventional theory. However, urbanization's positive effect on White status was greater than its positive effect on Black status and consequently the association between urbanization and White-Black inequality was *positive*. This finding contradicted both conventional theory and Blalock's own prediction of no effect.

Unlike his earlier work establishing the relationship between relative minority size and racial inequality (Blalock 1956; 1957), the results of this study did not inspire much in the way of additional research. This is probably because Blalock did not advance a satisfactory explanation of the unexpected finding of a positive relationship between urbanization and inequality. Thus, the finding may have been viewed by many as an anomaly which could not be reconciled with the prevailing theory. As we shall note below, however, Blalock's findings can be explained with new hypotheses developed from ecological theory. For example, we will argue that inequality will tend to increase with the onset of urbanization because it introduces a more complex division of labor and a more highly differentiated status structure which carries greater structural possibilities for inequality. We will also argue that sectoral changes associated with urbanization — namely the shift from unskilled and skilled manual occupations and toward white-collar occupations with higher formal education requirements — promotes greater racial inequality by amplifying the consequences of Black educational disadvantage and by drawing White women into labor market as competitors for jobs and occupational position.

Brown and Fuguitt (1972) extended Blalock's research by investigating racial inequality in nonmetropolitan cities of the South. Using cross-sectional data from the 1960 Census of Population, they found strong support for Blalock's "minority size" or "competition" hypothesis. Their study was notable because they decomposed the effect of minority size on racial inequality into separate "component" effects on occupational status for Whites and Blacks. To do this, they measured occupational inequality by differences between the percentages of White men and Black men at or above selected points in the occupational hierarchy (e.g., the White-Black difference in the percentages employed in white-collar or higher status occupations).[3] They then showed that percent Black in the local area had positive effects on both components of the measure of inequality (i.e., positive effects on the percentages of both Whites and Blacks in higher status occupations) and that a net positive effect on inequality resulted because the effect of minority size on White status was larger than its effect on Black status.

This analytic strategy provided a more complete understanding of the dynamics of racial stratification. It also provided a new opportunity to distinguish between theories which make similar predictions about the net effect of a particular variable on inequality but different predictions about the variable's effects on White and Black status considered separately.

A later study by Elgie (1980) was notable because it was the first to examine racial inequality in a sample of nonmetropolitan areas using longitudinal data (i.e., 1950, 1960, and 1970). The major focus of Elgie's study was on the impact of industrialization on racial inequality in education, occupation, and income.[4] He used factor analytic methods to develop indices of four aspects of industrialization: community size, educational status, manufacturing orientation, and agricultural scale and then used the resulting factor scores to predict racial inequality in decade-specific, cross-sectional analyses.[5]

Elgie found only limited support for the so-called "thesis of industrialization" which predicted racial inequality would fall as industrialization increased. The predictions were supported in his regression analyses of educational inequality. However, the predictions were not supported in his regression analyses of occupational inequality and income inequality. Moreover, he found that effects which did support the "thesis of industrialization" were attenuated or even reversed altogether when relative minority size was included as a predictor in the analyses. Thus, he concluded that the results did not confirm the traditional expectation that industrialization promotes reductions in racial inequality. Nonetheless, Elgie cautioned that it "would perhaps be premature to conclude that southern modernization has had limited distributive consequences." We will not be so cautious.

Elgie's study was significant in at least two respects. One is that his findings regarding the effects of industrialization closely paralleled Blalock's findings regarding the effects of urbanization. Like Blalock, Elgie presented evidence that a structural variable which traditionally had been viewed as likely to promote reductions in racial inequality did not do so. Elgie's study was also significant because it anticipated the potential advantages of analyzing longitudinal data to test theories of racial stratification. Unfortunately, his analysis did not fully exploit this opportunity as it did not include analyses of changes in inequality. However, in arguing that it would be "premature" to dismiss the thesis that industrialization reduces inequality, Elgie clearly implied that cross-sectional analysis might not be adequate to assess the hypothesis and that direct analyses of change over a longer time frame might be needed. We directly address that need in the present study.

Another notable study of racial inequality in nonmetropolitan areas was Semyonov and Scott's (1983) analysis of occupational inequality using data for a sample of 40 nonmetropolitan places with populations between 25,000 and 50,000 in Mississippi and South Carolina in 1970. Unlike Brown and Fuguitt (1972) and many others, Semyonov and Scott reported that percent Black had a negative effect on the relative representation of Whites in higher status occupations (i.e., professional and managerial occupations) and a positive effect on the relative representation of Whites in lower status occupations (e.g. service occupations). This combination of effects would seem to imply that relative minority size has a negative on racial occupational inequality. It is important to view these results cautiously, however, because no other study, including a follow-up study on racial occupation differences in metropolitan areas by the same principle authors (Semyonov, Hoyt, and Scott 1984), has reported a similar pattern of effects implying a negative relationship between relative minority size and racial occupational inequality.

One potential explanation for the anomalous findings reported by Semyonov and Scott is that they used relative odds ratios to measure occupational differences between Whites and Blacks. To be specific, their dependent variables were ratios of White males' odds of employment in a given occupational category to Black males' odds of employment in that same occupational category.[6] Caution must be exercised before interpreting ratios of this sort as indicators of inequality because they measure relative group access to occupations without taking account of where those occupations stand in local occupational hierarchies (Fossett and Swicegood 1982; Fossett and South 1983; Fossett 1984).[7] By way of example, sales and clerical jobs might rank in the top 30 percent of the status hierarchy in one community and only in the top 50 percent in another. If racial stratification functions to reserve the best *available* jobs in the local community for Whites, relative odds ratios for sales and clerical jobs might differ across the two communities even when the ratio of Whites to Black in the top 30 percent of jobs is identical in both communities.

In our view, the most compelling theories of racial stratification are those which argue that racial stratification systems function to reserve the best available jobs for Whites. Thus, we do not see relative odds ratios of the type just considered as being well-suited for evaluating these theories because they do not measure race differences in access to ranked positions in the local occupational structure. Our analyses here rely instead on measures of racial inequality which directly acknowledge and reflect the ordinal- and interval-level status dimensions of occupations.

Extensions of Previous Research

These earlier studies by Blalock (1957; 1959), Brown and Fuguitt (1972), Elgie (1980), and Semyonov and Scott (1983) established a tradition of comparative research on inequality in nonmetropolitan areas. They pointed to the relevance of ecological/structural theory for explaining variation in racial inequality in nonmetropolitan communities and their empirical and theoretical work helps frame the agenda for future research. We draw heavily on this previous body of work (and related research focusing on metropolitan areas) and have incorporated many of the more successful theoretical orientations and methodological strategies found in this literature into the present study.[8] However, we have also attempted to advance beyond these previous efforts in order to better test ecological and structural theories of racial inequality. We briefly note some of the more significant ways in which we extend previous research as follows.

We give careful attention to the measurement of occupational inequality in light of the fact that findings in previous studies have varied depending on the measure of occupational inequality adopted. We believe we were able to develop more refined measures that well suit the needs of our study. We briefly note the major conceptual issues regarding the measurement of occupational inequality and occupational status in Chapter 3 and provide extended discussions of these issues in Appendices A and B.

We also extend previous research by examining the effects of a wider range of potential structural determinants of inequality. Space limitations dictate that we discuss only the structural determinants included in the final analyses in this monograph and one or two additional ones that are of special theoretical interest. It is fair to state, however, that we considered many more independent variables that we are able to directly discuss in this monograph and that the number and range of variables we examined significantly exceeds the number and range of factors considered in previous studies.

Finally, the most important way we extended previous research is by gathering longitudinal data from six separate censuses spanning five decades and directly estimating panel models of change in racial inequality. This is a significant methodological improvement which advances the literature beyond the cross-sectional models found in previous studies. The attractive properties of using longitudinal data to estimate panel models of change have been authoritatively described elsewhere (e.g., Finkel 1995; Kessler and Greenberg 1981; Tuma and Hannan 1984) and thus we need not catalog them at length. However, we will take this opportunity to stress the following three points. The panel design we use provides a larger sample size which allows us to more easily detect and more reliably estimate the effects of factors which influence inequality;[9] It allows us to assess whether the effects of determinants of inequality estimated from cross-sectional data have been stable over time; And, most importantly, it allows us to directly model change in inequality and more rigorously assess theories which previously have only been tested via analysis of cross-sectional data.

Determinants of Inequality in Local Areas

Previous theory and research in the ecological tradition has linked racial inequality to many different structural characteristic of communities. A partial listing includes the relative size of minority populations (Blalock 1957; Brown and Fuguitt 1972; Frisbie and Neidert 1977; Wilcox and Roof 1978), industrial and occupational composition (Blalock 1956; 1957; Frisbie and Neidert 1977; Jiobu and Marshall 1971; Spilerman and Miller 1976; Turner 1951), economic growth (Farley and Hermalin 1972), unionization (Hill 1974), urbanization (Lyson 1985; Martin and Poston 1976), industrialization (Elgie 1980), and population size (Blalock 1956; 1957; Glenn 1963; 1964; 1966). In this section we review and elaborate arguments linking these and other community characteristics to racial inequality.

We should note that our review discusses several variables which ultimately were not directly included in our final empirical analyses. Some theoretically interesting variables were excluded from the final models because they were conceptually and/or empirically collinear with other predictors. Other variables were excluded because preliminary analyses revealed that their effects were weak or inconsistent. Nevertheless, we discuss hypotheses relating to them in the interests of thoroughness and because it has implications for the interpretation of our final empirical models.[10]

Minority Size

Ecological theory has long linked the size of the minority group to minority and majority status levels and majority-minority status inequality. We discuss several hypotheses relating to minority group size including: (a) the "competition" hypothesis which links relative minority size to intergroup competition, prejudice, and discrimination, (b) the "resource" hypothesis which links relative minority size to minority political and economic power, (c) the "composition" hypothesis which links relative minority size to intergroup inequality and group status levels in situations with multiple, ranked minorities, (d) the "overflow" hypothesis which links relative minority size to minority status levels, (e) the "semi-separate minority economy" hypothesis which links absolute minority size to the emergence of a minority subeconomy, and (f) the "White gains" hypothesis which links relative minority size to discrimination.

As we shall see, several of these hypotheses "overlap" in the sense that their predictions about the relationship between minority size and majority-minority inequality are similar. In other cases, the hypotheses generate distinctly different predictions. However, it is important to recognize that even when the predictions differ *they are not mutually exclusive.* Indeed it is logically possible that all of these hypotheses could be correct at some level, although we believe some are more compelling than others.

Relative Minority Size: The Competition Hypothesis

Hawley (1944), Williams (1947), Allport (1954), Blalock (1956; 1957; 1967), and others have advanced what we term the "competition hypothesis." This argument sits squarely in the ecological tradition of competitive ethnic relations (Park 1950; Olzak and Nagel 1986) and holds that greater relative minority size is associated with higher levels of racial inequality because it provokes a conservative response by the majority group as members of this group attempt to protect their privileged position in the face of a potential threat from a large minority population. Minority threat has been linked to relative minority size in two ways. One is that minority populations may

have greater potential capability to successfully mobilize and eliminate racial inequality when their relative size is large. The other is
that effective minority mobilization to eliminate racial inequality will
have greater adverse consequences for majority status when relative
minority size is large.[11]

Wilcox and Roof (1978) outlined the competition hypothesis as a
causal chain in which (a) greater relative minority size leads to
greater perception of minority threat on the part of the majority,
(b) greater perception of threat by the majority promotes greater levels of in-group solidarity and greater prejudice against out-groups,
(c) greater majority prejudice leads to increased discrimination
against out-groups by the majority, and (d) increased discrimination
leads to greater majority-minority inequality. This reasoning has
long been supported in "reduced form" ecological models reporting
positive effects of percent Black on racial inequality (Blalock 1957;
Frisbie and Neidert 1977; Glenn 1963; 1964; Turner 1951; Wilcox and
Roof 1978). Fossett and Kiecolt (1989) have provided additional support for this theory based on individual-level contextual analyses of
White racial attitudes which indicate that relative minority size has a
positive effect on Whites' perception of power threat from minorities
and a negative effect on Whites' acceptance of principles of racial
integration. Glaser (1994) presents similar evidence from individual-
level contextual analyses which document that relative minority size
has sizable effects on Whites' attitudes toward racial charged political
issues such as the pace of civil rights movement and government
efforts to help Blacks.

Relative Minority Size: A Demographic Resource

Under some circumstances, group influence over the distribution
of social and economic rewards is likely to be at least partly a function
of numbers and thus larger relative group size becomes a potential
resource which might enable a group to garner a larger share of social
and economic rewards. In such circumstances, a negative relationship between minority size and inequality would be expected. This
"resource" aspect of relative minority size has not been emphasized in
prior theory and research because majority control over the distribution of rewards has been largely taken for granted. The assumption
of complete majority effectiveness in protecting group advantage thus
leads to the presumption that minority size will affect inequality primarily or solely through its impact on majority actions (e.g., majority
discrimination). In contrast, possible practical advantages which
might accrue to the minority based on greater relative size have been
assumed to be of secondary importance if not negligible altogether.

It may be that this view should be reconsidered in light of important structural changes in the American political system in recent decades. Specifically, voting rights legislation and civil rights legislation enacted in the 1960s may have changed the social environment for Blacks in the American South in ways that may have enabled them to convert relative size into a resource, at least under certain conditions and for certain outcomes. For example, voting rights reforms in the 1960s enabled Blacks to register and vote in substantial numbers after many decades of being effectively disenfranchised (Alt 1995; National Research Council 1989) and the number of Black elected officials in the South increased dramatically after 1965 (National Research Council 1989:238).

The percentage Blacks among all elected officials in the South was still less than 5% as recently as 1985 and, relative to their representation in the population, Blacks in the rural South are especially underrepresented. For example, in 1985, local governments were headed by Whites in 61 of 82 majority-Black counties (National Research Council 1989:239). Nevertheless, the "single most important determinant of Black candidates' success is the racial composition of the electoral jurisdictions: the higher the Black percentage of the voting-age population, the higher the probability of the election of a Black to office" (National Research Council 1989:239). Statistical models estimated by Engstrom and McDonald (1981) indicate that under district election formats representation of Blacks on city councils closely follows the representation of Blacks in the district population and even under less favorable "at-large" election formats, the representation of Blacks tracks the racial composition of the community and approaches 25 percent when Black representation in the population reaches 50 percent.

Black underrepresentation among elected officials continues. However, this should not obscure the facts that there have been very dramatic increases in Black representation among elected officials and that these increases are most evident in areas where the relative size of the Black population is large (O'Hare 1986). Thus, voting rights reform fundamentally changed the nature of electoral politics in the South. It enhanced the potential for Blacks to exert greater influence in elections and created the possibility that Blacks could potentially determine leadership of local governmental bodies in areas with majority Black populations. Research on urban areas suggests that greater minority size not only leads to greater Black representation among elected officials but presumably also increases Black representation in political patronage positions and public employment (Karnig and Welch 1980).

The "resource" hypothesis predicts a negative relationship between relative minority size to majority-minority inequality. This is quite different from the "competition" hypothesis which predicts a positive relationship. It is important to remember, however, that the two hypotheses are not mutually exclusive. Greater minority size can elicit a conservative response by the Whites to preserve racial advantage even as it simultaneously enhances the minority's capacity to challenge the racial stratification order in the political sphere. Insight into the question of whether both effects or only one or the other are present may be gained by considering their different implications for the shape of the minority size-inequality relationship.

Blalock (1967) has argued that the competition hypothesis implies that the relationship between relative minority size and inequality should be positive but nonlinear. Specifically, Blalock predicts that inequality should increase with minority size but by smaller amounts at higher levels of minority size.[12]

In contrast, the resource hypothesis implies that the relationship between relative minority size and inequality should be negative and nonlinear. The nonlinear relationship will take the form of a backward facing "S" curve. In this, inequality would be high when percent minority is low (i.e., below 20 percent) and increases in minority size would have only small negative effects on inequality. However, as minority size moves into the range where the minority population begins to approach a numerical majority in the electorate (i.e., in the range of 40-60 percent) the slope of the relationship would become steeply negative as increases in minority size moves the group closer to an effective voting majority and generates greater negative effects on inequality. Then, once an effective voting majority is achieved in the electorate, further increments in minority size become irrelevant and have only small negative effects on inequality.

When the predictions of the "competition" and "resource" hypotheses are considered jointly (on the assumption that both effects are operating), they imply that the overall relationship between minority size and inequality will be a downward opening parabola. At low levels of minority size the resource effect is negligible and inequality increases steadily as minority size increases. Then, perhaps in the range of 20-40 percent minority, the resource effect begins to strengthen and counteract the competition effect. Finally, at some point in the range of 40-60 percent minority the resource effect begins to overwhelm the competition effect and the relationship begins to turn down.

Previous studies have only reported positive, monotonic relationships between relative minority size and inequality. While this provides evidence for the competition effect, it does not rule out the resource effect because the two hypotheses are not so strongly specified as to precisely predict the shape of the final relationship.[13] Also, both hypotheses might be correct, but the competition effect might be stronger than the resource effect such that the ultimate impact of the resource effect on the final relationship is minor.

The availability of longitudinal data provides an additional opportunity to look for evidence of both effects. The key, of course, is that the resource effect should have been weaker (perhaps even nonexistent) before 1960 and stronger after 1960 and Civil and Voting Rights legislation. Assuming the competition effect has been largely constant over time, this would imply that the positive effect of relative minority size on inequality would substantially weaken over time, possibly to the point that it turns negative at higher levels of relative minority size after 1960.

Relative Minority Size and Multiple Minority Groups

The competition hypothesis has been extended to situations with multiple minority groups. In such situations, the majority's sense of threat to its privileged position is thought to be a function of the combined sizes of all minority groups. In one sense, the majority is seen as responding to its own relative size and is more likely to define competition for scarce rewards along group lines when its own relative size is small rather than when any particular minority group is large. Thus, the combined presence of multiple minorities may provoke a conservative response from the majority even when the relative size of each minority group considered separately is small.

This scenario implies that each minority is affected both by its own relative size and by the relative size of other minority groups. An important study by Frisbie and Neidert (1977) has provided evidence consistent with this prediction. They performed a comparative analysis of inequality between Anglos (i.e., non-Hispanic Whites) and Blacks and inequality between Anglos and Hispanics in metropolitan areas from the southwestern United States. Using data for males in 1970 they found that the relative size of the Hispanic population had a positive effect on Anglo-Hispanic inequality and that the relative size of the Black population had a positive effect on Anglo-Black inequality. Significantly, they also found that percent Black had a positive effect on Anglo-Hispanic inequality and that percent Hispanic had a positive effect on Anglo-Black inequality.

A question here is whether the majority will be equally sensitive to the presence of all minority groups and whether its response to a perceived threat will be uniform across all minority groups. Theory is not well developed in this area but one distinct possibility is that the majority might be more sensitive to the presence of some minorities than others; perhaps because of greater cultural differences, higher "visibility," separatist goals of the minority group, prior history of conflict, or yet other factors. Frisbie and Neidert (1977), for example, suggest that Anglos are more tolerant or accepting of Hispanics than Blacks. If so, Anglo perception of minority group threat might be more sensitive to growth in the Black population than growth in the Hispanic population. Assuming the majority response to perceived threat is uniform across minority groups, Anglo-Black and Anglo-Hispanic inequality would both be more strongly influenced by the relative size of the Black population than the Hispanic population. If the majority response is stronger against less tolerated groups, the relative size of the Black population would still have stronger effects than the relative size of the Hispanic population, but both effects would be stronger for Anglo-Black inequality (i.e., the effect of percent Hispanic on Anglo-Hispanic inequality would be weaker than its effect on Anglo-Black inequality).

Previous theoretical and empirical work in this area is limited and deals with multiple *ethnic* minorities. The potential complications of considering multiple minorities defined along gender lines as well as ethnic lines is as yet unexplored. One possible scenario that warrants attention is as follows: (a) majority men perceive women and Blacks in the labor force as a competitive threat and (b) majority men are more tolerant of majority women than of Black men and thus their response to the perceived "global" minority threat is disproportionately channeled against Black men. In this situation, the movement of White women in the labor force would potentially have greater adverse consequences for Blacks than for women. This possibility is also considered in more detail later in this section.

Relative Minority Size: Composition Effects

To this point we have focused on the potential impact relative minority size may have on inequality via its effect on the *severity* of racial stratification. The competition hypothesis linked relative minority size to prejudice and discrimination by the majority; the resource hypothesis linked relative minority size to the minority's capacity to counter majority discrimination. Here we identify another effect of minority size which we term the "minority composition" effect. This effect has important consequences for both minority and majority status levels. Furthermore, in situations where the population includes *multiple, ranked* minority groups, the composition effect has consequences for inequality between groups. This hypothesis can be summarized in two statements. The first is that, all else equal, changes in the relative sizes of groups can affect average status levels for different groups even when rank-order stratification relations among groups are fixed and unchanging. The second is that, all else equal, changes in the relative sizes of groups can affect average status differences between groups even when rank-order stratification relations among groups are fixed.

The implications of relative minority size in the multiple minority situation can be developed from graphical analysis presented in Figures 2.1-2.6. These figures build on Horowitz's (1985) graphical representation of "ranked" and "unranked" ethnic groups and extends the analysis to the multiple minority group situation. We draw on this graphical representation to discuss the quantitative implications of the intergroup relations depicted. The example developed here designates three groups A, B, and C which in Figure 2.1 are depicted as being equal in relative size (i.e., each is one third of the total population).[14] The Y-axis in the charts registers percentile location in the cumulative status distribution for the total population and extends from 0 to 100. The X-axis registers percentage population shares for the three groups beginning first with Group A and then proceeding to Group B and Group C. By definition the population shares begin at 0 and must sum to 100. The graph thus depicts group population shares at each status percentile.

Figure 2.1 depicts a situation where the three groups are "unranked." In this situation, group representation at any status level is equal to the group' representation in the total population which is approximately 33.3 percent. The group means on status are each equal to 50.0, the mean status percentile for the total population (MSP$_T$), and are denoted by points a, b, and c (for MSP$_A$, MSP$_B$, and MSP$_C$, respectively) on the right hand Y-axis.[15] Figure 2.2 depicts a different situation with a majority group and two "unranked" minority groups. Here ranking of minority groups relative to the majority is "complete;" all members of the majority group have higher status than all members of the minority groups. The minority groups are "unranked" relative to each other and are equally subordinate to the majority group. In this situation, the top status percentiles are filled by the majority group whose mean status "a" is 83.3. The two minority groups share the remaining status ranks equally based on their proportionate share of the combined minority populations. Their mean status levels "b" and "c", respectively, are both 33.3.[16]

Majority-minority inequality can be represented by differences in mean status percentiles (DMSP) is given by a–b (for DMSP$_{AB}$) and a–c (for DMSP$_{AC}$) which are both 50.0 (i.e., 50.0 = 83.3–33.3). In

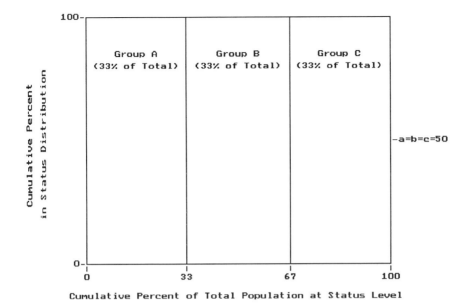

FIGURE 2.1 Unranked Ethnic Groups

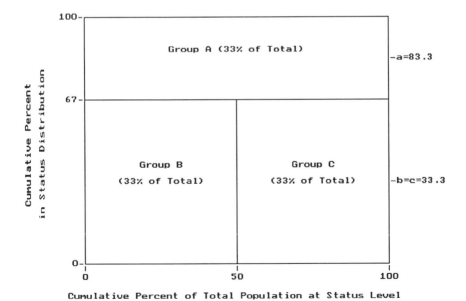

FIGURE 2.2 Unranked Minority Groups

situations like this where majority-minority ranking is complete (i.e., there is no overlap between minority and majority status distributions) and both minority groups are equally subordinate, the majority's status advantage over minorities is at its maximum and changes in the relative size of any group *do not affect* status comparisons among groups. The minority-majority comparisons will always be 50.0 and the minority-minority comparison will always be 0.0, regardless of the relative sizes of the groups.[17]

The situation is more complex when minority groups are "ranked" and have different relations to the majority. This might occur when the majority is less tolerant of one minority group and discriminates more severely against it; for example, when one minority group is a more recent and less acculturated immigrant group. Figure 2.3 depicts a situation of this sort where there is a dominant majority — Group A — and two ranked minority groups — Groups B and C, where Group B is less subordinate to the majority and Group C is more subordinate. Group percentages in the population are as previously stated (i.e., 33.3 percent for each group). Rank subordination is complete in the sense that group status distributions do not overlap as all members of Group A rank above all members of Group B who in turn rank above all members of Group C. Consequently, group status means reflect the midpoints of the percentile ranges occupied by each group and the status means a, b, and c are 83.3, 50.0, and 16.6, respectively. Majority-minority inequality is given by a–b and a–c which are 33.3 and 66.7, respectively, and reveal less inequality between the majority and the more tolerated minority than between the majority and the less tolerated minority.

One consequence of moving to a multiple minority situation is that the logical range of majority-minority status inequality is expanded. As mentioned above, the maximum possible difference between groups on mean status percentiles is 50 in the two group situation. In the multiple, ranked minority situation the difference may exceed 50. For example, in Figure 2.3 the difference between the mean status percentiles for Groups A and B is 66.7. In fact, the logically possible maximum value for inequality can approach 100 under extreme circumstances.[18]

Another consequence of moving to a multiple minority situation is that changes in relative group size now affects inequality comparisons among groups. The effects of changes in group size are illustrated by comparing Figures 2.4, 2.5, and 2.6 to Figure 2.3. In Figure 2.3 each group comprises one third of the total population. Figure 2.4 depicts the changes that result when Group C increases in size until it represents 50 percent of the total population while the other two

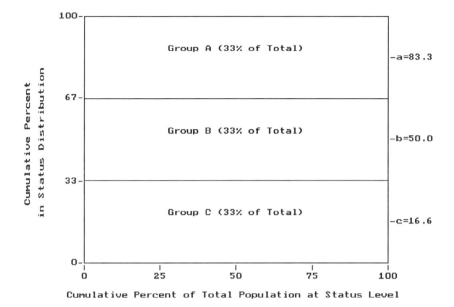

FIGURE 2.3 Ranked Minority Groups

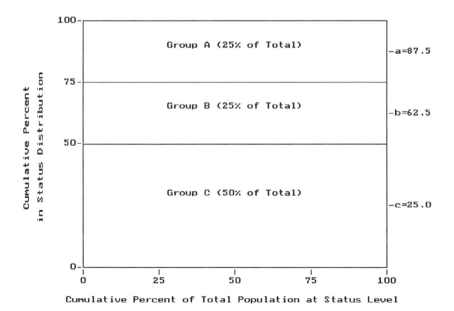

FIGURE 2.4 Increase in Relative Size of Group C

groups do not increase in size and thus fall to 25 percent of the population. Figure 2.5 depicts the changes that occur when Group B increases and Figure 2.6 depicts the changes that occur when Group A increases.

These different scenarios of demographic change have surprisingly different implications for group status and intergroup inequality. For example, when compared with initial conditions depicted in Figure 2.3, the increase in the size of the more subordinate minority (Group C) depicted in Figure 2.4 leads to *increases* in the mean status level for all three groups. Group A's mean status increases from 83.3 to 87.5; Group B's mean status increases from 50.0 to 62.5; and Group C's mean status increases from 16.6 to 25.0. Furthermore, the resulting demographic change *reduces* inequality between the majority group and the minority groups and it *increases* inequality between the two minority groups. The mean status difference between Groups A and B (i.e., a–b) falls 8.3 points from 33.0 to 25.0 and the difference between Groups A and C (i.e., a–c) falls 4.2 points from 66.7 to 62.5. In contrast, the mean status difference between Groups B and C (i.e., b–c) rises 4.1 points from 33.4 to 37.5.

When the less subordinate minority (Group B) increases in size as depicted in Figure 2.5, the consequences are substantially different from those just discussed. Compared to the initial conditions depicted in Figure 2.3, the mean status for Group A *increases* from 83.3 to 87.5 while the mean status for Group C *decreases* from 16.6 to 12.5. In this case, there is no effect on the mean status for Group B. But note that this is not a necessary result.[19]

The consequences for intergroup inequality also are quite different; in this situation *all* intergroup comparisons become more *unequal*. The increase in the relative size of Group B causes the mean status difference between Groups A and B (i.e., a–b) to *increase* by 4.2 points from 33.3 to 37.5. It causes the mean status difference between Groups A and C (i.e., a–c) to *increase* 8.3 points from 66.7 to 75.0. And it also causes the mean status difference between Groups B and C (i.e., b–c) to *increase* by 4.2 points from 33.4 to 37.5.

Finally, the scenario depicted in Figure 2.6 where the majority (Group A) increases in relative size leads to yet a different pattern of consequences relative to the initial conditions given in Figure 2.3. Here the mean status levels for all three groups *decline*. The mean status for Group A falls 8.3 points from 83.3 to 75.0; the mean status for Group B falls 12.5 points from 50.0 to 37.5; and the mean status for Group C falls 4.2 points from 16.7 to 12.5. At the same time, some intergroup comparisons become more equal while others become less equal. The increase in the relative size of Group A causes the mean

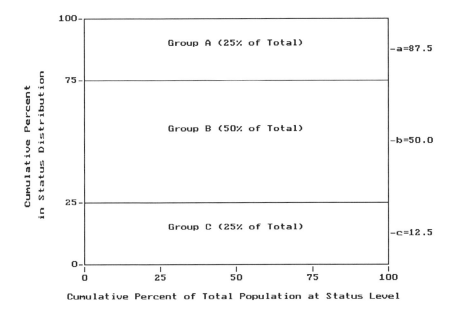

FIGURE 2.5 Increase in Relative Size of Group B

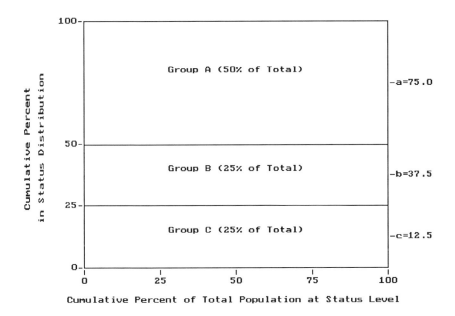

FIGURE 2.6 Increase in Relative Size of Group A

status difference between Groups A and B (i.e., a–b) to *increase* by 4.2 points from 33.3 to 37.5. It causes the mean status difference between Groups A and C (i.e., a–c) to *decrease* by 4.2 points from 66.7 to 62.5. And it causes the mean status difference between Groups B and C (i.e., b–c) to *decrease* by 8.3 points from 33.4 to 25.0.

In general, group differences in mean status percentiles are usually (but not always) subject to change when the relative sizes of the different groups change. To this point we have assessed the impact of changes in ethnic composition based on graphical analysis and intuitive calculations. These work well enough in the examples presented here because the rank-order stratification depicted in Figures 2.3-2.6 represent the simple extremes (i.e., no overlap and complete rank-order inequality). However, the impact of changes in group size on group status means and intergroup differences in mean status are more complex and difficult to assess when rank-order stratification relations between groups are not so simple (i.e., when the group status distributions overlap). In this situation, relations are not so easily depicted graphically and intuitive calculations based on graphical analysis are no longer convenient.

Fortunately, we have discovered simple analytic expressions which provide a basis for precisely determining the impact of changes in relative group size on group means on status percentiles. The relevant results are summarized in Equations 2.1-2.3.

$$\mathrm{MSP_A} = 50 + (\,P_B\,\mathrm{ND_{AB}} + P_C\,\mathrm{ND_{AC}}\,)\,/\,2, \qquad\qquad [2.1]$$

$$\mathrm{MSP_B} = 50 + (\,P_A\,\mathrm{ND_{BA}} + P_C\,\mathrm{ND_{BC}}\,)\,/\,2,\ \mathrm{and} \qquad [2.2]$$

$$\mathrm{MSP_C} = 50 + (\,P_A\,\mathrm{ND_{CA}} + P_B\,\mathrm{ND_{CB}}\,)\,/\,2, \qquad\qquad [2.3]$$

where MSP denotes a group's mean status percentile, ND is Lieberson's (1975) index of net difference — a measure of rank-order inequality between two groups (the measure and its computing formula are discussed at length in Appendix A), and P indicates each group's proportionate representation in the total population.[20]

The number 50, which appears in all three equations, represents the mean status percentile that a group will have under conditions where all groups are represented at all status levels according to their population proportion (i.e., under conditions of exact equality in group distributions as depicted earlier in Figure 2.1). Thus, these equations show that a group's mean status percentile will deviate from 50 based on its rank-order stratification relations with other groups (as represented by the net difference index) and the relative sizes of the different groups (as represented by proportion of population).

We find Lieberson's index of net difference to be an attractive measure for representing rank-order stratification relations among groups. Technically, it is a nonparametric measure of group difference which is mathematically tractable. Conceptually, it does a good job of capturing the kind of rank-order patterns predicted by queuing perspectives on ethnic stratification (Lieberson 1980; Thurow 1969). Ethnic queuing perspectives argue that ethnic stratification systems function to disproportionately reserve the top positions in the status hierarchy for the dominant group. ND fits this notion nicely because it summarizes comparisons between two groups' distributions on an ordered characteristic and registers the extent to which members of one group systematically rank above members of another group when members of the two groups are randomly paired. A maximum value of 100 indicates strict or complete rank-order stratification wherein all members of one group rank above all members of the second group; a value of -100 indicates the reverse. A value of 0 indicates no rank order-stratification in the sense that members of one group are equally likely to be ranked higher or lower than members of the other group. Values between these extremes indicate partial rank-order stratification. The reason the situations depicted in Figures 2.1-2.6 can be readily analyzed using graphical methods and intuitive calculations is that the rank-order stratification relations between groups in these examples are assumed to be either strict and complete rather than partial (i.e., the ND scores are either -100 or 100) or absent altogether (i.e., ND scores of 0).

The relationships specified in Equations 2.1-2.3 provide a simple basis for determining how changes in the relative sizes of each group will affect each group's mean status percentile. Once the rank-order stratification relations between groups summarized by ND are known (either through empirical analysis or by assuming particular values for a "what if" analysis), it is a simple matter to use these equations to assess the consequences that changes in relative group size will have for group means on status percentiles. All that is needed is to take the initial group proportions and compute the result and then take the new group proportions and compute the new result. Alternatively, difference terms for P_A, P_B, and P_C can be "plugged" into Equations 2.4-2.6 to obtain the result directly. (The previously discussed examples developed from Figures 2.1-2.6 can be confirmed in this way.)

Obviously, if the impact of changes in relative group size on group means for status percentiles can be assessed precisely, only a little more work is needed to assess the similar impact on group differences in mean status percentiles (DMSP). The relevant analytic results are presented in Equations 2.4-2.6 which were developed by substituting the right-hand sides of Equations 2.1-2.3 for the terms MSP_A, MSP_B, and MSP_C (as relevant) and then reorganizing and simplifying terms.[21]

$$DMSP_{AB} = MSP_A - MSP_B$$

$$= \{ (P_A + P_B) \, ND_{AB} + P_C \, (ND_{AC} - ND_{BC}) \} / 2 \qquad [2.4]$$

$$DMSP_{AC} = MSP_A - MSP_C$$

$$= \{ (P_A + P_C) \, ND_{AC} + P_B \, (ND_{AB} + ND_{BC}) \} / 2 \qquad [2.5]$$

$$DMSP_{BC} = MSP_B - MSP_C$$

$$= \{ (P_B + P_C) \, ND_{BC} + P_A \, (ND_{AC} + ND_{AB}) \} / 2 \qquad [2.6]$$

As before, once the rank-order stratification relations between groups (summarized by ND) are known, it is a simple matter to use these equations to assess the consequences that changes in relative group size will have for group differences in mean status percentiles. All that is needed to do this is to take the initial group proportions and compute the result and then take the new group proportions and compute the new result. Alternatively, difference terms for P_A, P_B, and P_C can be "plugged" into Equations 2.4-2.6 to obtain the result more directly. (Again, the results for the previously discussed examples developed from Figures 2.1-2.6 can be confirmed using these equations.)

Unfortunately, the consequences that follow when the relative sizes of different groups change do not lend themselves to simple summarization. The reason for this is that the magnitude and even the direction of the impact of these changes on a particular group mean status percentile or a particular group difference in these means depends on the initial sizes of the groups and the initial pattern of the pairwise rank-order stratification relations between the groups (i.e., the initial ND scores). This said, at least two important generalizations can be established with these equations.

The first is that *changes in relative group size may affect mean status levels for different groups even when rank-order stratification relations among groups are fixed and unchanging.* This is directly clear from Equations 2.1-2.3 so long as at least one of the ND terms in each equation is not 0 (in which case the system reduces to a two rather than three group situation in terms of ethnic stratification).

Thus, this generalization applies in situations with either ranked or unranked minority groups.

The second is that *changes in relative group size may affect mean status differences between groups even when rank-order stratification relations among groups are fixed and unchanging.* Again, this is directly clear from Equations 2.4-2.6. However, this is true *only* in the case of multiple, ranked minority groups (i.e., only in cases where all three ND terms in each equation are not 0) . Stated another way, if there is only one minority group, or if there are multiple minority groups but they are not ranked, changes in relative group size do not affect group differences in mean status.

Generally speaking, the impact of changes in relative group size on mean status differences between groups is greater when: (a) the rank-order stratification relations between groups are severe (i.e., the ND scores for the pairwise group comparisons are closer to 100 or – 100 than to 0), and (b) the changes in relative group sizes are large. An example may help illustrate the point.

Consider an ethnically stratified system which includes a dominant group and several minority groups. If all minority groups are treated the same relative to the majority (i.e., the majority discriminates against non-majority groups in a uniform fashion), changes in the relative sizes of the different groups do not affect group differences in mean status. The reason for this is that, as a practical matter, the separate minority groups can be considered as a single minority population. This renders relative group size irrelevant because majority-minority differences in mean status percentile are unaffected by changes in relative group size in the two-group situation. This can be seen from the following equations which summarize the relevant relations for the *two*-group situation only.[22]

$$MSP_A \quad = 50 + P_B ND_{AB} / 2, \qquad\qquad [2.7]$$

$$MSP_B \quad = 50 + P_A ND_{BA} / 2, \text{ or}$$

$$\qquad\qquad = 50 - P_A ND_{AB} / 2, \qquad\qquad [2.8]$$

$$DMSP_{AB} \quad = MSP_A - MSP_B$$

$$\qquad\qquad = 1/2\ ND_{AB} \qquad\qquad [2.9]$$

Now assume instead that the minority groups are immigrant groups that immigrated at different times and that the majority discriminates more severely against groups that arrived most recently (e.g., because they are less acculturated), a situation of multiple ranked minority groups will hold. In this situation, the relative sizes of the different groups will have consequences for group differences in mean status percentiles.

For example, growth in the relative size of the most recent immigrant group will tend to reduce the mean status difference between the majority group and earlier immigrant groups. This demographic effect generates a "ladder of immigrants" pattern of ethnic mobility. In this pattern, new immigrant groups who are discriminated against most severely enter at the bottom of the ethnic hierarchy (i.e., they assume the position of Group C in Figure 2.3). As their relative numbers increase, the status positions for all other groups increase and inequality between the other groups is reduced (as seen in the previously discussed comparison of Figures 2.3 and 2.4).[23] In turn, the recently arrived immigrant group may subsequently experience upward mobility when they are "replaced" at the bottom of the ethnic hierarchy by yet newer immigrant groups. In many ways this scenario is consistent with the mobility experiences of successive waves of European immigrant groups.

A different situation arises in situations where minority groups are ranked and the "less-subordinate" groups expand in size. This is the situation considered in the earlier discussion of Figures 2.3 and 2.5 which may be considered to be parallel the situation, common in many contemporary urban areas, where Asians, Hispanics, and Blacks are all present in significant numbers and the Asian and Hispanic populations are growing faster than other groups. To establish the parallel with the analytic example discussed earlier, Asians, Hispanics, and Blacks must be considered ranked minority groups with Blacks being the "more-subordinate" minority group and Asians and Hispanics being "less-subordinate" groups. This characterization is supported by Kirschenman and Neckerman's (1991) study of employer attitudes which reported employers prefer Anglo (i.e., Non-Hispanic White) and Asian applicants over Hispanic applicants and Hispanic applicants over Black applicants. It is also supported by Frisbie and Neidert's (1977) study of Anglo, Black, and Hispanic status inequality in southwestern metropolitan areas and Tienda and Lii's (1986) study of status inequality between Anglos, Asians, Hispanics, and Blacks.

In this case, growth in the relative size of either the Asian or Hispanic populations (or both populations) would tend to *increase* status differences between Anglos and Blacks whereas growth in the Black population would tend to *reduce* status differences between Anglos and Hispanics and Anglos and Asians.[24] The resulting changes would be greatest when the differences in minority disadvantage are large (i.e., when Blacks are subject to significantly more rank-order stratification relative to Anglos than are Asians and Hispanics) and when the changes in group size are large.[25]

This last example has only limited practical implications for our empirical analysis since we focus on nonmetropolitan areas of the South where ethnic relations are Black-White. However, a different ranked-minority group scenario involving White men, Black men, and women may be relevant. If White women and Black women represent minority groups that are subject to discrimination but not necessarily to the degree experienced by Black men, then the "composition" hypothesis predicts that the increasing representation of women in the labor force may have contributed to increased status differences between White men and Black men. Again, this expectation follows from our previous discussion of the comparison of Figures 2.3 and 2.5 which show that when a "less-subordinate" minority group increases in relative size it elevates the status of the majority group, lowers the status of the "more-subordinate" minority group, and increases the status difference between the majority group and the "more-subordinate" group.[26]

This possibility will be considered in greater detail below. For the moment, we note that the potential for a composition effect might be large because the proportionate representation of women in the labor force has increased dramatically over time. The one thing mitigating against a large composition effect is that rank-order comparisons between White men and women (especially White women) have historically been smaller than rank-order comparisons between women and Black-men and the maximum composition effect is realized when these are both large.

Before leaving this discussion of "composition" effects we take a moment to stress that predictions about composition effects on group status means and group differences in status means computed from Equations 2.1-2.6 assume that rank-order stratification relations among groups are fixed and unchanging. This obviously should not be taken for granted in empirical settings since rank-order stratification relations between groups may be affected by changes in relative group size. Indeed, "competition" or "resource" effects associated with changes in relative minority size might lead to changes in the rank-order stratification relations among groups. If so, "composition" effects resulting from changes in relative minority size would be different from those implied by Equations 2.1-2.6; that is, they might be "amplified" or "dampened" depending on how rank-order stratification relations among groups are affected.

42

The Overflow or Spillover Hypothesis

The "overflow" hypothesis argues that the minority group's average status tends to increase as its relative size increases. This is based on the assumption that minorities first fill the bottom ranks of the occupational hierarchy and then "overflow" or "spillover" into higher ranks (Spilerman and Miller 1976).[27] Predictions of minority status gains from overflow are consistent with the ideas just discussed; indeed they are a special case of the "composition" effects we outlined above. The previous analysis has just established that overflow effects may be predicted in situations involving a single majority and a single minority and in situations involving multiple, unranked minority groups (since this reduces to a single-minority situation when considered in terms of ethnic stratification). Specifically, it can be predicted that an increase in the minority group's relative size raises the minority's average status. Of course, it also raises the majority's average status by an equal amount, thus status differences between the majority and minority do not diminish. Nevertheless, the minority group does attain a higher average status level.

When the situation involves multiple, ranked minority groups, the possibilities for overflow effects are more complicated and difficult to summarize. One thing can be said; increases in the minority group's relative size may logically have positive, neutral, or negative effects on the minority group's average status level. The potential impact of a given change in relative minority size can be computed under different scenarios by working with Equations 2.1, 2.2, and 2.3 provided earlier. Detailed analysis (not shown here) indicates that the effect of increases in relative minority size on average minority status depends on the initial relative sizes of the different groups and the initial rank-order inequality patterns among the groups.

If the group in question is a "more-subordinate" minority (i.e., it is ranked below the majority group and below other minority groups), an increase in the group's relative size always increases its average status and overflow effects are thus positive.[28]

On the other hand, if the group in question is a "less subordinate" minority (i.e., if it ranks below the majority group but above other minority groups), overflow effects on mean status may be positive, negative, or neutral. If groups ranking above the minority in question are larger than groups ranking below it, increasing relative size for the minority tends to raise its mean status. If the reverse is true, increasing relative size tends to lower the minority's mean status. If groups ranking above and below the group in question are approximately equal in size, changes in the minority's relative size tend to have little effect on the group's mean status. These generalizations hold only when the group in question has an advantage over the lower ranked minority that is approximately similar to the group's disadvantage relative to the majority. As these circumstances vary, overflow effects may also vary.

Equations 2.1-2.6 can be used to directly assess these effects. But overflow effects in the multiple, ranked minority situation are complicated and the various possible effects cannot be easily summarized other than to note that the impact of a change in the relative size of the minority group will vary depending on the initial group composition and rank-order stratification relations (i.e., the initial levels of P_A, P_B, P_C, ND_{AB}, ND_{AC}, and ND_{BC}).

It is also important to realize that our predictions about possible overflow effects (and composition effects generally) are developed in the context of an analytic model and that certain conditions must be met before our predictions should be expected to hold in empirical systems. One of these conditions is that the local occupational structure is substantially independent of the ethnic mix in the local population. This justifies the assumption that workers compete for positions in an occupational structure rather than the occupational structure being tailored to provide jobs to workers. Thus, for example, we assume that local demand for professionals, clerical workers, laborers, etc. is not determined by the ethnic mix but rather emerges in response to changes in the local economy such as when a new steel mill opens up or a bank closes.

Another condition which needs to hold for our predictions regarding overflow effects to be plausible is that the racial stratification system functions primarily to reserve the best available jobs for the majority rather than to keep minorities out of specific occupational categories (as would be the case in an occupational caste system). A final condition which needs to hold is that the demand for labor is sufficiently strong that all ethnic groups are drawn into the local economy. If these conditions are not approximated, our predictions about overflow effects may not be relevant.

Finally, it is important to remember that, as with composition effects generally, the overflow hypothesis assumes that rank-order stratification between majority and minority remains constant as relative minority size changes. This assumption may not be appropriate. Previous research investigating the "competition" hypothesis suggests that increasing minority size is instead likely to lead to increased rank-order stratification between majority and minority (i.e., increased discrimination against minorities). As noted earlier, this effect increases majority-minority *inequality* by lowering minority status and increasing majority status. Thus, the negative competition effect on minority status could possibly counter a positive composition effect on minority *status*. That is, if rank-order stratification increases when relative minority size increases, the expected increase in mean minority status under the overflow effect may be muted or even reversed altogether. Thus, while analytic models support the predictions of the overflow hypothesis under certain conditions, the potential positive effect of "overflow" on minority status might be overwhelmed in an empirical setting by the increased discrimination resulting from the competition effect.

Absolute Minority Size and a Semi-Separate Minority Economy

This hypothesis holds that a large minority population provides the possibilities for the emergence of separate or semi-separate Black professional and entrepreneurial classes serving a primarily Black clientele and potentially providing more favorable employment opportunities for Black workers. This hypothesis is similar in many ways to "enclave economy" theory (e.g., Light 1972; Portes and Manning 1986; Portes and Jensen 1989; Wilson and Martin 1982) although many enclave economy hypotheses are developed against a presumed backdrop of voluntary immigration and barriers associated with acculturation as well as discrimination and are thus less directly applied to the experience of Blacks in America.

There are at least two components to notions connecting minority size to the development of a semi-separate Black economy. One is the relationship between minority size and the capacity of the minority population to sustain minority-owned businesses and professional services. The other is the relationship between minority size and the strength of minority solidarity which directs minority consumers, workers, entrepreneurs, and professionals to satisfy their needs within the minority sub-economy rather than the broader economy.

Given discrimination by majority consumers, a minority business and professional class cannot emerge until there is a sufficiently large minority consumer base to sustain them. This implies a positive effect of *absolute* minority size on minority status as, all else equal, larger minority populations can sustain a larger number of higher status specialized entrepreneurs and professionals. It also implies a negative effect of absolute minority size on majority-minority inequality. Obviously, this results in part because size permits a high-status segment to emerge in the minority population. In addition, there may be a negative effect on majority status levels as minority consumers would then trade less frequently with majority business owners and professionals.

Breton (1964) has argued that greater absolute minority size also may facilitate the emergence and/or persistence of a distinctive minority subculture with more complete institutional structures and stronger internal solidarity. This can potentially contribute to the growth of minority businesses and professional services since a distinctive minority subculture creates demand for services not provided in the majority economy and greater solidarity within the minority community increases the likelihood that its members will trade within the minority subeconomy for noneconomic reasons. These expectations imply that *absolute* minority size should have a positive effect on minority status and a negative effect on minority-majority inequality.

Anticipating our specification of empirical models reported below, we note that it is not appropriate to include absolute minority size in regression models which include both relative minority size (i.e., percent minority) and *total* population size since these two variables perfectly determine the absolute size of the minority population. However, while absolute minority size cannot be directly included, its effects will be bound up in the effects of total population size (when relative size is controlled). Thus, theory of a semi-separate minority economy predicts that total population size should have positive effects on minority status and negative effects on majority-minority inequality. As we will see momentarily, other theoretical perspectives also suggest these predictions.

Relative Minority Size: White Gains

The "White gains" hypothesis traces to the work of Dollard (1937) and more recently Glenn (1963; 1964; 1966). The argument is easily summarized; Whites derive social, economic, and political advantages from the subordination of Blacks and other minority groups and thus material incentives are central to the creation, maintenance, and defense of racial stratification, discrimination, and inequality. Unlike Marxist and other class-based perspectives (Bonacich 1980; Cox 1948; Reich 1981) which hold that White elites are the primary beneficiaries of discrimination, the White gains perspective argues that nontrivial gains also accrue to the White working and middle classes and that Whites' material interest in discrimination are thus broad based.

The White gains perspective provides a ready explanation for why Whites would resist efforts to end discrimination and promote equality; such efforts will have significant negative consequences for Whites including reduced political power, reduced access to education, diminished occupational attainments, and lowered income. The basis for this expectation is simple; redistribution of zero-sum goods to bring about equality necessarily entails status losses for advantaged groups.

The "composition" hypothesis introduced earlier fits nicely with the White gains perspective and the combination of the two ideas provides a powerful basis for predicting that Whites' stake in and defense of racial stratification (resistance to equality-promoting efforts) is likely to be greater in areas where the relative size of the Black population is large. In a nutshell, the composition hypothesis predicts that the negative impact of integration (i.e., successful equality-promoting efforts) on White status will be most severe in areas where the relative size of the Black population is large.

The structural underpinnings of this relationship can be summarized in the following equations which hold in the simplified two-group situation where Whites and Blacks are the only groups.[29]

$$MSP_T \quad = 50$$

$$= P_W MSP_W + P_B MSP_B \qquad [2.10]$$

$$DMSP_{WB} \quad = MSP_W - MSP_B \qquad [2.11]$$

$$MSP_W \quad = MSP_T + P_B DMSP_{WB} \qquad [2.12]$$

$$MSP_B \quad = MSP_T - P_W DMSP_{WB} \qquad [2.13]$$

Equation 2.12 shows that the positive deviation of Whites' mean status from the average for the overall population is a product of the relative size of the minority population and the magnitude of the status difference between the two groups.[30] Thus, for any given level of status inequality, White gains increase in direct proportion to the relative size of the minority population, and, for any given level of minority presence, White gains increase in direct proportion to the magnitude of the majority-minority status difference.

This means that integration (i.e., successful equality-promoting efforts) will *reduce* Whites' average status by the amount $P_B DMSP_{WB}$ and, for any given level of status advantage, the expected status losses for Whites will be greatest in areas where the relative presence of the minority population is large. This suggests that the documented positive relationship between relative minority size and White reticence to embrace various aspects of racial integration (Fossett and Kiecolt 1989) can readily be interpreted in terms of "realistic" material conflict (Fossett and Kiecolt 1989; Glaser 1994).

Women as a Competing Minority Group

As noted earlier, the ethnic stratification system in southern, nonmetropolitan areas is typically seen as a single-minority situation organized around the Black-White dichotomy. An important question, however, is whether minority groups defined along gender lines are analytically interchangeable with minority groups defined along racial and ethnic lines. If this is even partially the case, then inequality between Black and White men in the South may be affected by the increasing representation of women in the labor force via "competition" effects and/or "composition" effects.

The possibility of "composition" effects was mentioned earlier and rests on the assumption that women are situated in an intermediate position between White men and Black men in majority-minority stratification relations. Given this, an increase in the relative number of women would increase the mean status difference between White men and Black men with the magnitude of the effect depending on the size of the increase in the relative number of women and on the severity of the rank-order stratification relations among the three groups. Growth in the representation of women in the labor force has been considerable and could sustain a large composition effect. However, rank-order inequality between White men and White women on occupational status is modest compared to either rank-order inequality between White men and Black men or inequality between White women and Black men. This muted contrast limits the potential composition effect.

We have argued that women (especially White women) rank after White men and ahead of Black men in intergroup stratification relations. Some might argue that the ranking of the two minorities should be reversed on grounds that sexism is more pervasive and virulent than racism. If this were true, Black men would rank intermediate between White men and women in the status hierarchy and increasing representation of women in the labor force would *reduce* mean status differences between White men and Black men.[31]

The possibility that Black men might rank ahead of women in labor market demand queues is not wholly implausible. The feminist movement has not been able to achieve judicial and legal successes comparable to those accomplished by the Civil Rights movement (Marshall 1986) and legislation continues to be used to segregate occupations along gender lines while legislation segregating workers by race has long been overturned (Roos and Reskin 1984). Additionally, research shows that industrial unions have been slow to accord women protection from employer discrimination comparable to that they have provided Black men (Baron and Bielby 1984; Leonard 1985).

Still, the basis for assuming White women rank ahead of Black men is stronger.[32] One reason for this conclusion is that we assume intragroup racial solidarity tends to override solidarity based on gender. Given this, White women are more likely to be afforded access to positions of authority and decision making in order to consolidate power and resources within the ethnic group. Occupational comparisons between White men, White women, and Black men are consistent with this assumption; rank-order status inequality between White men and White women is small compared to rank-order inequality between White men and Black men and rank-order inequality between White women and Black men.

Another reason justifying the assumption that racism tends to be more salient than sexism is that, while women and Black men both pose a competitive threat to the advantaged position of White men, Black men pose the greater threat because women's material gains are shared within the ethnic group via familial relationships and thus gains accruing to White women indirectly benefit White men while gains accruing to Blacks do not.

Szymanski (1977) was among the first to argue that movement of women into the labor force is likely to have adverse effects on the status of Black men. The basis for his argument was that women were at least partially functional substitutes for Black men in the labor force and thus entry of women into the labor force provides employers an alternative to Black men for hiring in especially service, sales, and clerical jobs. Similar reasoning underlies the composition hypothesis outlined earlier in this chapter.

Villemez (1977) argued against Szymanski's hypothesis on grounds that women and Black men do not work in or compete for the same jobs and therefore they are not functional substitutes. If correct, this position undercuts the "composition" hypothesis because it assumes the key feature of the gender and race stratification systems is that it reserves high status occupations for the majority. This implies that the gender and race composition of occupations is not fixed in the long run and may change depending on the changing race and gender composition of the labor force and the changing status of the occupation.

We discount Villemez's objection to possible "composition" effects because occupation distributions for White men, women, and Black men overlap considerably even though occupational segregation between the groups is high. In and of itself, this establishes the plausibility of the composition hypothesis. The possible response that the

measured overlap is simply a function of measurement error in occupational categories (i.e., that more refined categories would show only
trivial overlap) can be countered in two ways. First, no study shows
anything approaching zero overlap between occupation distributions
between women and Black men no matter how detailed the occupational categories. Second, the sex composition of occupations varies
over time and cross-sectionally across areas (Reskin and Roos 1990).
This indicates that women are *potential* functional substitutes even
though they may be highly segregated at any given time or place.
Accordingly, composition effects associated with the increasing representation of women in the labor force are plausible.

Growth in women's representation in the labor force also may
affect inequality through a "competition" effect. That is, Frisbie and
Neidert's (1977) application of the competition hypothesis to the
situation with multiple ethnic minorities could be adapted to the
situation with multiple minorities defined by gender and ethnicity.
In this scenario, increasing representation of women in the labor force
should increase White men's perception of status threat. This in turn
should increase their prejudice and discrimination either against *all*
minority groups or against selected minority groups and ultimately
increase majority-minority inequality.

The key assumption in adapting the competition hypothesis to
this situation is that majority men view the entry of women into the
labor force as potentially threatening. Such an assumption is justified because (a) occupational distributions for White men and women
(especially White women) overlap indicating direct competition,
(b) even if occupational overlap is limited, men are likely to view
women as *potential* competitors so long as women desire entry into
traditionally male-dominated occupations, and (c) women's educational attainments generally equal (or even exceed) those of men's.
Thus, the movement of women into the labor force represents the
growth of a competing minority that is highly skilled as well as potentially numerous.

Three issues are then central to the competition hypothesis' prediction that the entry of women into the labor force affects inequality
between White men and Black men. Does perceived competition from
women promote prejudice and discrimination by White men? If so, is
the effect potentially important? If so, is the resulting prejudice and
discrimination structured narrowly along gender lines or does it generalize to all minority groups?

The question of whether White men's perception of a status
threat from women is associated with greater gender prejudice by
White men has yet to be investigated. However, this seems likely

since previous research has shown Whites' perception of a status threat from ethnic minorities to be associated with prejudice by Whites (Fossett and Kiecolt 1989).

Whether the consequences of this effect for prejudice and discrimination are likely to be important is a function of two things — the magnitude of the perceived status threat and the strength of White men's conservative response. The magnitude of the perceived status threat is presumably related to the size of the increase in women's representation in the labor force and thus could be considerable. The response by White men to a competitive threat from women might not be as strong as their response to a competitive threat from Black men, primarily because the benefits of status gains by women, as noted above, are more likely to benefit White men indirectly (via marital, familial, and kin relationships).

Frisbie and Neidert's (1977) study of relative minority size and majority-minority inequality in the multi-ethnic Southwest has shown that majority response to relative minority size is generalized rather specific to each minority group. That is, Blacks are affected by the relative size of the Hispanic population as well as their own and vice versa. Tienda and Lii's (1987) analysis of the effects of Asian, Hispanic, and Black relative size also presents evidence consistent with the idea that majority response to minority size is general rather than group-specific. In view of this, it is reasonable to assume that White men would respond to competition from women in a general way rather than strictly along gender lines and thus that Black men would likely be adversely affected by the growing presence of women in the labor force.

Manufacturing Concentration

A number of studies have reported a negative association between the level of manufacturing employment and racial inequality (e.g. Blalock 1956; 1957; Elgie 1980; Frisbie and Neidert 1977; Jiobu and Marshall 1971; Spilerman and Miller 1976; Turner 1951). Several arguments have been advanced for this finding. First, manufacturing industries are capital intensive, a fact which makes discrimination potentially costly since it returns on capital investments will be reduced when workers are not assigned to manufacturing jobs based on skills and ability (Franklin 1968). Conventional models posit that labor and capital investments interact in contributing to productivity and profit (i.e., the production function is multiplicative). This implies that unqualified workers are especially costly in manufacturing enterprises. The desire to maximize profits thus presumably encourages employers and managers to forego discriminatory practices in favor of maintaining a qualified work force (Franklin 1968:371).

Second, manufacturing industries typically produce goods for export to distant rather than local markets. Consumers of the finished product have little or no association with the workers producing the product so consumer prejudice is less likely to be an important consideration in the hiring, retention, and promotion of workers in manufacturing industries. This is a distinct contrast to business, professional, and personal services and sales where consumer prejudice may exert powerful effects on hiring. Similarly, compared to other industries, manufacturing involves less intimate interaction among workers and thus the impact of worker prejudice on hiring and retention of workers is blunted.

Third, occupational structures within manufacturing industries tend to be organized into well defined mobility channels where hiring and promotion decisions are likely to be rationalized to a greater degree than in other industries where the prevalence of nepotism and other forms of particularism is pronounced (Spilerman and Miller 1976; Piore 1975). This results in part because manufacturing industries tend to be more heavily unionized and unions structure relations between workers and employers promoting accountability in employment and promotion decisions. Racial inequities in union membership and in efforts on behalf of members are not unknown (Beck 1980; Hill 1974), but the incorporation of minorities is likely to evolve because the effectiveness of unions partly depends on their success in minimizing racial divisions among workers in order to maintain overall solidarity in bargaining with owners and managers. Accordingly, previous research has shown that race discrimination tends to be less extensive in unionized plants (Ashenfelter 1972; 1973; Leonard 1985).

Relatively few studies have examined the effect of manufacturing on racial inequality in southern nonmetropolitan areas. However, the broader literature focusing on the impact of industrialization in nonmetropolitan areas suggests that the impact of new manufacturing industries is not always salutary and notes that, even when welcome effects are observed, they may come at a high price to the community (e.g., subsidies and tax breaks) and often are short lived (Colclough 1988; Falk and Lyson 1988; 1989; Summers 1986; Summers et al 1976; Tickamyer and Duncan 1990). They note that nonmetropolitan areas of the South tend to receive mature industries which are seeking to minimize labor costs by relocating to low-wage, *nonunionized* areas. To the extent that such relocations create higher skilled, better paying jobs in the destination communities, these positions often are filled with "imported" workers from outside the community who have critical skills and training needed to qualify for the positions. Since the "new" workers are likely to be White, the impact can actually *increase* racial inequality. Consistent with this scenario, Colclough (1989) has reported that, greater industrialization was associated with increased racial inequality in income in Georgia.

Conceivably, this short-run effect might later give way to long-term "leveling" effects. Perhaps, over time workers in skilled positions might increasingly be drawn from the pool of indigenous workers who initially enter the new industry in unskilled positions, but then gain access to on-the-job training and within-firm promotion ladders. Unfortunately, plants which relocate in rural areas to take advantage of low cost labor often move on after a relatively short stay to new locations outside the United States where wages are even cheaper. Thus, long-term effects of industrialization, if they exist, may never have the chance to take hold. Furthermore, Blumer (1965; 1990) has argued that assumptions that industrialization will disrupt and undermine traditional ascriptive relations are questionable and that its intrinsic effects may in fact be *neutral*. Thus, in his view "[i]ndustrialization provides the occasion and sets the stage for changes in the traditional order; it does not determine or explain what takes place in that traditional order" (Blumer 1990:102).

White-Collar Employment

Occupational structure may affect racial inequality by affecting labor demand since occupations vary in their rewards, skill requirements, their functions, and their social relations. Even relatively crude traditional distinctions between white collar, blue collar, and farm occupations may have implications for inequality. Compared to unskilled manual occupations in the farm and blue-collar categories, white-collar jobs have traditionally been higher status with better working conditions, higher wages and benefits, and better job security. Competition for these jobs is intense and several factors work against minority men in this competition.

One is that skill requirements for white-collar jobs are higher and this favors Whites who have greater access to formal schooling and greater access to human capital in informal settings (e.g., socialization with the family) and on the job. Another aspect of skill requirements is that women (especially White women) are strong competitors for white-collar occupations by virtue of their high levels of education. By comparison, minority men are more likely to compete successfully against women for unskilled manual occupations where physical strength, stamina, and tolerance of dirty and hazardous working environments are often requirements. Thus, a shift from farm and blue-collar occupations to white-collar occupations tends to draw greater numbers of women into the labor force to the detriment of minority men.

Finally, the job functions and social relations of work for white-collar occupations work do not favor minority men. White-collar jobs generally have greater autonomy in decision making, frequent face-to-face interaction, greater authority and responsibility, greater likelihood of interacting with majority individuals from a position of status equality or superiority, and greater likelihood of interacting with majority women concentrated in gender-typed, white-collar occupations. Traditional racial caste norms prescribe against employment of Black men in occupations with these characteristics. Thus, we expect shifts toward white-collar employment to have a positive effect on racial inequality.

Demand for Educated Labor

The above discussion introduces the notion that the occupational mix has consequences for the demand for formally educated labor. For example, shifts in the occupational mix from skilled and unskilled manual occupations to white-collar occupations elevates the demand for workers with greater formal education; presumably because professional, managerial, sales, and clerical functions have higher *intrinsic* educational requirements. The fact that white-collar workers have considerably higher educational attainments than workers in skilled and unskilled manual occupations is consistent with this view.[33]

Heightened demand for educated workers might affect racial inequality in several different ways. One common assumption is that the long run effect of increasing prevalence of occupations with high skill and education requirements is to reduce racial inequality because it creates greater competitive pressures to reward labor on the basis of education and skills rather than race and other ascriptive criteria. This hypothesis is a variant of the familiar thesis of modernization which argues that, in contrast to pre-industrial societies, stratification structures in industrial societies emphasize achieved over ascribed characteristics due to an internal logic that gives great weight to the goals of maximizing productivity and economic growth.

This traditional view is rooted in several strains of classical sociological theory. However, other scenarios can be identified where increasing demand for workers with greater formal education and training does not necessarily lead to reductions in racial inequality. Three are considered here.

The first scenario is one wherein the *intrinsic* linkage between education and occupation is seen as relatively weak and the linkage between education and occupation is instead thought to reflect a transformation of racial and class stratification systems from systems of overt discrimination based on ascription to systems of institutional discrimination based on education. This scenario questions the presumption that the increasing emphasis on education in occupational stratification is solely a function of intrinsic performance requirements of occupations. It suggests instead that rules linking educated workers to "good" jobs are in part a means of reproducing race and class inequalities in situations where direct ascriptive allocation is difficult to maintain or is blocked altogether.

This view assumes, of course, that the majority exercises disproportionate control over hiring decisions and is advantaged with respect to education. In this situation, the majority embraces a system of allocating jobs according to education because it produces an occupational advantage for the majority. One test of the credibility of this thesis is to consider the question of whether the majority would continue to embrace the policy of allocating jobs on the basis of education if the minority had higher average education. An affirmative answer negates the thesis while a negative answer supports it. A related test of the credibility of this thesis is to consider the question of whether the majority and minority would swap job distributions if they were to somehow swap education distributions. A negative answer suggests that the intrinsic link between education and occupation is weak rather than strong.

The other two scenarios accept the premise that increasing emphasis on education in occupational stratification is a response to *intrinsic* requirements of a changing occupational mix, but they do not necessarily assume that this trend will promote reductions in racial inequality. One recognizes that Black education disadvantages have been and continue to be severe and thus the transition from stratification by ascription to stratification by achieved characteristics such as education might have no impact on racial inequality or might even lead to increases in inequality.[34] Still, this view sees fundamental change in the nature of racial stratification in occupation; that is, the direct role of race is removed from the economic system and driven elsewhere (e.g., into the educational system).

Yet another possibility is that the stratification system could shift partially in the direction of stratification on the basis of education and training yet still retain an ascriptive component wherein lesser rewards are given to Black human capital stocks. For example, education could increasingly determine occupation but the "rules" for converting education into occupation could remain more favorable for Whites and thus maintain the White advantage in occupation.

Blumer (1965; 1990) has argued that modern industrial stratification structures can easily retain such ascriptive features in the short and medium run, and possibly even in the long run. Research on the American stratification system indicates that even in the modern era where education is an important stratifier for both Whites and Blacks, Black returns to education are markedly lower than those for Whites (Jencks 1977; Blau and Duncan 1967). Thus, if increasing prevalence of occupations with higher education requirements dampens the ascriptive component of stratification and ultimately leads to reduced inequality, it would seem the reductions in inequality are slow in coming.

In light of these different possibilities, the most compelling advance prediction is that increasing demand for educated labor will have either no effect or a positive effect on racial inequality. Perspectives arguing for a negative effect on racial inequality are less plausible because they do not specify the time frame within which reductions in inequality should be realized. They also are unclear about whether such reductions in inequality are inevitable or whether large degrees of stratification by ascription can be retained.

Education Differences and Occupation Inequality

Education plays a role in occupational attainment and education differences between Blacks and Whites are large. It is therefore reasonable to expect that White-Black education differences have important implications for racial occupational inequality. Unfortunately, the matter is considerably more complicated and this seemingly simple and obvious conclusion may easily be overdrawn.

Fossett (1988) has discussed this issue in some detail. We summarize three points from his paper here. The first point is that large education differences between groups sometimes have little or no consequence for occupational inequality between the groups. When stratification systems distribute rewards equally to all groups on the basis of achieved characteristics such as education, group differences in education may contribute significantly to group differences in occupation. However, when rewards are distributed directly on the basis of ascribed characteristics such as race, or when "returns" to achieved characteristics such as education vary across groups, education may not have an important *causal* role in occupational attainment and even large education differences between groups may have limited implications for occupational inequality. In other words, majority-minority education differences have no implications for occupational inequality until the minority begins to receive significant status returns to education.

The second point is that an accurate assessment of the impact of group differences in education on occupational inequality requires knowledge of race differences in the education-occupation relationship. Unfortunately, the required data — separate education by occupation by race tabulations for each local area — are not available for counties. Without such tabulations it is not possible to determine whether occupation depends strongly on education and, if so, whether the relationship is the same for Blacks and Whites. Thus, there can be no empirical basis for accurately assessing the extent to which White-Black occupation differences are due to group education differences and how this has changed over time.

The third point is that many comparative studies have attempted to estimate the impact of race differences in education on occupational inequality using a strategy that is flawed and yields estimates that are subject to large upward bias. Specifically, they have correlated measures of occupational inequality with measures of educational inequality and then interpreted the positive association as evidence that the education differences *cause* the occupation differences. This methodology is fundamentally flawed because *the impact of group education differences on occupational inequality cannot be inferred from the aggregate-level correlation between inequality in education and inequality in occupation* (Fossett 1988).

One reason for this is that knowledge of aggregate education differences between two groups is not sufficient to establish the impact that the education difference has on occupational inequality.[35] This will depend quite critically on the occupation-education relationships for each group. Since the race-education-occupation relationship varies across areas and over time, the impact of the education difference on occupational inequality also varies across areas and over time; often in ways that are counterintuitive.[36]

Another reason is that the correlation of occupational inequality with educational inequality is spuriously inflated because conditions that produce race inequality in education (e.g., prejudice and discrimination) also produce race inequality in occupation. In fact, analysis reported by Fossett (1988) suggests that this dependence on common causes accounts for most of the association between the two variables. Thus, a *causal* interpretation of the strong correlation between inequality in education and inequality in occupation is untenable.

The conclusion we must reach then is that presently available methods do not allow us to assess the impact of race differences in education on racial occupational inequality in the context of a comparative analysis at the county level. The detailed, area-specific race by education by occupation tabulations needed to make an accurate assessment of this relationship are not available and strategies used in previous research have been shown to yield biased and highly misleading results.

Education Differences and Inequality Reconsidered

Education differences between majority and minority are routinely presumed to be an important factor contributing to racial occupation inequality. This is a straightforward conclusion when the education differences are large and the minority is able to convert education into higher status occupational attainments. However, minorities often are not able to convert education into occupation attainments with the same kind of success observed for the majority group. When this is the case, large education differences do not necessarily have important implications for group differences in occupation.

One obvious reason for this is the role of discrimination in the labor market. Increasingly the role of discrimination is discounted on the assumption that discrimination is less prevalent today than in the past. While this is not wholly implausible, quantitative, longitudinal data on discriminatory behavior do not exist which would permit a careful and rigorous assessment of the hypothesis. Whatever the trend, however, there is ample evidence from in-depth interviews, direct observation, and field studies to document the fact that discrimination continues to persist at significant levels (Kirschenman and Neckerman 1991).

It is also important to note, that moderate forms of discrimination can produce important occupation differences between majority and minority groups *even when jobs are allocated on a strict merit system*. For example, prejudiced employers can hire and promote only "qualified" job candidates but routinely choose from among "qualified" applicants on the basis of race and other ascribed characteristics. If "ties" occur often among qualified job applicants, a "ties-go-to-Whites" ascription rule would meet intrinsic education requirements for positions (i.e., no White is hired or promoted over a more qualified Black) and still produce substantial levels of racial occupational inequality.

The potential importance and persistence of this form of discrimination should not be underestimated. Even the most optimist neoclassical economic theories of labor markets provide no basis for expecting competitive forces to eliminate discrimination of this sort; no job is filled with an under-qualified worker so employers who discriminate do not bear any particular burden. Legal sanctions also are likely to have little influence since present day anti-discrimination laws and judicial interpretations make it very difficult for individuals to pursue complaints of discrimination unless an clear difference in qualifications is involved. Indeed, this pattern of discrimination cannot be established by examining any single case. Instead, it requires evaluation of a statistical pattern over many hiring and promotion decisions and such patterns are increasingly difficult to use in discrimination complaints.

Merit-Based Stratification or Institutional Discrimination?

Another issue that is relevant to discussion of the impact of racial education differences on racial occupation inequality is the degree to which the relationship between education and occupation reflects merit-based stratification. Too often this connection is simply presumed when alternative interpretations are plausible. For example, the link between education and occupation may reflect a system of institutional discrimination which functions to reproduce race and class inequalities. With this in mind, Lieberson (1985:164-168;186-187) has argued that the causal connection between education and labor force outcomes should not be interpreted naively. As Lieberson points out, the "basic" cause underlying racial inequality is the desire of the majority to establish and maintain a position of privilege and advantage. This basic cause may express itself in different ways. These not only include systems of overt race discrimination, but also systems of institutional discrimination which generate outcomes "acceptable" to the majority group.

Recent decades have seen a steady dismantling of formal systems of "overt" racial discrimination in the educational, economic, and political arenas. The effectiveness of informal systems of "overt" discrimination has also been reduced. Lieberson argues that it does not necessarily follow that racial stratification has been eradicated. In fact, he sees this as unlikely. Instead, the basic forces originally giving rise to formal and informal systems of overt discrimination are likely to lead to a reformulation of the racial stratification system in a new guise. That is, the majority's desire to maintain its advantage is likely to be expressed in new social forms when previous means of fulfilling this goal are blocked.

One possibility is that systems of institutional discrimination will evolve to replace systems of overt discrimination. In this, the majority may relinquish systems of overt discrimination and accept stratification principles based nominally on education *so long as the new system preserves the majority's occupational advantage.* This line of reasoning suggests the possibility that the connection between education and occupation only partially reflects stratification by achievement based on the "intrinsic requirements" of occupations. Instead, the education-occupation link may be fostered *in part* by a reformulated strategy of racial stratification wherein majority occupational advantages are maintained via a process of institutional discrimination based on education.

This hypothesis need not imply that "intrinsic" education requirements are unimportant to the occupation-education relationship. Undoubtedly, occupational attainments are partly determined by a process which matches "qualified" individuals to jobs based on the requirements of the occupations. However, it would be naive to assume that this is the *sole* basis for the correlation between occupation and education especially given the well-documented history of ascriptive stratification based on race, sex, and class in both education and occupation.[37]

It is difficult to distinguish between the situation where a system of racial stratification is in transition from overt discrimination to institutional discrimination based on education and the situation where a system of stratification is in transition from ascriptive stratification to merit stratification. However, insight into the forces at work may be gained by pondering the question, "Is it plausible that the education-occupation relationship would remain unchanged if the education distributions of Blacks and Whites were reversed?" That is, if Blacks gained an advantage in education comparable to that enjoyed by Whites, would they likewise gain a comparable advantage in occupation?

A strongly affirmative answer to this question implies that the education-occupation relationship primarily reflects a relationship between merit and "intrinsic" job requirements. A negative or partially negative answer to this question implies that the current connection between education and occupation is "tolerated" by the majority because it produces "acceptable" outcomes (i.e., majority occupation advantage).

In our view, it is highly implausible to assume that White and Black occupational inequality would be reversed or even sharply reduced if Whites and Blacks were to exchange education distributions. Thus, on these grounds the linkage between occupations and education should be seen as at least partially reflecting a process of institutional discrimination wherein a putatively "objective rule" of occupational stratification sustains an evolving racial stratification system.

Again, this does not imply that a link between "intrinsic" occupation requirements and individual education is completely absent; only that this association does not fully dominate allocation mechanisms based on race, sex, class, kinship, and other ascriptive criteria. The degree to which this is or is not the case revolves around the question of the extent to which the minority could in fact dislodge the majority from the upper segments of the occupational hierarchy by acquiring more education. We know of no evidence to suggest that this is presently the case.

Before leaving this point it is important to acknowledge that, while the transformation of the racial stratification system from overt discrimination to institutional discrimination may enable the majority to maintain its advantage in the short run, it is nevertheless an important change which may weaken the majority's ability to maintain their advantage in the long run. Once education becomes the "nominal" basis of allocating rewards, the link between race and occupation is indirect rather than direct and the majority's advantage is made more precarious. The problem for the majority is that, once the connection between education and occupation becomes institutionalized, it may be difficult to change this stratification mechanism should it fail to produce majority advantage in occupation. Instead, the battle ground in the struggle to maintain majority advantage in occupation shifts to the educational system and out of the economy.

Economic Growth

Several arguments hold that economic growth promotes or facilitates reductions in race inequality. One standard argument is that minorities rank lower in the hiring queue and are thus hardest hit when employment falls during recessions (Thurow 1969). Another is that the relative position of minority groups is likely to advance during periods of growth because the costs to employers of discrimination are greater when competition for qualified workers is keen (Becker 1957; Beck 1980; Reich 1981). A third argument is that dominant groups are more willing to accept *relative* concessions to minorities when economic growth permits them to do so and avoid absolute status declines or even enjoy absolute status increases (Coleman 1971). Yet another argument is that dominant groups are likely to adopt more tolerant attitudes toward minorities during periods of affluence rather than during recessions when competition for scarce resources is heightened (Farley and Hermalin 1972).

The link between economic growth and inequality is widely accepted, but evidence for a strong effect beyond short-term cyclical fluctuations is limited. The strongest empirical support is found in studies which note that racial inequality tends to increase during recessions and decrease during periods of economic expansions (Farley and Hermalin 1972) and studies that report a negative relationship between annual economic performance (e.g., employment rates) and racial inequality (Beck 1980; Reich 1981).

Surprisingly, however, there is little empirical data to show that periods of economic growth produce *permanent* or long-term changes in majority-minority inequality. Indeed, the case can be made that, major shifts in *relative* racial inequality in the United States have not tracked the movement of the economy so much as changes in the political and judicial spheres (e.g., civil rights and equal opportunity legislation). Possibly, sustained economic growth may have facilitated changes in these arenas. However, this kind of link between the economy and racial inequality is more indirect and tenuous than is commonly supposed.

One problem in evaluating hypotheses linking economic growth to lower racial inequality is that they are not well specified. For example, the appropriate measurement of economic growth is not made clear. Many studies measure economic growth by employment rates. This is a short-term measure which, as the last decade has clearly shown, is conceptually distinct from real growth in income and wages.[38] Employment rates has fluctuated in a low-to-moderate range while wages and income have been stagnant. Even when growth in income and wages is considered, it is not necessarily clear what kind of income growth is most likely to promote reductions in racial inequality. Is it absolute income growth; relative (percentage) income growth; relative intergenerational income growth (e.g., relative to parent's income); growth relative to normative expectations (e.g., growth exceeding expected growth); or something else?

This question should not be taken lightly. By all quantitative measures, economic growth over the past century has been phenomenal. Present day generations live far better in material terms than past generations; most families with incomes below the official poverty line today enjoy material comforts that middle-class families of a century ago could not have imagined. Yet anxiousness and insecurity about material well-being is pervasive. One likely explanation for this is that the subjective response to economic growth is as much a function of expectations as actual income and that each generation's expectations about income and status adapt quickly to historical trends in economic growth and prevailing standards of material well being. If this is the case, then the impact of economic growth on interethnic economic competition is less straightforward and may not be closely tied to simple measures such as changes in "real" median family income or aggregate employment levels.

Theories linking economic growth to racial inequality also are unclear about the functional form of the causal relationship. Is the effect reversible? If reversible, is it symmetric (i.e., are the effects of expansion and contraction be similar in size and duration)? Which is more important, short-term (i.e., cyclical) growth or long-term growth? What are the time lags for the effect? Does the first year of an expansion have the same effect on inequality as year five?

Almost all empirical studies focus on the effects of short-term economic growth (e.g., employment rates) and use model specifications which imply that the effects of economic growth on racial inequality are reversible, symmetric, and fully realized within a short time lag (i.e., less than a year). *This conventional specification implies that economic growth does not have important long-term, cumulative effects on racial inequality.* Short-term growth is cyclical and thus by definition reductions in inequality which might occur during a period of economic growth are destined to be *fully* reversed when the inevitable recession occurs. If successful economic policy were to reduce the average level of unemployment or the time spent in recession, *average* inequality over long time-spans would indeed fall. However, the original level of high inequality would always return in times of peak recession and in that sense, *permanent* change in inequality would not be achieved.

Economic growth can only produce long-term change in inequality when the conventional specification of the effect is discarded and alternatives are considered. For example, if the effects of economic growth were irreversible, periods of growth would exert a "ratchet" effect leading to ever-diminishing inequality.

A more plausible scenario is that the effect of economic growth is reversible, but asymmetric, and that each year of an expansion or contraction exerts an independent and additional effect on inequality.[39] Asymmetry would occur to the extent that inequality might increase more rapidly during the first year of a recession than it decreases during the first year of an expansion. If so, growth cycles with equal durations of recession and expansion would create a saw-toothed pattern of steadily increasing inequality. However, assuming each year of an expansion or a recession has an independent, cumulative effect on inequality, then inequality could be reduced over the long run if periods of expansion lasted longer than periods of recession and recessions were not too severe.

This introduces the idea that sustained, long-term economic growth has effects that are equally if not more important than the current state of the short-term business cycle. While this distinction between long-term and short-term growth receives little explicit discussion in the literature, it is potentially important for two reasons. First, since long- and short-term growth can move in different directions, failure to consider both might make it difficult to estimate the effect of either. Second, long-term growth becomes the more relevant policy tool for producing long-term reductions in inequality.

The nature of causal lags and possible nonlinear effects has also been neglected in discussions of the effects of economic growth on inequality. The literature is not specific about how long periods of economic growth must be before an effect on inequality is to be expected or about how much time must elapse before the effect is fully realized. Likewise the literature is not clear about whether the effects of economic growth and decline are linear; for example, whether the first year of an expansion (contraction) has the same effect as the fifth year of an expansion (contraction).

Queuing theories (e.g., Thurow 1969) imply effects on inequality via a "first fired, last hired" dynamic. This suggests short causal lags and no cumulative effects. That is, the impact of increased employment on inequality is realized quickly (within a year) and subsequent years of full employment have little or no effect. Theories which argue that economic growth creates greater competition among employers for qualified workers and thus penalizes employers who discriminate (Becker 1957) and theories which argue that the majority is more tolerant of minorities and less diligent in protecting its advantage during periods of increasing affluence (Coleman 1971; Farley and Hermalin 1972) imply lagged and cumulative effects of economic growth. Effects on majority tolerance and discrimination are likely to be small initially, but may slowly build during long, sustained expansions. Thus, later years in an expansion would be more important than early years. However, the majority's conservative response during a contraction would likely be realized rapidly and build to its maximum effect more quickly.

The issues we have discussed to this point speak to how theories linking economic growth to reduced racial inequality might be refined and the effect might be specified more precisely. Heistand (1964) has called for a more fundamental questioning of the basic idea that economic growth necessarily leads to reductions in racial inequality. He argues that long-term economic growth is likely to be at least as beneficial to majorities as to minorities, so gains resulting from economic growth do not necessarily reduce *relative* inequality between groups.

In fact, there is little quantitative evidence to suggest show that majority tolerance of relative status gains for minorities increases during periods of economic growth. Negative effects of employment levels on inequality in time-series analyses (Beck 1980; Reich 1981) simply do not sustain the conclusion that economic growth fundamentally alters the racial stratification order. Historical examples, such as the mass deportation of the Mexican-origin population during the depression era suggest that interethnic conflict and discrimination does increase during economic contraction. But there are also many historical examples where extended periods of economic growth were not accompanied by important reductions in racial inequality.

Heistand's criticism can be further developed by pointing out that interethnic competition over social and economic rewards is often a zero-sum game. In particular, interethnic competition for rank positions in status hierarchies is zero-sum. For one individual or group to move up, another individual or group must move down (holding group size constant). When this dimension of competition is important — that is, when individuals and groups strive to maintain rank position rather than to obtain a certain absolute level of a reward — there is no theoretical reason to assume that economic growth will reduce interethnic competition. The logic of the argument that it should do so would appear to be based on the assumption that the majority becomes less concerned with and less defensive of relative position once it achieves certain absolute levels of economic security and material standard of living. The theoretical and empirical basis for this assumption, at least in such a simple form, is weak to say the least.

In sum, evidence supporting theories linking economic growth to reductions in racial inequality is surprisingly weak and theoretical specifications of this effect are not well developed. The distinction between long-term and short-term growth is one that may be particularly important and it remains to be seen whether either has important consequences for trends in racial inequality.

Urbanization

Several theoretical arguments suggest that urbanization should exert a negative effect on racial inequality (Blalock 1959; Elgie 1980). One is that urbanization is associated with greater differentiation in work activities (a more complex division of labor) each with specialized requirements for performance. Presumably, this then promotes greater emphasis on skills and abilities over ascribed characteristics in occupational attainment processes. A complementary perspective suggests that minority economic opportunities are better in urban areas because job opportunities are more varied than in rural areas where employment tends to be concentrated in agriculture (Hathaway, Beegle, and Bryant 1968; Lyson 1985).

Another view is that, like industrialization and modernization, urbanization is a disruptive force that undermines the stability of traditional normative orders based on ascription. Urban centers are seen as centers of social and cultural innovation which foster new, non-traditional ideas (Ford 1977:8) including modern values promoting stratification on the basis of achievement rather than ascription. In sum, then, ecological theory argues that traditionalism and resistance to change are undermined in urban areas (Ford 1977; Willits, Bealer, and Crider 1982; Wilson 1986) and thus, by implication, that racial inequality is more easily maintained in nonmetropolitan areas.

Surprisingly, empirical research has yet to establish that urbanization reduces racial inequality. To the contrary, the limited research to date suggests the opposite. For example, Blalock (1959) reports positive relationships between urbanization and different types of inequality using cross-section data for a sample of 150 southern counties in 1950. Similarly, Wilcox and Roof (1978) find that the effect of urbanization on inequality diminished when relative minority size is taken into account. Finally, like Blalock, Elgie (1980) reports a positive relationship between urbanization and racial inequality using data for southern counties in 1950, 1960, and 1970. These researchers all note the possibility that possible negative effects of urbanization on racial inequality are undermined in the South where racial prejudice and discrimination are deeply entrenched in the social system.

Elgie (1980) has noted that critics of the thesis of industrialization have argued that there is no logical necessity for industrialization to produce universalism. Instead, decline of ascriptive stratification is only one among many possible outcomes. It is also possible that urbanization and industrialization can be adapted to a strongly entrenched racial stratification order (Blumer 1965; Stokes and Harris 1978). Indeed, in the short-term it may be rational for even racially neutral employers to accept the economic inefficiencies of racial discrimination in order to avoid social and economic retaliation from dominant group workers and in order to cater to the preferences of prejudiced consumers (Blalock 1959; Oster 1975; Welch 1967). Thus, the assumption that an underlying logic of industrialization and urbanization must inevitably overcome the short-term social, political, and economic costs of major alterations to the social order should not be taken for granted.

Another point that must be considered is that the transition to an urban industrial order brings increased status diversity. There are more occupational roles in the social order and the degree of separation between the middle ranks and the bottom ranks of the status hierarchy may well increase in the short run. As will be discussed below, this creates a structural opportunity for larger inequalities to emerge between the minority and the majority. Thus, urbanization may indirectly promote inequality due to its impact on the complexity of the status hierarchy.

Community/Labor Market Size

Several studies have reported a negative relationship between population size and racial occupational inequality (Glenn 1963; Lagory and Magnani 1979; Martin and Poston 1972; 1976). The general structure of theories predicting such a relationship is quite similar to that for theories predicting a negative relationship between urbanization and racial inequality. This is not surprising because community size and urbanization are positively correlated for nonmetropolitan counties. However, size is conceptually and empirically distinct from urbanization and several specific arguments for a negative effect on inequality have been advanced.

One hypothesis is that large social systems tend to develop bureaucratic structures needed to coordinate more complex production and market systems and this generates promotes more rational and efficient use of labor (Treiman 1970). A related argument is that competitive pressures are greater in larger labor markets and force employers to emphasize achieved characteristics over ascribed characteristics. Yet another argument is that nondiscriminating employers find it easier to overcome the social obstacles (e.g., sanctioning by other employers) to hiring minority labor in larger labor markets (Oster 1975). Finally, the greater diversity of cultural and social groups in large population centers is thought to breed greater tolerance for cultural heterogeneity (Wirth 1938).

On the one hand, these arguments are supported by research showing that Whites living in larger communities tend to express greater levels of support for racial integration (Abrahamson and Carter 1986; Fossett and Kiecolt 1989; Wilson 1986). However, Breton (1964) and Hwang and Murdock (1988) have noted that large population size facilitates the emergence of distinct, "institutionally complete" subcultures which can promote particularism rather than universalism. These arguments can be reconciled by noting that large size may promote greater tolerance in secondary relations such as the labor force while simultaneously affording greater structural capacity for particularism in primary relations (Hwang and Murdock 1988).

Status Diversity

Status diversity is critical to the potential for inequality to arise. Following Blau (1977), occupational inequality between groups cannot arise unless the status structure is sufficiently diversified to admit the possibility of inequality. For example, extreme status inequality between groups cannot arise in a community if its occupational structure is essentially homogenous with respect to socioeconomic status (e.g., if everyone is a peasant). This is an important consideration in nonmetropolitan counties of the South as the categories of farmer and farm laborer dominated most local occupation distributions as recently as 1940.[40]

There was, however, a dramatic transformation of the economies of nonmetropolitan counties between 1940 and 1990. Agricultural employment declined sharply and employment in service, manufacturing, and trade increased dramatically. Consequently, status diversity in the occupational structure increased and with it came greater structural potential for status inequality between groups. If race prejudice and rank-order ethnic stratification rules remained constant, increases in overall status diversity would be followed by increased status inequality between Blacks and Whites.

This prediction further calls into question traditional expectations regarding the impact of population size and urbanization on racial inequality. The emergence of large urban centers is likely to lead to greater diversification in the status structure and thus increase the structural potential for inequality. Moreover, the period of greatest status diversity should occur during the transition phase from a rural to an urban economy. Before the transition, status diversity is low as most people work in a small number of low status farm occupations. After the transition, status diversity is higher due to the more complex mix of low, middle, and upper status urban occupations. However, the peak in status diversity occurs *during* the transition because the occupation mix includes both rural occupations and urban occupations. Thus, urbanization and size would tend to have a nonlinear effect on inequality through status diversity.[41] Inequality rises during the transition from rural to urban, falls back once the urban transition is complete, and stabilizes at a level of inequality greater than that originally observed.

This reasoning closely parallels Kuznet's (1955) argument that inequality in the overall income distribution first rises and, then falls as economies undergo major structural transformations. His argument distinguishes between inequality between workers in the same sector of the economy and inequality between workers in different sectors of the economy. Whenever the economy changes from being dominated by one sector (e.g., agriculture) to being dominated by another (e.g., manufacturing), and the two sectors have different wage levels, inequality peaks during the transition because inter-sectoral inequality is maximized. Inequality will then fall when the transition is complete because inter-sectoral inequality will return to being negligible. Whether inequality is lower or higher after the transition compared to before is then determined by whether the emerging sector is characterized by greater intra-sectoral wage inequality than the declining sector. The Kuznet's argument applies here with the understanding that sectors of the economy which dominate in rural areas (e.g., agriculture) are characterized by lower status jobs than sectors which dominate in urban areas (e.g., manufacturing, financial and commercial, trade, etc.)

Proximity to a Metropolitan Area

Ecological theory holds that innovations in technology, ideas, and other cultural changes tend to originate in urban centers and then diffuse to nonmetropolitan areas (Hawley 1971). In light of this, nonmetropolitan areas which are near metropolitan areas have been predicted to have lower levels of inequality because they are more likely to be exposed to the presumably more universalistic norms of metropolitan areas. This argument is plausible because previous research has found that attitudes of racial tolerance are more prevalent in metropolitan areas (Fossett and Kiecolt 1989, Wilson 1986) and because metropolitan areas exercise disproportionate influence over subregional channels of information distribution (e.g., electronic and print media) and regional economic activity. Nevertheless, it has yet to be shown that the diffusion of ideas and behavior patterns to nonmetropolitan areas proceeds more rapidly in areas near metropolitan centers. It also remains to be shown that norms and behavior patterns relating to racial stratification diffuse as rapidly as styles, fashions, and aspects of culture less directly tied to economic status.

Semyonov (1983) has argued against this traditional ecological perspective and has suggested instead that inequality may be more pronounced in nonmetropolitan counties located close to metropolitan areas. He reasoned that, due to recent patterns in the relocation of manufacturing and other industries, nonmetropolitan communities distant from metropolitan centers are likely to develop occupational and industrial structures which offer greater opportunities for employment. In contrast, nonmetropolitan communities neighboring large metropolitan areas are more likely to be suburbs with economies dominated by locally-oriented service industries with lower status jobs. Consequently, inequality should be less prevalent in nonmetropolitan areas which are not adjacent to metropolitan areas because of the different kind of economic development taking place in these areas.

Indigenous Labor Supply

Ecological theory holds that tensions between minority and majority are likely to increase when job competition is more severe. Population pressure is a potential source of increased job competition and is thus predicted to foster greater intergroup competition and inequality. Population pressure can be conceptualized in terms of indigenous labor supply — the balance between the relative sizes of cohorts entering and exiting the labor force. Population pressure and competition are greater when the entry labor cohorts are larger than exit cohorts (i.e., when job candidates outnumber available jobs).

Poston and White (1978) reported that indigenous labor supply had a strong negative effect on net-migration in nonmetropolitan communities; that is, the greater the relative size of entering cohorts, the greater the impact of population pressure on job competition and the greater the volume of out-migration. These important effects on net-migration suggest the potential importance of indigenous labor supply for racial inequality.

With this, we conclude our review of potential determinants of racial inequality in southern, nonmetropolitan areas. We now turn to a brief discussion of selected methodological issues before introducing our empirical analyses.

Summary

We began this chapter by acknowledging previous research investigating racial inequality in nonmetropolitan areas of the South. While it goes without saying, we nevertheless take the opportunity to again note that we owe a significant debt to those who have preceded us and upon whose work we build.

We then devoted the remainder of the chapter to reviewing specific hypotheses linking structural characteristics of communities to racial inequality. The variables we identified as likely structural determinants of inequality included: relative minority size, industrial structure (manufacturing concentration), occupational structure (white-collar employment), structural demand for educated labor, urbanization, status diversity, labor market size, indigenous labor supply, women's participation in the labor force, economic growth, proximity to a metropolitan area, and indigenous labor supply. This is the list of "likely suspects" which guides our efforts to develop statistical models predicting variation in inequality across areas and over time (the results of which are presented in Chapters 4 and 5). Perhaps the strongest case is made for the effects of relative minority size where the "competition" hypothesis and the "White gains" hypothesis make particularly strong predictions that relative minority size will have a positive effect on racial inequality and where the "resource" hypothesis makes a prediction that after 1965 the adverse consequences of the "competition" and "White gains" effects may diminish.

As a concluding note we point out that not all of the variables listed above are directly represented in our final statistical models. The primary reasons for this are that our exploratory modeling efforts revealed that some variables simply did not have important effects on inequality (e.g., proximity to a metropolitan area) while other variables were empirically and/or conceptually redundant (e.g., white-collar employment and structural demand for educated labor). Thus, we were forced to strike a balance between the goal of directly testing as many hypotheses about the determinants of racial inequality as was feasible and the goal of developing stable and trustworthy models which would permit such tests. The next two chapters carry us forward to the later chapters where the results of these modeling efforts are discussed. These two intervening chapters present an overview of our research design and measurement strategies and an overview of basic trends in inequality and structural characteristics of local areas.

Notes

1. Technically, these studies were based on random samples of *all* counties. Under random sampling, however, most would have been non-metropolitan.

2. This study was a follow-up to a previous metropolitan-level analysis (Blalock 1956).

3. Measuring inequality in this way has certain limitations (Fossett

and South 1983), but nevertheless it can be quite useful when appropriate precautions are taken (e.g., multiple cut points are used).

4. The dependent variables in Elgie's study were measures of equality rather than inequality. However, we describe the results in terms of inequality to maintain consistency in our discussion.

5. The factor names were derived from variables loading high on each factor: community size (log of population 0.89); educational status (percent with less than 5 years of education -0.94); manufacturing orientation (percent employed in manufacturing 0.81); and agricultural scale (value of products sold per farm 0.83).

6. Turner (1951) also used relative odds ratios to measure White-Black differences in employment in an analysis of inequality in metropolitan areas.

7. This point is discussed in more detail in Appendix A.

8. Related research focusing on metropolitan areas and cities is very extensive. Some important examples include Blalock (1956), Glenn (1964; 1966), Frisbie and Neidert (1977), Jiobu and Marshall (1971), Hill (1974), and Wilcox and Roof (1978).

9. In other words, the use of multiple observations over time yields more efficient parameter estimates and greater power in statistical tests.

10. For example, if two variables are collinear and only one is included in the model, the included variable may be subject to more than one interpretation.

11. This will be discussed in more detail in a later section dealing with the "White gains" hypothesis.

12. This would imply that the relationship between percent minority and inequality would best be captured when percent minority is subjected to a square root transformation.

13. For example, a positive monotonic relationship between inequality and relative minority size might result if the competition effect is strongly positive, the resource effect is weakly negative, and both effects are linear.

14. Extension to n-group situations is straightforward.

15. The mean status percentile (MSP) for a group is given by $\Sigma(SP_i g_i/G)$ where i is an index for status percentile running from 0 to 100, SP_i is the status percentile for status category i, g_i is the number persons in the specified group in status category i, and G is the total number in persons in the specified group.

16. Group A is evenly distributed over status percentiles 100.0–66.6. Thus, the mean status percentile for its members is 83.3. Similarly, members of Group B and Group C are evenly distributed over status percentiles 66.6–0.0 and have status means of 33.3.

17. The majority (i.e., Group A) always occupies the top ranks ranging from percentile 100 to percentile $100-P_A$ where P_A denotes the population share of Group A. Its mean status percentile is given by the average of these

two end points and is thus equal to $(100+(100-P_A))/2$. The minority groups occupy the ranks ranging from percentile $100-P_A$ to percentile 0. Thus, their mean status percentile are given by $(100-P_A)/2$. The difference between these two amounts is 50.

18. For example, when group rankings are strict (i.e., no overlaps) inequality between the majority and the more disadvantaged minority (i.e., Groups A and C) will approach 100 as the population percentage for the less disadvantaged minority (Group B) approaches 100.

19. This result occurs in the present example because Groups A and C were initially equal in size. In other situations, the mean for Group B might increase or decrease depending on the initial relative sizes of the three groups.

20. The order of the subscripts for ND are important as they dictate the sign of the measure (e.g., $ND_{BA} = -ND_{AB}$).

21. Thus, for example,

$$
\begin{aligned}
DMSP_{AB} &= MSP_A - MSP_B \\
&= \{ 50 + (P_B\,ND_{AB} + P_C\,ND_{AC}) / 2 \} \\
&\quad - \{ 50 + (P_A\,ND_{BA} + P_C\,ND_{BC}) / 2 \} \\
&= \{ P_B\,ND_{AB} + P_C\,ND_{AC} - P_A\,ND_{BA} - P_C\,ND_{BC} \} / 2
\end{aligned}
$$

(the next step is based on the fact that $ND_{AB} = -ND_{BA}$)

$$
\begin{aligned}
&= \{ P_B\,ND_{AB} + P_C\,ND_{AC} + P_A\,ND_{AB} - P_C\,ND_{BC} \} / 2 \\
&= \{ (P_A + P_B)\,ND_{AB} + P_C\,ND_{AC} - P_C\,ND_{BC} \} / 2 \\
&= \{ (P_A + P_B)\,ND_{AB} + P_C\,(ND_{AC} - ND_{BC}) \} / 2
\end{aligned}
$$

22. The result for the group difference in mean status given in Equation 2.9 is obtained as follows.

$$
\begin{aligned}
DMSP_{AB} &= MSP_A - MSP_B \\
&= \{ 50 + P_B\,ND_{AB} / 2 \} - \{ 50 + P_A\,ND_{BA} / 2 \} \\
&= P_B\,ND_{AB} / 2 - P_A\,ND_{BA} / 2
\end{aligned}
$$

(the next step is based on the fact that $ND_{AB} = -ND_{BA}$)

$$
\begin{aligned}
&= P_B\,ND_{AB} / 2 + P_A\,ND_{AB} / 2 \\
&= (P_A + P_B)\,ND_{AB} / 2
\end{aligned}
$$

(in the two-group situation $P_A + P_B = 1.0$, thus)

$$= ND_{AB} / 2$$

Thus, the difference in mean status is equal to 1/2 ND regardless of the relative sizes of the two groups.

Please note, however, that this relationship is a special case which holds *only in the two-group situation*. When there are multiple ranked minority groups, $DMSP_{AB}$ cannot be determined from ND_{AB}.

23. With some effort it can be shown that the results obtained in this example hold generally. Due to space limitations we do not present the proof here as each result requires a separate proof.

24. If Whites and Blacks took the role of Groups A and C, respectively, and Asians and Hispanics took the role of Group B, in Figures 2.3 and 2.5, an increase in the percentage of Asians and Hispanics would increase Anglo's mean status, lower Black's mean status, and increase the mean status difference between Anglos and Blacks.

25. Equations 2.4 and 2.5 make it clear that the maximum impact occurs when *both* rank-order stratification relations involving the less advantaged minority are large. The reason for this is that, if either of the rank-order stratification relations involving the intermediate group are small, then the situation begins to approximate a single-minority situation instead of one involving multiple, ranked minorities. As noted earlier, changes in relative group size have no implications for mean status differences in the single-minority context.

26. Again, with a little effort these can be shown to be general results.

27. This can be recognized as a variant of the ethnic queuing theories advanced by Lieberson (1980) and Thurow (1969).

28. As noted in Equation 2.3, MSP_C, the mean status percentile for the lowest ranked minority group, is equal to $50 + (P_A ND_{CA} + P_B ND_{CB}) / 2$. If the minority increases in relative size, changes in P_A and P_B must be negative. Since ND_{CA} and ND_{CB} also are negative by definition (in this example), MSP_C must increase.

29. In situations with multiple, ranked minority groups, these relationships are more complex but can be similarly derived with only slightly more effort. We discuss the simpler two-group scenario because the substantive point is the same and the presentation is more convenient.

30. This relationship was first noted in Fossett and Kiecolt (1989).

31. Analysis not shown here suggests that if women were at the bottom of the status hierarchy, increases in their relative number would tend to push both White men and Black men up in the status distribution. Furthermore, the increase in status would be greater for Black men and, thus, the mean difference in status between White men and Black men would narrow.

32. Whether women should be subdivided on race is an open question. Unreported analyses of rank-order occupation comparisons show White women and Black men both have an advantage over Black women. Thus, Black women suffer a double minority status. The practical significance for our study is limited, however, because the representation of women in the labor force primarily reflects behavior of White women since they greatly outnumber Black women in most counties in our sample.

33. For example, in 1960, 91 percent of professionals, 63 percent of managers, 71 percent of clerical workers, and 55 percent of sales workers had a high school education. The corresponding percentages for crafts workers, operatives, and laborers were 36, 26, and 18, respectively (US Bureau of the Census 1963 [Subject Report on Occupations]).

34. Majority-minority education differences have been narrowing over time. Nevertheless, occupational inequality could increase if status differences between education groups were increasing faster than racial education differences were narrowing. For example, if initially each year of education was worth an average of 2 status points and the majority advantage in education averaged 4 years, an average 8 point majority status advantage would result. If the education advantage then narrowed to 3 years and the status return to education *increased* to 3 points, the majority status advantage would *increase* to 9 points.

35. There is one exception to this generalization: aggregate education differences can provide a basis for estimating the impact of education differences on occupational inequality if the race-education-occupation relation is known and is known to be identical in all areas.

36. For example, historically, large education differences had little consequence for occupational inequality because education did not play an important role in Black occupational attainments. Education differences today are smaller but ironically their implications for inequality are potentially greater because education now plays a more important role in Black occupational attainment.

37. For example, in 1960 71 percent of clerical workers had at least a high school degree. In contrast, the corresponding figure for the presumably more demanding and better rewarded managerial occupations was only 63 percent. The most plausible explanation of this is not that clerical jobs were more demanding of education, but rather that these occupations were strongly sex-typed and had a high proportion of women employees. That is, women in the labor force are strongly selected on education and had higher percentages with a high school degree yet were disproportionately concentrated in strongly sex-typed occupations.

38. Growth in real incomes and wages may be more likely during periods of full employment, but the past two decades show it is by no means certain.

39. Conventional specifications imply that an increase in unemployment which marks the onset of a recession leads inequality to shift to a higher level and that inequality then stays at that level regardless of whether the recession lasts one year, five years, or longer.

40. No doubt socially meaningful status gradations existed within the farm categories. However, these status differences were not similar in magnitude to the status differences between persons in farm occupations and persons in nonfarm occupations such as professional and managerial occupations, other white-collar occupations, and skilled crafts workers.

41. This prediction is similar to Lenski's (1966) prediction that inequality is greatest during the early phases of transition from agricultural to industrial economies. It is also similar to Kuznet's (1955; 1963) prediction that *intra*group inequality will increase when economies undergo sectoral transformations associated with economic growth.

3

Measurement Issues

In this chapter we review our strategies for measuring racial occupational inequality and its potential determinants. Additionally, we describe the sample we use in our analysis and touch on several secondary methodological points. We have tried to limit our discussion here to the minimum needed to adequately describe our procedures and have relegated detailed discussion of methodological issues to Appendices A-C. Even so, many readers may prefer to skim this chapter or defer reading it so they may proceed directly to Chapter 4 which presents analyses of how inequality in southern, nonmetropolitan counties has changed since 1940.

Occupational Inequality

Our study focuses on occupational inequality in local areas; what its level is, how it varies from area to area, and how it changes over time. While inequality on other aspects of socioeconomic attainment (e.g., education, income, home ownership, etc.) also merit examination, we believe occupation is an especially important stratification outcome to consider. Salary, wages, fringe benefits, and other "material" rewards flow directly and indirectly from occupational position as also do "subjective" rewards such as respect, authority, prestige, and working conditions. There can be no doubt that occupation has wide-ranging consequences for life chances, life experiences, and material well being. It is a fundamental stratification outcome and this is why competition among individuals and groups for occupational position is so keen.

Several practical concerns also factor into our decision to focus on occupational inequality. The most important of these is that occupation has been tabulated by race and sex for southern counties in each of the six census years from 1940 to 1990. In contrast, earnings data were not tabulated by race and sex at the county level before 1970 and income data for persons and families were not tabulated by race and sex before 1960.[1]

Another important practical concern is that occupational status is one of the most reliable and stable indicators of socioeconomic attainment (Zimmerman 1992). By comparison, annual income and earnings are somewhat less reliable indicators of long-term life chances because they often vary greatly from one year to the next (Featherman 1980; Solon 1992; Zimmerman 1992). The year-to-year stability of occupation is especially valuable in the present context where we are tracking trends in inequality from one decade to the next based on single-year observations that are ten years apart.

The final practical consideration we mention here is that occupation data are tabulated for persons in the civilian labor force and thus register stratification outcomes generated by the dynamics of the local economy and local labor market. In contrast, income tabulations for counties include data for persons not in the labor force including retirees, the disabled, inmates of institutions, members of the armed forces, and other special populations whose primary sources of income (e.g., social security, pensions, social welfare transfers, military salaries, etc.) do not reflect local labor market dynamics.

We use two different indices to measure racial inequality in distribution across occupation categories. The first is Lieberson's (1975) index of net difference (ND) which measures inequality between groups based on the assumption that occupations can be *rank ordered* in terms of socioeconomic status. The second is the mean difference in socioeconomic status (SD) which measures inequality based on the assumption that occupations can be *scaled* on a socioeconomic status continuum.

The theories guiding our research predict that White-Black occupation differences are generated by a process of racial stratification and that they will therefore confer a systematic, status advantage to one group. In view of this, we have chosen measures that are well suited for summarizing systematic group advantage and which will not give off "false" signals for racial inequality when occupations differences in fact reflect only racial segregation and differentiation (i.e., unranked differences). We review conceptual issues relevant to this measurement goal and the merits of the different measures that have been used in previous research in Appendix Chapter A. There we show that the index of net difference (ND) and the mean status difference between Whites and Blacks (SD) are both attractive measures which meet relevant criteria for measuring ordinal and interval inequality.

The computing formulas and the properties of these (and other) measures are discussed in Appendix A. Thus, we need note only a few of their more important characteristics here. The index of net difference has a logical range which runs from −100 to 100. In the present context, a score of 100 indicates that, in random pairings of Whites and Blacks, Whites always rank above Blacks on occupation. A score of −100 indicates the reverse, and a score of 0 indicates that Whites rank below Blacks as often as they rank above Blacks. As a rule of thumb, net difference scores between 0 and 10 indicate relatively low levels of inequality; scores between 10 and 25 indicate medium levels of inequality; scores between 25 and 40 indicate high levels of inequality; and scores above 40 indicate extremely high levels of inequality.

The mean status difference (SD) between Blacks and Whites is obtained by first calculating mean status levels for White men (SES_W) and Black men (SES_B) based on their separate occupation distributions and then taking the difference between the two group means. We used Nam-Powers socioeconomic status scores to scale occupation on a status continuum for the purpose of computing group means. (We also used these scores to rank order occupations for the purpose of computing the index of net difference.) Nam-Powers scores reflect an occupation's standing relative to other occupations based on the income and education attainments of persons employed in the occupation. Specifically, the Nam-Powers score for a given occupation represents the average of the occupation's percentile scores on income and education relative to other occupations. (Nam-Powers scores are discussed in more detail in Appendix Chapter C.)

Status scores for individual occupations have a logical range of 0 to 100. Because the scores are averages of two percentile scores (i.e., for income and education) which are highly correlated, they are roughly comparable to percentile scores.[2] Thus, the maximum logical range for the White-Black differences in mean status is approximately −50 to 50 and the mean difference indicates the approximate percentage of the total labor force that must be "crossed over" to travel from one group's mean to the other group's mean.[3] In view of this, White-Black differences in mean status can be roughly interpreted using the following rule of thumb: differences of between 0 and 5 points indicate relatively low levels of inequality; differences of between 5 and 12.5 points indicate medium levels of inequality; differences of between 12.5 and 20 points indicate medium levels of inequality; and differences of more than 20 points indicate extremely high levels of inequality.

We report both the index of net difference and the mean status difference in the descriptive analyses reported in Chapter 4. However, we rely solely on the mean status difference for the multivariate regression analyses reported in Chapters 5 and 6. Space does not permit us to report parallel analyses for both measures and this is unnecessary in any event as the two are highly correlated in our sample and thus yield similar results.[4] Ultimately, we decided to focus on the mean status difference in the regression analyses because it is constructed from separate White and Black status levels which can themselves be modeled in order to better clarify how inequality arises.

Selected Independent Variables

We will be somewhat briefer in summarizing the strategies used to measure the independent variables. For those who are interested, Appendix C provides a more detailed discussion of the operationalization of these measures. One point we should make here is that we considered many alternative approaches to measuring the independent variables based on theoretical considerations and as required to best capture each variable's relationship with our dependent variable of occupational inequality. The strategies we ultimately adopted either were the most successful of those considered, or were among the most successful and were attractive on other counts as well (e.g., ease of interpretation).

Relative minority size was measured by percent Black in the county population. In regression analyses, this variable was subjected to a square root transformation to better capture its nonlinear relationship with inequality. This rescaling takes account of the fact that the effect of fixed increases in percent Black (e.g., increments of 5 points) are less important in counties where percent Black is large.

Female labor force share was measured by the percentage female for the total labor force. We also considered a similar measure computed separately for White women only, but it provided no additional useful information.

Manufacturing concentration was measured by the percentage of the total labor force employed in manufacturing industries. We also considered measuring this separately for durable- and nondurable-goods manufacturing. However, the distinction proved unimportant and we do not use it here.

White-collar employment was measured by the percentage of the total labor force employed in white-collar occupations. Between 1940 and 1970 this included the major categories of professionals, managers, sales workers, and clerical workers. For 1980 and 1990 this included the major categories of executives and managers, professional specialists and technical, sales, and administrative support workers.

Urbanization was measured by the percentage of the total county population residing in urban areas.

Labor force size was measured by the natural logarithm of the total labor force for the county. The natural log transformation was used to better capture its nonlinear relationship with inequality. This rescaling takes account of the fact that the effect of fixed increases in labor force size (e.g., increments of 100 workers) are less important in counties where the labor force is large.

Economic growth was measured in two ways. Long-term economic growth was measured by *labor force growth* as given by change in the natural logarithm of total labor force size. Short-term economic growth was measured by *percent employed* for the total civilian labor force.

Indigenous labor supply was measured by expressing the difference between the size of age cohorts poised to enter (e.g., persons 10-19 years of age) and age cohorts poised to leave the labor force (e.g., persons 55-64 years of age) to the size of age cohorts in the prime years of labor force participation (i.e., persons 20-64 years of age) (adapted from Poston and White 1978). We computed the measure using data for males only because female labor force participation rates changed dramatically between 1940 and 1990. However, alternative measures based on the total population were in fact highly correlated with the measure we used.

Status diversity was measured by the mean absolute deviation in socioeconomic status for the employed labor force. This was computed by assigning Nam-Powers socioeconomic scores to the occupation distribution for the total labor force. It indicates the average absolute status difference between randomly selected pairs of workers. We also computed a second measure of occupational diversity based on 1 minus the gini index of concentration for the distribution of persons across occupation categories.

Demand for education was measured in two ways. One was the expected demand for high school graduates. The other was the expected demand for mean years of completed schooling. Both were obtained by the method of indirect standardization. In this method, the education distributions for occupations at the national level in 1960 were used to estimate differences between occupations in their "intrinsic" requirements for education. These differences were then used to compute the "expected" education distributions for local areas based on their occupation distributions in each decade. The resulting scores indicated the extent to which the local occupation mix was dominated by occupations with high demands for education. The 1960 national occupation-education distribution is used as the standard for the computations because this decade was near the middle of our period of observation, but the results would have changed little if another decade had been adopted as the standard.

Units of Analysis

Our theoretical interest focuses on community-level stratification systems in the nonmetropolitan South. We use nonmetropolitan counties to delimit such systems. Obviously, the match between conceptualization and unit of analysis is not perfect here; counties sometimes overbound and sometimes underbound community structures in nonmetropolitan areas. However, counties have a proven track record in previous research and superior alternatives are not available. To the extent that the use of counties introduces error to our analysis, the error should be largely random in nature and will create a conservative bias *against* finding significant effects. Alternative units that we considered (e.g., nonmetropolitan cities, minor civil divisions) are no better in this regard and often are significantly worse. Moreover, , they carry the additional disadvantage of having considerably less data available. In sum, while counties only approximately represent community-level stratification systems, their advantages are considerable and far outweigh their disadvantages, especially when counties are compared with realistic alternatives.

Initial Sample

We randomly sampled (without replacement) counties of the census South until we obtained 300 nonmetropolitan counties which met the Census Bureau's criteria for tabulating occupation data separately by race and sex for each decade from 1940 to 1990.[5] To be considered as nonmetropolitan, counties could not be classified as metropolitan at any time between 1940 and 1990. We focused only on the South because census tabulations were not available for the Black populations of nonmetropolitan counties outside the South over the full time period covered by our study.

In drawing our initial sample of 300 counties, we rejected many counties (141 in all) which were randomly selected and met our sample criteria (i.e., were nonmetropolitan) but did not meet the Census

Bureau's specified criteria for publishing separate labor force and occupations tabulations for the Black population in one or more decades. These publication criteria are based on population thresholds which varied across decades. For example, in 1960 — the decade for which these criteria were most stringent, separate labor force and occupation tabulations for the Black (i.e., Nonwhite) population were not published for counties where the total Black population numbered fewer than 1,000 persons. Consequently, counties with small Black populations, resulting either from having small populations overall or from having low Black proportions in counties with larger overall populations, are not represented in our sample.

We computed descriptive statistics and correlation matrices using selected variables for which data were available for the 141 counties which were excluded from the analysis on this basis. These analyses (not reported here) indicated that these counties were not obviously different from the counties included in the sample. For example, their means for manufacturing concentration, unemployment, growth rates, etc. appeared to be similar to those observed for counties included in the sample. The same was true for correlations among these variables. There was one important but hardly surprising exception. The means for the excluded counties were decidedly lower for percent Black and for population size — the two main factors determining whether the Black population met the threshold for publishing the data for Blacks separately in census tabulations. Other than this expected difference, we could find no evidence that our analysis sample was markedly unrepresentative of southern, nonmetropolitan counties.

Nevertheless, we take a conservative position and stress that our sample is not representative of *all* southern, nonmetropolitan counties; it underrepresents counties with small Black populations. Thus, since the dynamics of racial inequality may well be different in such counties, we are careful to stress that our results do not generalize to these counties.

Analysis Sample

As we moved from initial data collection to descriptive analysis and later to multivariate modeling efforts we found it necessary to impose additional restrictions on the sample. These can be summarized as follows. We required that the Nonwhite population be at least 80 percent Black to insure that tabulations for the census racial category of "Nonwhite" (used in 1950 and 1960) could be reasonably used to index the Black population. Fourteen counties from our initial sample of 300 were lost based on this restriction.[6] We also required that the White population be at least 80 percent non-Hispanic to insure that White occupation distributions were not biased toward lower status occupations by the inclusion of Hispanics who were recorded as Whites and not reported separately for nonmetropolitan counties prior to 1970. Six additional counties were lost based on this restriction. Finally, we required that the county have a minimum of 150 Black men in the civilian labor force in each decade to insure that the samples used to generate the census occupation tabulations were adequate to sustain analysis. Two additional counties were lost based on this restriction.

In addition to these systematic sample refinements, we also excluded two counties from the analysis sample because they had extreme scores on change in percent Black which dramatically influenced the results of multivariate regression analyses. Beaufort, South Carolina had a very large increase in percent Black between 1940 and 1950 which appears to result from the establishment of a large military installation. Union, Kentucky had a very large increase in percent Black between 1960 and 1970 that may have resulted from the establishment of a job training facility.[7] When these counties were included in the regression analyses they exerted unusual influence which *exaggerated* the effects of changes in percent Black. We excluded them because they represented highly unusual situations which made them quite different from "typical" communities which experienced much smaller decade-to-decade changes in percent Black due to less exceptional patterns of migration.[8]

Finally, nine counties from our initial sample were lost because separate occupation and labor force tabulations for the Black population were inexplicably not published for the county in one or more decades (even though the county met the Census Bureau's stated criteria for publishing separate tabulations by race).

Altogether our final sample used for performing statistical analyses totaled 267 cases with complete data for all six decades. This yields a maximum sample size of 1,602 cases in "pooled" analyses (based on 267 cases observed at six points in time).

The sample restrictions we imposed are justified on grounds that it helped insure the validity of the measures of inequality and the robustness of the analysis results. When we included these cases in our analyses, the substantive findings rarely changed (with the exception noted above when the two cases with extreme values on change in percent Black were included). However, model errors of prediction were larger due to increased measurement error in the dependent variables. Additionally, the regression results were less consistent across decades because the impacts of some of the problems we were coping with via sample restrictions change from one decade to the next due to changes in census procedures.[9] For example, if we include counties with complex ethnic structures (i.e., substantial numbers of Hispanics, Asians, Native Americans, or other groups) our measures of White-Black inequality are biased *down* in decades where these groups are included with Nonblacks and are biased *up* in decades where these groups are included with Nonwhites.

Miscellaneous Methodological Issues

We encountered several miscellaneous methodological problems which warrant brief mention. Many were common to other cross-sectional studies of racial inequality and have previously been noted in the research literature. Others, however, were associated with the analysis of change in inequality over time and have not to our knowledge been noted in previous studies. Here we try to note some of the more important of these methodological problems so future investigators will be wary of them and we indicate how we dealt with them. Other concerns are also discussed in Appendix Chapter C.

Changes in Census Race Categories

Racial and ethnic categories used in the census have changed with every census. Four different definitions of the Black population were used in census materials between 1930 and 1990. In 1930 and 1940 the designation Negro was used; in 1950 and 1960 the designation was Nonwhite; in 1970 the designation was Black; and in 1980 and 1990 the designation was Black or African American.[10] To insure that these changes did not affect our Black-White comparisons across areas or over time, we included counties in our final analyses only when the racial breakdown of the population effectively included only Blacks and Whites. Thus, we excluded areas where Hispanics, American Indians (Native Americans), Asian Americans, or other non-Black ethnic minorities were present in significant proportions. More specifically, we excluded counties where other Nonwhite minorities comprised more than twenty percent of the Nonwhite population in 1980, or where Hispanics comprised more than twenty percent of the White population in 1980. These sample restrictions were noted earlier and were necessary to insure that data for non-Whites primarily reflected Blacks and that data for Whites (often obtained by subtracting data for Blacks from data for the total population) primarily reflected non-Hispanic Whites.

Changing Occupation Categories

Detailed census occupation categories changed with each census between 1940 and 1990. Major census occupation categories were relatively stable between 1940 and 1970 (though not entirely). However, the changes in major occupation categories between 1970 and 1980 were significant and greatly complicated descriptive analysis of group occupation differences over time. We dealt with these changes by constructing occupation distributions for 1980 and 1990 that conformed to the major categories used in the 1970 census so we could use comparable major occupation categories for all decades. We accomplished this by mapping detailed 1980 occupation titles onto detailed occupation titles for 1970 using a conversion table taken from census publications (US Bureau of the Census 1989) and then aggregating to 1970 major categories. Thus, we were able to build our own "1970-category" occupation tables for 1980 and 1990 to obtain a consistent occupation scheme for descriptive analysis.

We conducted detailed methodological analyses examining the impact of using different approaches to measuring occupation. Some of the relevant results are presented in Appendix Chapter B. Here we make two points. The first is that changes in occupation categories between 1970 and 1980 do not create serious problems for measuring inequality between groups over time. The second is that representing 1980 and 1990 occupation distributions using 1970 broad categories is not problematic because the vast majority of detailed occupation titles for 1980 and 1990 map into 1970 major categories in a straightforward and unambiguous way.

Changes in the Sample Universe for Occupation Tabulations

The sample universe for local area occupation tabulations has changed over time. One change was that the minimum age for inclusion in the tabulations increased from 14 and above in 1940 and 1950 to 16 and above in later decades. Another, potentially more important, change is that the 1940 tabulations included members of the armed forces while later decades were limited to the employed civilian labor force. We examined changes in occupation status, occupational inequality, and total labor force to determine if changes between 1940 and 1950 were distorted by these shifts in census procedures. Insofar as we could determine, the impact was minimal for the counties in our sample.

Relative versus Absolute Status

Nam-Powers status scores measure status at a particular point in time. The education and income rankings of occupations which serve as the basis for developing the scores are decade-specific and, thus, the scores measure *relative* not "absolute" status. We call attention to this fact, but we do not see it as a limitation. Notions of "absolute" occupational status are not well developed and are not the focus of our analysis. Future studies might attempt to develop status scores which can be compared over time in some absolute sense by ranking occupations based on income and education rankings pooled over a broad time frame (e.g., 1940-1990). At present, however, there is no accepted basis for evaluating the status of an occupation apart from its decade-specific historical context.

The computing methodology for Nam-Powers status scores dictates a mean of near 50 for the total civilian labor force for the nation in each decade. This national mean cannot change appreciably over time because the status scores are recalibrated each decade. However, status means for local areas, regions, and sociodemographic subgroups can change over time. These changes reflect changes in regional and subgroup integration into the national occupational structure. Changes in the mean status score for a region, county, or demographic subgroup indicate how the occupation distribution for that subpopulation is changing relative to the national status structure. Differences across majority and minority groups indicate how they compare to each other in this regard.

Measuring Status from Major Occupation Categories

We performed methodological studies to determine whether the use of major-category occupational data affected the reliability of our measurements of status and status inequality. For earlier decades (1940-1960), county-level occupation data were available only in major-category form. However, intermediate- and detailed-category tabulations also were for available for 1970, 1980, and 1990.

We used detailed data for 1980 and 1990 to compare measures of status and inequality computed from broad occupation categories to measures computed from detailed occupation categories. The most important finding that emerged from our analyses was that measures based on major categories consistently *underestimate* status inequality between Black and White men. This is not surprising. Measures of inequality developed from major-category occupation data implicitly treat individuals in the same major occupation category as having identical status scores. Of course, this is not the case and inequality that exists *within* major categories is missed.

For example, in 1980 White-Black inequality measured by the mean status difference computed using data for 504 detailed categories averaged 16.5 for the counties in our sample whereas the same measure computed using data for 12 major categories averaged 13.3. Thus, the measure based on broad categories underestimated the level of inequality by almost 20 percent on average. The extent of variation in inequality from county-to-county was also underestimated by approximately 20 percent as the standard deviations of the county-level inequality scores was 4.0 for measures computed using detailed occupation categories and 3.2 for measures computed using major categories.[11] Nevertheless, the correlation between inequality scores computed using detailed categories and major categories was 0.843 which indicates that essential variation in inequality across areas *is* captured by measures based on major categories.[12]

In sum, measures based on major categories underestimate the *level* of inequality, but are reasonably reliable and can be used to investigate differences in inequality across areas and over time. Undoubtedly, measurement based on more detailed data would show *greater* advantages for White men. However, since major category data are used throughout, this factor is essentially constant across areas and over time. Thus, there is little reason to believe that *trends* in inequality between White men and Black men, area differences in inequality, or trends in inequality over time in any given area, are misleading. To the contrary, the major category data appear to do a good job of capturing cross-area and over-time variation in inequality. Further discusion of this and related measurement issues is provided in Appendix B.

Census Sampling Rates

Occupational distributions, industry distributions, and other key census tabulations were based on complete count data in the 1940 census but have been based on sample data in every subsequent census. As an added complication, the sampling procedures have varied from one census to the next. Thus, for example, occupation tabulations were based on sample rates of approximately 16 percent in 1950, 25 percent in 1960, 20 percent in 1970, and between 16-50 percent in 1980 and 1990.[13] Obviously, the reliability of measures developed from sample tabulations tends to be better in years where the sampling fraction is larger. This is suggested by the results of detailed analyses (not reported here) which show that the relationships among variables are stronger for decades where the sampling rate is higher, especially for 1940 where tabulations were based on complete counts. On the whole, however, the attenuation of associations among variables in decades with lower sampling rates appears to be modest and we could not find any evidence to indicate that differences in sampling rates across census years influences our substantive findings in any important way.[14]

Heteroskedastic Regression Residuals

One technical problem associated with decade-to-decade variation in the sampling rates is that it contributes to heteroskedasticity in the residuals of our multivariate regression analyses. The reason for this is that measures developed from tabulations based on smaller samples are less reliable and thus tend to have larger average residuals in regression analyses.

This problem is further compounded by the fact that, net of sampling considerations, the dispersion of regression residuals varies with county population size and percent Black. Heteroskedasticity is connected to population size because stratification outcomes involve random as well as systematic factors and the impact of random factors can more easily distort outcomes in small populations (thus leading to less predictable outcomes and larger average residuals in regression analyses). Similarly, heteroskedasticity is connected to percent Black because, controlling for population size, it determines the size of the Black population and thus the reliability of measured outcomes for this group.

Together these three factors (i.e., census sampling rates, population size, and percent Black) combine to create a fairly complex pattern of heteroskedasticity in the residuals of our regression analyses. As a result, the technical assumptions of regression analysis are not met and conventional procedures for assessing the statistical significance of the estimated effects of independent variables are rendered inappropriate. To address this problem we calculated decade-county-specific estimates of the standard error of the White-Black difference in mean status. This statistic serves as a direct measure of the reliability of the dependent variable which we then used to estimate weighted (generalized) least squares regressions which take account of heteroskedasticity and yield more appropriate significant tests. Additionally, we used robust regression techniques (Hamilton 1992) to insure that our results were not distorted by outliers which may result due to the less reliable measurements for counties with small samples.

Summary

This concludes our review of issues relating to measurement of the variables used in our analysis. We turn now to a descriptive analysis of how inequality and its potential determinants are distributed across southern, nonmetropolitan counties and how they have changed over time.

Notes

1. Income data for families *and unrelated individuals* is tabulated by race in 1950. Family income is problematic because it varies with family structure which varies by race over time. This problem is made worse when unrelated individuals are combined with families.

2. By construction, percentile scores follow a rectangular distribution with a mean of 50 and a standard deviation of 28.9 (calculated from a formula provided in Freund 1962:146). In individual-level data for 1980, the mean and standard deviation for Nam-Powers status scores are 51 and 26.

3. In the two group situation, the logical range of group differences in mean percentile scores is −50 to 50. Nam-Powers status scores are the average of two percentile scores (one for education and one for income) and group differences in mean status will thus have a *maximum* logical range of −50 to 50 when the two percentile scores are perfectly correlated (and less otherwise). The logically possible range is greater in local areas and in multi-group situations, but this is possibility is not realized in our data.

4. The two measures correlate at 0.92 or higher in every decade.

5. As defined by the Census Bureau, the South includes the following states: Alabama, Arkansas, Delaware, Florida, Georgia, Kentucky, Louisiana, Maryland, Mississippi, North Carolina, Oklahoma, South Carolina, Tennessee, Texas, Virginia, and West Virginia. The census South also includes Washington, DC, but it is entirely metropolitan.

6. As noted below, occupation tabulations for the Black population were based variously on "Negro," Nonwhite, and Black. The presence of significant numbers of "Nonblack" Nonwhites thus affected changes in measured occupation inequality. This sample restriction primarily affected counties in Oklahoma where Nonwhite data often included a high proportion of Native Americans. The restriction was applied based on 1980 data. Persons in the "other" race category were not included among Nonwhites if they were of Spanish origin. Nonwhites thus included Blacks, Asian and Pacific Islanders, Native Americans, and other Nonwhites who were not of Spanish origin. In several counties, persons of Spanish origin identified themselves as "other" on the race question at a high rate in 1980 where in previous years this fraction had been very small.

7. We could not confirm this speculation using readily available secondary data sources. It seems a plausible guess, however, as by 1970 about 65 percent of the Black population consisted of youths living in group quarters but few were represented in the most common settings for young adults living in group quarters (i.e., military, institutional, and college settings).

8. One indication of how unusual these two counties are is that in robust regression analyses they were given "robust weights" of near zero which effectively drops them from the analysis.

9. For example, inclusion of Hispanics in occupation data for Whites biased measures of White status downward and inclusion of other non-White groups in occupation data for Blacks tended to bias Black status upward. Together they biased measures of White-Black status inequality downward.

10. This is only a crude summary. See the documentation for each census to examine more detailed changes in the census procedures used to determine respondent's race.

11. We also computed inequality using the thirteen broad categories adopted in the 1980 census. The mean and standard deviation were 11.8 and 3.1, respectively, which indicated that it underestimated the level of inequality by almost 30 percent and the variability in inequality by almost 25 percent.

12. The correlation between inequality computed from 504 detailed categories and 13 circa-1980 broad categories was 0.85.

13. The intended sampling fraction in 1980 varied between 16 percent (1 in 6) for enumeration districts with 2,500 or more inhabitants to 50 percent (1 in 2) for enumeration districts with less than 2,500 inhabitants. Therefore, depending on the mix of enumeration district size within a county, the sampling fraction can range from 16 percent to 50 percent. The actual fractions are reported in appendix tables to the published census volumes and often vary considerably from area to area.

14. One possible exception is that the levels of explained variance in our regression analyses are lower in more recent decades where sampling fractions tend to be smaller. This result is discussed in more detail in Chapter 5.

4

Trends in Inequality

In this chapter we review trends in socioeconomic inequality between Whites and Blacks from 1940 to 1990 in southern, nonmetropolitan areas. We begin with a brief examination of trends in educational inequality and income inequality. After that we turn to our main focus — trends in occupational distribution and occupational inequality. Finally, we conclude the chapter with a review of trends for selected structural characteristics of southern nonmetropolitan areas.

Educational Inequality

Detailed education data were not reported separately by race for nonmetropolitan counties until 1950 and were not reported separately by sex for Blacks until 1970. Accordingly, our analysis of trends in education begins in 1950 and is limited to a review of data for men and women combined. Fortunately, combining data for men and women is not a significant problem because trends in education for men and women tend to be very similar *within* racial groups.

Table 4.1 presents data documenting trends in levels of educational attainment for Whites and Blacks and trends in White-Black educational inequality. We measured level of education by the average number of years of schooling completed for members of the group. We calculated these figures separately for each county in our sample. Thus, the descriptive statistics in Table 4.1 summarize the distribution of these county-specific aggregate measures (e.g., medians reported in Table 4.1 refer to medians of the county-specific scores for average years of schooling completed).

The data reveal that educational attainments for Whites in southern nonmetropolitan counties were low in 1950 but increased

TABLE 4.1 Inequality in Educational Attainments, 1950-1990

Variable	N	Mean	SD	IDR	P_{10}	P_{50}	P_{90}
Mean Years of Education for Whites*							
1950	267	8.3	0.9	2.1	7.2	8.3	9.3
1960	267	9.0	0.8	2.0	8.0	9.0	10.0
1970	267	9.7	0.7	1.8	8.8	9.7	10.6
1980	267	10.7	0.7	1.6	9.9	10.7	11.5
1990	267	11.7	0.6	1.5	11.0	11.7	12.5
Mean Years of Education for Blacks*							
1950	267	4.9	0.9	2.3	3.8	4.8	6.0
1960	267	5.7	0.9	2.1	4.6	5.8	6.8
1970	267	6.9	0.8	2.1	5.9	6.9	8.0
1980	256	8.6	0.8	1.9	7.7	8.6	9.6
1990	267	10.1	0.6	1.5	9.4	10.1	10.9
Net Difference for Education Whites-Blacks							
1950	267	49.7	14.7	36.3	31.8	50.9	68.1
1960	267	45.3	15.0	38.9	26.0	46.7	64.8
1970	267	39.3	14.0	36.0	21.1	40.6	57.1
1980	256	30.2	12.8	33.0	14.9	30.9	47.9
1990	267	26.0	11.4	28.6	12.0	26.6	40.6

Note: N refers to the number of counties in the sample; Mean refers to the sample mean; SD refers to the sample standard deviation; IDR refers to the sample interdecile range (i.e., P_{90}–P_{10}); P_{10} refers to the 10th percentile case in the sample distribution; P_{50} refers to the median or 50th percentile case in the sample distribution; and P_{90} refers to the 90th percentile case in the sample distribution.

*Mean number of years of schooling completed were computed separately for Whites and Blacks in each county. This table reports descriptive statistics for these means (e.g., P_{50} for mean years of education for Whites represents the median in the distribution of the county-specific scores on mean education for Whites).

rapidly over the next four decades. In 1950, the level of education for White adults (i.e., persons aged 25 and older) was only 8.3 years in the "typical" county in our sample (i.e., the White education level for the median or 50th percentile county in our sample was 8.3 years).[1] This figure climbed approximately 3.4 points over the next four decades and stood at 11.7 years by 1990.

Education levels for Blacks started out at an even lower level but followed a stronger upward time trend. In 1950 the level of edu-

cation for Blacks in the typical county was only 4.8 years, but this
figure increased by 5.3 points to stand at 10.1 years in 1990.

In relative terms, improvements in educational attainment were
substantially greater for Blacks than Whites. The 5.3 point increase
in the Black education level for the typical (i.e., median) county
between 1950 and 1990 represents a gain of 110.4 percent. In contrast, the 3.4 point increase in the White education level for the typical county represents a substantial but clearly smaller increase of
40.9 percent.

Since education increased faster for Blacks than Whites, educational inequality between Whites and Blacks fell sharply over time.
We measure inequality between the White and Black education distributions in each county using Lieberson's (1975) index of net difference. A score of 0 on this index indicates equality between the
groups. Specifically, it indicates that, when randomly chosen Whites
and Blacks are compared on education, Blacks are as likely to rank
above Whites as below.[2] The logical range of the measure is from a
maximum of 100 which results when all Whites have higher educational attainments than all Blacks to −100 which indicates the
reverse.

By this indicator racial inequality in education was extremely
high in 1950; the score for the typical county in our sample was 50.9.
Furthermore, the 10th percentile score (P10) of 31.8 indicates that
fully ninety percent of the counties had ND scores above 31.8. Thus,
in 1950 there were few areas where the magnitude of educational
inequality was even moderate much less low. Clearly the dominant
feature of the distribution of scores is the consistently large advantages Whites had over Blacks in education in the counties in our
sample. That does not mean, however, that educational inequality
was uniform from area to area. To the contrary, ten percent of the
counties had scores above 68.1. Thus, the interdecile range (IDR) for
the inequality scores for education was 36.3, a figure which indicates
considerable variation in inequality across areas. The variation, however, is from high inequality to extremely high inequality.

White-Black educational inequality declined rapidly over time.
The net difference score for education fell from a typical (i.e., median)
value of 50.9 in 1950 to 26.6 in 1990. To be sure, inequality in education was still relatively high in most counties in 1990, but the score
for the typical county had fallen by almost one half over the four decades. The variability in inequality across areas declined to a certain
extent but it continued to be substantial (e.g., the interdecile range in
1990 was 28.6).

Such a strong and steady trend of convergence in White and

Black education levels might suggest that racial income and occupation comparisons would also be characterized by substantial movements toward equality. As we shall see, however, this was not the case.

Family Income

Census data on income distributions were not available in any form for nonmetropolitan counties before 1950. Similarly, income distributions for nonmetropolitan counties were not tabulated separately by race and sex for individuals until 1970. Income for families has been tabulated separately by race since 1950 so we use these data to examine trends in inequality between the White and Black income distributions. As we will note below, however, these data are less than ideal because they are strongly affected by trends in family structure.[3] Data summarizing these trends are presented in Table 4.2.

The summary statistics presented here show that family income in the typical county (i.e., the median county in our sample) increased with each decade for both Whites and Blacks. The percentage gains were especially large between 1950 and 1970. Over this period, the sample median for White income increased by 157 percent and the sample median for Black income increased by 184 percent. After 1970 income growth slowed for both groups. Between 1970 and 1990, the sample median for White income increased by about 20 percent and the sample median for Black income increased by about 21 percent. For Blacks, the inflation-adjusted median family income in the typical county actually fell between 1980 and 1990.

In contrast to educational inequality which fell sharply over time, White-Black inequality in family income did not decline significantly over time. The net difference score for the comparison of White and Black income distributions was never lower than 36.4 for the typical county (i.e., the sample median) in any decade between 1950 and 1990. Furthermore, in every decade, at least ninety percent of the counties in our sample had net difference scores of 22.0 or higher.

The finding that the white advantage in income was high throughout the period does not mean that it was uniformly high in all areas. To the contrary, the magnitude of inequality varied widely across counties in every decade. This is indicated by the fact that the interdecile range for the net difference scores was never smaller than 24.4 in any decade. In short, inequality was high everywhere, but it was exceptionally high in some areas compared to others.

TABLE 4.2 Inequality in Family Income, 1950-1990

Variable	N	Mean	SD	IDR	P_{10}	P_{50}	P_{90}
White Median Family Income [1990 Dollars]							
1950	267	9,529	2,719	6,843	6,335	9,294	13,178
1960	267	16,828	3,579	9,623	12,092	16,590	21,715
1970	267	24,055	3,585	9,450	19,182	23,905	28,631
1980	267	25,921	3,558	8,872	21,263	26,081	30,135
1990	267	28,940	4,520	10,889	23,606	28,668	34,495
Black Median Family Income [1990 Dollars]							
1950	267	4,383	1,564	3,270	2,544	4,309	5,814
1960	267	7,523	2,205	5,799	4,988	7,045	10,787
1970	267	12,760	3,177	8,452	9,080	12,239	17,532
1980	241	15,527	3,182	8,284	11,672	15,177	19,955
1990	266	15,644	4,152	10,377	10,880	14,784	21,257
Net Difference for Family Income White-Black							
1950	267	40.7	11.7	29.3	26.4	40.4	55.7
1960	267	49.2	12.4	32.7	32.7	49.3	65.3
1970	267	42.3	11.5	28.8	27.8	42.8	56.6
1980	241	36.0	10.7	26.9	22.0	36.4	49.0
1990	266	40.3	10.4	24.4	28.6	40.9	53.0

Regarding trends in inequality, the pattern is easy to summarize; the index of net difference score for the typical county in our sample in each decade was no lower in 1990 than it had been some forty years earlier in 1950. Examination of the decade-to-decade changes shows that White-Black inequality on family income increased significantly in the 1950s, fell in the 1960s and 1970s, and then increased again in the 1980s. The index of net difference for the typical county increased by 8.9 points between 1950 and 1960, fell by 6.5 points between 1960 and 1970, fell again by 6.4 points between 1970 and 1980, and then increased by 4.5 points between 1980 and 1990.

These data overwhelmingly contradict conventional wisdom that racial inequality in income has been steadily diminishing over time. Furthermore, it is clear from these data that the sizeable narrowing of human capital differences between Whites and Blacks that took place between 1950 and 1990 apparently has had only limited consequences (if any) for White-Black income inequality in the nonmetropolitan South.

This said, we must note that trends in income and income inequality should be interpreted cautiously. Income tabulations for 1950 included families *and* unrelated individuals while tabulations for 1960 and later included only families. Possibly this change in census methodology exaggerated the apparent increase in inequality between Whites and Blacks observed for the 1950s. However, this methodological issue does not have any bearing on the fact that inequality in family income did not decline substantially after 1960.

A different and more complicated issue to address is the extent to which trends in family income inequality are affected by important changes in family structure that are occurring at the same time. Family income is strongly affected by family structure; on average, husband-and-wife families have much higher incomes than other family types. The percentage of families that are husband-and-wife families has declined significantly and steadily in recent decades. The trend is readily apparent for both Whites and Blacks, but the changes have been particularly dramatic for Black families. This raises the possibility, then, that the continuing high level of inequality in income between White and Black families we observe in our data is attributable, in part, to differential trends in family structure.

This issue should not be ignored, but at the same time it should not be naively used to "explain away" the stubborn persistence of racial income inequality. The causal connections between family income and family structure are complicated. Trends in Black family structure have almost certainly been influenced by changes in the relative economic opportunities available to Black men. Thus, family structure is best seen as endogenous to the trends not exogenous. That is to say, trends in family structure are best seen as being at least partly determined by many of the same factors that are shaping income inequality. Feedback loops and indirect linkages connecting family structure and income inequality are likely such that it would be inappropriate to view trends in income inequality as "dependent" on family structure in any simple way. Untangling these reciprocal causal connections would require detailed analysis of complex longitudinal models and this has yet to be undertaken.

What is clear from this discussion is that interpretations of trends in family income are open to debate. Some of the ambiguities could be avoided if we could track income inequality for individuals as well as families. Unfortunately, we cannot do this for the nonmetropolitan counties in our study because the requisite data do not exist for the earlier decades in our study period. This is one of the reasons why we see the data on occupation as being more attractive for tracking trends in White-Black inequality over time in nonmetropolitan counties.

Occupation

Occupational inequality is the major focus of our study. It is an important stratification outcome and it has been tabulated separately by race and sex for individuals employed in the civilian labor force at the county level since 1940. This latter fact means that the data for occupation afford the possibility of tracking long-term trends in racial inequality. In view of this, we describe trends in occupational attainment and occupational inequality in some detail.

Occupational attainments and intergroup inequality on occupation can be examined in many different ways. One way is to examine detailed occupation distributions to see how they change over time. It is not feasible to perform such an analysis separately for each county. However, we perform such an analysis by aggregating the separate occupation distributions for the counties in our sample to obtain one summary occupation distribution for these counties. Table 4.3 presents the percentage occupation distributions for race and sex groupings derived from the "combined" occupation distributions for each decade from 1940 to 1990. The occupation categories used in the table are major groupings which can be maintained across time.[4]

The occupation categories are listed in order of status ranking as determined by Nam-Powers socioeconomic scores which reflect the education and income attainments of the incumbents of the detailed occupations in the broad category.[5] The rank ordering of occupations here is a rough approximation because the relative status positions of broad occupation categories, while somewhat stable over time, are not perfectly so.

This fact is illustrated in Figure 4.1 which depicts trends over time in the socioeconomic status levels of broad occupation categories.[6] The data show that the professional and managerial categories consistently have high socioeconomic status. The sales and crafts categories have lower but above average status levels. The operative, service, and nonfarm laborer categories are next lowest on average status. Finally, the farm laborer and domestic service (private household worker) categories have the lowest average status.

For the most part the relative standings of the major occupation groupings on socioeconomic are stable over time. Only two groupings, farmers and clerical workers, change position significantly between 1940 and 1990. The status of farmers (or more accurately, farm owners and farm managers) was initially very low in the 1940s and 1950s but it increased significantly after 1960. Closer inspection of the data reveals that this is a real trend, not an artifact of changes in census procedures or peculiarities of the Nam-Powers methodology for

TABLE 4.3 Occupation Distributions by Race, Sex, and Decade for Southern Nonmetropolitan Counties, 1940-1990

Occupation Category	Males						Females					
	1940	1950	1960	1970	1980	1990	1940	1950	1960	1970	1980	1990
White												
Professionals	3.5	4.8	7.2	9.8	11.2	12.6	18.1	14.3	13.7	14.4	16.0	19.1
Managers	8.3	9.6	11.7	11.8	11.9	14.6	5.2	5.5	4.9	4.3	6.5	9.7
Skilled Craft Workers	9.3	15.0	19.5	23.9	25.7	22.9	0.6	1.1	1.2	2.3	2.5	2.3
Clerical & Sales Workers	7.3	9.2	11.6	11.7	11.7	11.4	22.4	31.9	34.2	35.6	38.3	37.2
Operatives	14.9	18.9	22.4	21.9	20.1	18.9	23.1	24.9	26.5	24.6	17.5	12.4
Service Workers	2.4	2.5	3.4	5.1	6.3	7.5	8.8	10.1	11.7	14.0	15.5	15.8
Nonfarm Laborers	5.9	5.8	5.7	6.1	7.7	7.7	0.9	0.7	0.5	1.3	1.8	1.8
Farmers	34.1	25.6	13.8	6.3	4.4	3.0	4.7	1.8	1.6	0.7	0.6	0.5
Farm Laborers	14.2	8.5	4.7	3.3	2.0	1.5	9.2	7.0	2.2	0.8	0.7	0.4
Domestic Workers	0.1	0.1	0.1	0.1	0.0	0.0	7.2	2.6	3.6	2.1	0.7	0.6
Black												
Professionals	1.2	1.6	2.5	3.3	4.3	4.8	4.7	7.4	8.5	10.3	11.0	10.9
Managers	0.5	0.9	1.1	2.0	3.0	4.2	0.5	1.1	1.0	1.1	1.8	3.3
Skilled Crafts Workers	2.3	4.2	6.9	13.5	15.8	16.1	0.0	0.2	0.2	1.1	1.9	2.0
Clerical & Sales Workers	0.4	0.9	1.5	3.1	4.9	6.5	0.4	1.6	2.0	6.1	13.7	18.3
Operatives	7.4	15.0	21.5	29.8	32.7	21.3	2.0	6.3	7.4	21.8	30.5	29.0
Service Workers	3.1	4.1	7.0	10.2	12.1	13.9	5.1	11.4	15.3	22.0	27.0	28.1
Nonfarm Laborers	14.2	17.0	21.2	20.7	18.9	17.2	0.7	1.0	0.9	1.8	4.1	3.4
Farmers	38.0	33.9	15.5	3.9	1.9	1.2	7.5	5.9	2.7	0.0	0.2	0.2
Farm Laborers	31.3	21.9	22.0	12.9	6.0	3.9	31.2	23.5	10.7	3.6	1.6	1.0
Domestic Workers	1.5	0.6	0.6	0.6	0.2	0.1	47.8	41.6	51.3	32.1	8.1	3.7

Note: See Appendix B for a more detailed version of this table.

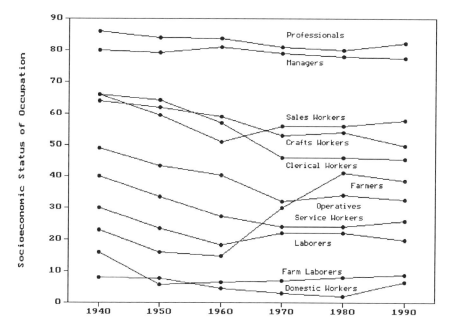

FIGURE 4.1 Socioeconomic Status Scores for Major Occupation
Groupings, 1940-1990.

computing status scores. The rise in the status scores for farmers and
farm managers came about because the education and income
distributions of persons employed in this category increased strongly
relative to the rest of the labor force. This was connected to two parallel trends, the emergence of large-scale, capital-intensive farming
enterprises and the decline of smaller "family" farms whose owners
typically had lower income and education attainments.

In contrast to farmers, the relative status of clerical workers
declined over time. In the 1940s and 1950s, the income and education
distributions of workers in this category ranked lower than those of
professionals and managers but were comparable to those of workers
in the crafts and sales categories and substantially higher than other
groups. After 1960 clerical workers began to compare less favorably
with crafts and sales workers. This resulted primarily due to a dete-
rioration of the relative income component of the socioeconomic status
score for clerical workers. Even so, clerical jobs continued to be solidly in the middle range of status positions and maintained a clear
advantage over the lower-status positions of operatives, service workers, laborers, and domestic workers.

The main point to be taken from this digression is that, with the exercise of appropriate care, the data presented in Table 4.3 provide a ready basis for evaluating how the distribution of Whites and Blacks across *ranked* occupation categories has changed over time.

Figure 4.2 presents the information in Table 4.3 in a graphical format which helps clarify the trends in distribution across different occupations for the different groups. One feature of these figures that we should note is that the Y-axis in each figure is scaled according to the square root of the percentage of the group employed in the occupation category. The square root transformation expands the lower portion of the scale relative to the upper portion. This helps improve the readability of the trends for occupations containing small percentages of the group. One consequence to bear in mind, however, is that vertical movement in the bottom half of the graph (where the scale is expanded) is exaggerated relative to vertical movement in the top half of the graph (where it is compressed).

The most dramatic trend in the panel for White males is the precipitous decline in representation in farm occupations between 1940 and 1990. In 1940 approximately 50 percent of White men were either farmers or farm laborers. By 1990 this had fallen to less than 5 percent. This trend was accompanied by considerable increases in the representation of White men in the professional and crafts categories and modest increases in representation in the managerial, clerical-sales, operatives, service, and nonfarm labor categories.

The representation of Black men in farm occupations also declined sharply between 1940 and 1990. In 1940, approximately 70 percent of employed black men were in farm occupations. By 1990 the figure was less than 6 percent. Over the same period Black men came to be increasingly represented in the crafts, operatives, and service categories. Their representation in the professional, managerial, and clerical-sales categories also increased over time but by a somewhat lesser amount than that observed for White men. The representation of Black men in all white-collar occupations combined increased significantly; it rose some 13.4 points from 2.1 percent in 1940 to 15.5 percent in 1990. However, over the same period the representation of White men in the white-collar occupations increased 19.5 points from 19.1 percent in 1940 to 38.6 percent in 1990. Thus, even as the representation of Black men in white-collar occupations was increasing, the *gap* between White men and Black men *expanded* from 17.0 percent in 1940 to 23.1 percent in 1990.

Our primary focus here is on occupation comparisons between White and Black men. Nevertheless, we briefly consider the trends in

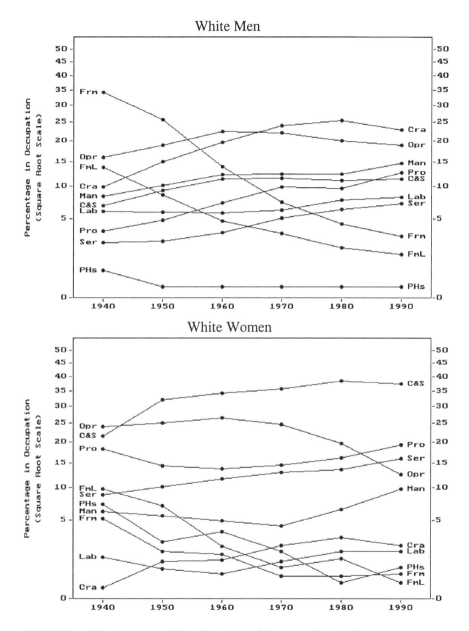

FIGURE 4.2 Percentage Distributions of Race and Sex Groups Across
Major Occupation Groupings by Decade.

Pro-professionals, Man-managers and administrators, C&S-clerical and sales,
Crf-crafts workers, Opr-operatives, Srv-service workers, Lab-nonfarm laborers, Frm-farmers, FmL-farm laborers, and PHs-private household workers.

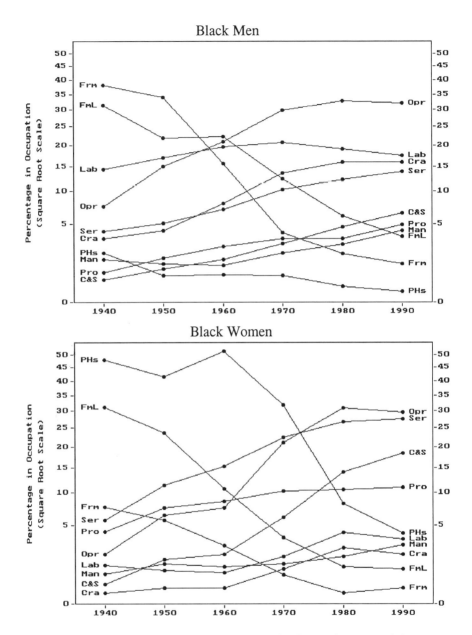

FIGURE 4.2 (Continued) Percentage Distributions of Race and Sex Groups Across Major Occupation Groupings by Decade.

Pro-professionals, Man-managers and administrators, C&S-clerical and sales, Crf-crafts workers, Opr-operatives, Srv-service workers, Lab-nonfarm laborers, Frm-farmers, FmL-farm laborers, and PHs-private household workers.

occupation distribution for White and Black women. These trends are dramatic and interesting in their own right. In addition, as we noted earlier in Chapter 2, the increasing representation of women in the wage labor force may have implications for racial inequality between White men and Black men and thus warrants at least brief review here.

Not surprisingly, the representation of White women in occupational categories in 1940 was much different from that of White men. White men were concentrated in the farm, operatives, and crafts categories; White women were concentrated in the operative, clerical-sales, and professional categories. White women's representation in white-collar occupations increased over the decades rising from 45.7 percent in 1940 to 66.0 percent in 1990. The clerical and sales categories accounted for most of this increase. The category of service worker was the only other category to show a significant increase. Declines were observed for operatives, farm laborers, and domestic workers.

Changes in occupational distribution for Black women were the most dramatic of the trends found in these data. In 1940 nearly four-fifths of all employed Black women were found in just two categories — farm laborer and private household worker. By 1990, less than 5 percent of employed Black women were found in these categories. Instead, Black women were concentrated in the operative, service, clerical-sales, and professional categories. Significantly, increases in the representation of Black women in white-collar and middle-status occupations was generally greater than the movement of Black men into these same categories. Thus, by 1990 63.5 percent of employed Black women were found in the top five occupation categories (i.e., operatives and above) compared to only 52.9 percent for Black men.

Mean Occupational Status

It is not practical to consider changes in detailed occupation distributions on a county-by-county basis. Instead, we must use summary measures of occupational status to describe trends in occupational distribution. Accordingly, Table 4.4 presents descriptive statistics for mean socioeconomic status by race and sex for the counties in our sample. The mean status scores are based on Nam-Powers socioeconomic status scores for occupations. As noted earlier, these scores reflect the income and education attainments of persons employed in the occupations. At any given point in time these scores measure relative status because the scores are recalibrated each decade to reflect changes in the income and education levels of workers

TABLE 4.4 Occupational Status, 1940-1990

Variable	N	Mean	SD	IDR	P_{10}	P_{50}	P_{90}
Mean Socioeconomic Status for White Males							
1940	267	39.0	6.8	16.8	31.0	38.2	47.8
1950	267	39.7	7.1	18.7	30.2	39.7	48.9
1960	267	45.5	5.5	14.3	37.9	45.7	52.2
1970	267	48.1	3.2	7.5	44.6	48.1	52.0
1980	267	48.9	2.6	6.1	45.8	48.9	51.8
1990	267	49.5	3.1	7.8	45.8	49.3	53.6
Mean Socioeconomic Status for White Females							
1940	267	53.9	5.9	14.0	47.0	54.2	61.1
1950	267	52.7	5.9	14.0	45.5	53.5	59.5
1960	267	49.9	4.0	9.7	45.5	49.9	55.2
1970	267	45.6	3.3	8.5	41.3	45.6	49.8
1980	267	47.8	2.6	6.5	44.4	47.9	50.9
1990	267	51.8	2.8	7.5	47.9	52.0	55.4
Mean Socioeconomic Status for Black Males							
1940	267	25.6	5.4	11.3	20.7	24.0	32.0
1950	267	24.4	5.4	13.0	18.2	23.5	31.2
1960	267	26.1	5.2	12.8	19.5	26.3	32.3
1970	267	31.9	3.9	9.1	27.1	32.3	36.2
1980	267	35.4	3.0	7.1	32.0	35.7	39.1
1990	267	36.7	2.8	6.6	33.6	36.5	40.3
Mean Socioeconomic Status for Black Females							
1940	267	18.7	2.9	6.7	15.6	18.3	22.4
1950	267	20.7	4.2	10.9	15.6	20.3	26.5
1960	267	20.4	4.5	11.2	14.9	19.9	26.1
1970	267	26.1	4.7	11.3	20.6	25.6	31.9
1980	267	34.9	3.8	9.0	30.4	35.0	39.4
1990	267	38.9	3.6	9.2	34.4	38.5	43.6

in different occupations. By their construction, the national average for Nam-Powers scores for the total labor force of the country will tend to be near 50 in any given decade. This value can thus provide a benchmark for interpreting trends over time.

    With this in mind, we see socioeconomic status for employed White males in the typical county in our sample converged on the national norm between 1940 and 1990. That is, as measured by Nam-Powers status scores the occupational standing of White men in southern, nonmetropolitan counties increased from 38.2 in the typical county in 1940 to 49.3 in 1990, a value which closely approximates the expected average for the national labor force. This trend reflects the increasing integration of the South into the national economy since World War II (McKinney and Bourque 1971) and the attendant massive redistribution of White men out of low status farm occupations and into higher status professional, managerial, sales, and crafts occupations. Most of the large 11.1 point improvement in relative status over the five decades occurred after 1950.

Socioeconomic status for employed Black males in the typical county in our sample also increased between 1940 and 1990. It increased by almost 12.5 points changing from an intitial value of 24.0 in 1940 to 36.5 in 1990. In comparison to the trend seen for White males, the increase in occupational status for Black males was delayed and did not begin until after 1960. As will be seen below, this delay relative to Whites resulted in a substantial increase in inequality between Whites and Blacks during the 1950s which was not reversed until 1980.

The lack of change in mean socioeconomic status for Black men between 1940 and 1960 highlights the relative nature of the Nam-Powers status scores and warrants a brief discussion of how this trend can be reconciled with the significant changes in occupational distribution for black men documented in Table 4.3 and Figure 4.2 introduced earlier. To be sure, the occupational distributions for Black men changed considerably during the 1940s and 1950s; the representation of Black men in the crafts, operative, and service categories increased while representation in the farm categories declined. From one point of view, this can be seen as an upgrading of occupational standing for Black men. However, from the point of view of their standing relative to other groups in the labor force, Black men did not improve their *rank-order* position in the occupational hierarchy. Occupational distribution in the nonmetropolitan South was changing and it carried Black men along with it. That is to say, in the 1940s and 1950s Black men simply maintained their rank-order position in a changing occupational structure.

The mean socioeconomic status for employed White women in the typical county in our sample fell steadily between 1940 and 1970. Overall, it fell by 8.6 points from an initial position of 54.2 in 1940 to 45.6 in 1970. This trend indicates that the occupational standing of White women relative to others in the labor force declined even as they were steadily shifting into clerical-sales and service occupations and shifting out of farm and private household occupations. The trend is so strong that, whereas employed White women in the typical county in our sample had a considerable status advantage over White men in 1940, this advantage was eliminated and reversed by 1970.

After 1970 the mean status for white women rebounded and the value for the typical county rose 7.1 points to stand at 52.1 in 1990 not quite 3 points above the typical score for white males. Examination of detailed data on occupation distributions (not presented here) yields insights into this trend in occupational status for White women. White women did indeed have a significant status advantage over White men in 1940 which disappeared by 1970. The pattern is not an artifact of census occupation categories or other measurement problems; it is quite real. The explanation for this trend is that White men in southern nonmetropolitan counties in 1940 and 1950 were concentrated in very low status farm occupations. Relatively few White women were in the wage labor force at this time and, in comparison with men, few of the women in the wage labor force were in the very low status farm occupations. They were instead concentrated in the middle-status sales-clerical and operatives categories.

Between 1940 and 1970 the representation of White men in the low status farm categories declined dramatically and their represent-ation in middle and upper status categories such as crafts and profes-sionals increased sharply. White women's representation in middle status categories of clerical-sales and operatives increased over this same period, but the upgrading of their occupational position was not as strong as that observed for White men during the same period. Furthermore, the representation of White women in the higher-status professional and managerial categories actually declined substan-tially between 1940 and 1970 while the representation of White men in these categories almost doubled. Thus, during the period where increasingly large numbers of White women were entering the labor force, the distribution of White women shifted strongly toward the middle-status clerical-sales, operative, and service occupations. With regard to relative status, these occupations rank well above the farm and laboring occupations where men were concentrated in 1940 but below the professional, managerial, and crafts occupations where men were coming to be increasingly concentrated over time.

The trend in occupation distributions for Black women is drama-tic and quite different from the trend observed for any other group. The mean socioeconomic status for Black women in the typical county was 18.3 in 1940, by far the lowest value observed for any of the groups. This figure increased 20.2 points, the largest increase observed for any group, to stand at 38.5 in 1990. Interestingly, most of this change (15.6 points) occurs in the 1960s and 1970s. The increase was dramatic by any standard. It can be traced to the shift

TABLE 4.5 Occupational Inequality, 1940-1990

Variable	N	Mean	SD	IDR	P_{10}	P_{50}	P_{90}
Dissimilarity for Occupation White Males-Black Males							
1940	267	36.7	11.0	29.2	23.1	34.9	52.3
1950	267	37.7	9.8	26.5	24.1	37.5	50.7
1960	267	44.8	7.0	17.4	36.1	45.1	53.5
1970	267	41.9	6.7	16.6	33.6	42.2	50.2
1980	267	37.1	6.2	16.2	28.9	37.1	45.1
1990	267	34.8	6.1	14.2	27.9	34.7	42.0
Net Difference for Occupation White Males-Black Males							
1940	267	31.2	16.3	42.9	10.4	29.4	53.4
1950	267	34.1	14.7	37.8	15.6	33.8	53.4
1960	267	44.6	12.3	31.2	28.3	45.9	59.5
1970	267	45.2	7.9	20.5	34.3	45.8	54.9
1980	267	39.8	7.7	20.1	28.9	40.6	49.0
1990	267	36.8	8.1	19.1	27.3	37.1	46.4
Mean Status Difference White Males-Black Males							
1940	267	13.4	5.7	15.0	6.6	12.7	21.5
1950	267	15.3	5.5	13.8	8.3	15.3	22.1
1960	267	19.4	5.0	12.4	12.8	19.5	25.2
1970	267	16.3	3.7	8.8	11.8	16.2	20.6
1980	267	13.5	3.1	7.9	9.8	13.7	17.6
1990	267	12.8	3.2	7.5	9.3	12.7	16.7

from massive concentration of Black women in the extremely low-status categories of farm laborer and domestic worker in 1940 to equally massive concentration in the middle- and lower-status categories of operatives, service workers, and clerical-sales workers in 1990. As a consequence, the mean socioeconomic status for employed Black women in the typical county went from being about 6.4 points below the comparable figure for Black men as recently as 1960 to being roughly equal by 1980. While this change is not a central focus of the present analysis, it is nevertheless a striking finding worthy of mention.

Differentiation and Inequality

Table 4.5 presents data documenting trends in occupational differentiation and inequality for the counties in our sample. Differentiation is distinct from inequality. It indicates only that occupation differences exist between groups; it does not necessarily imply that the differences are systematically patterned relative to the status rankings of occupations. We used the index of dissimilarity (D) to measure occupational differentiation between groups.[7] This index ranges from a minimum of 0, which occurs when groups have identical occupation distributions, to a maximum of 100, which occurs when groups do not have any occupations in common. The value of D indicates the minimum percentage of one group that would have to change occupations to make its occupational distribution identical to that of the other group.

Dissimilarity between the White male and Black male occupation distributions in the typical county increased slightly during the 1940s and moreso in the 1950s. It then fell steadily during the 1960s, 1970s, and 1980s. Dissimilarity in the typical county stood at 34.9 in 1940 and climbed to 45.1 by 1960, an increase of 10.2 points. It then fell by approximately the same amount over the course of the next three decades to stand at 34.7 in 1990. Thus, the typical level of dissimilarity for the counties in our sample in 1990 was scarcely different from what it had been in 1940 though it was significantly lower than the peak value of about 45 observed in 1960.

The dissimilarity score of 34.7 for the median county in our sample in 1990 indicates that at least 34.7 percent of Black men would have had to change occupations in order to make the relative frequency distributions for White men and Black men on occupation identical. It thus indicates that even as of 1990 Whites and Blacks are disproportionately concentrated in different occupations.

We also present summary data for two measures of occupational inequality — the index of net difference and the mean difference in socioeconomic status. Both are attractive measures of inequality (for more details see our discussion in Appendix A) and indicate the extent to which occupation differences between Blacks and Whites produce systematic advantage for one group relative to the other.

The index of net difference is a measure of ordinal inequality which requires only that occupations be rank ordered (not scaled) on status. It shows a strong trend of increasing inequality in the 1940s and 1950s. The value for the typical county in our sample increased by about 16.5 points from 29.4 in 1940 to 45.9 in 1960. The value observed in 1960 indicates that, if White men and Black men were randomly compared on status, the percentage of comparisons favoring White men would exceed the percentage of comparisons favoring Black men by 45.9 points.[8] The typical value of the index of net difference remained near this peak through 1970. It then declined by a total of 8.7 points in the 1970s and 1980s and stood at 37.1 in 1990. Significantly, the typical score in 1990 was some 7.7 points higher than the typical score of 29.4 observed in 1940.

We find an essentially similar pattern when occupational inequality is measured by the White-Black difference in mean socioeconomic status, an interval-level scaling of occupational status. Inequality in the typical county in our sample increased from 12.7 points in 1940 to 19.5 points in 1960, a total increase of 6.8 points. It then fell from this peak in subsequent decades and stood at 12.7 in the typical county in 1990. Thus, the mean status difference between Whites and Blacks increased during the 1940s and the 1950s, decreased afterwards, during the 1960s, 1970s, and 1980s, and stood at approximately the same level in 1990 as it had originally stood in 1940.

It is interesting to note that interarea variability in inequality declined steadily over time. For example, the interdecile range for the index of net difference fell in each decade starting at 42.9 in 1940 and ending at 19.1 in 1990. Likewise, the interdecile range for the mean status difference between White men and Black men fell steadily and precipitously from 15.0 in 1950 to 7.5 in 1990.

Several explanations for this trend are possible. One is that over time the areas in our sample became more similar on the structural characteristics which affect area variation in racial inequality. For example, as will be seen below, percent Black declined steadily over time and varied less across counties in 1990 compared to 1940.[9] Similarly, variation in women's labor force share and status diversity also declined substantially between 1940 and 1990.[10] Thus, at least in these respects, Southern nonmetropolitan areas became more homogeneous on structural characteristics affecting inequality. Alternatively, the effects of community characteristics on inequality may have become less important due to the effects of the passage and enforcement of federal equal opportunity legislation.

Declining area differences in inequality over time also might indicate that southern nonmetropolitan areas have been slowly but steadily integrated more tightly into national social and economic structures and that this has served to mute area differences in discrimination and inequality. For example, penetration and prevalence of mass media may have reduced regional, rural-urban, and local cultural differences. Similarly, improvements in communication and transportation may have increasingly integrated local areas into national and regional economies and reduced nonmetropolitan areas' isolation from and ability to deviate from national and regional business practices.

Graphical Representations of Inequality

Figure 4.3 helps clarify how the changing patterns for the differences between the occupation distributions for White men and Black men translate into trends in occupational inequality. This figure was prepared by aggregating the data for the counties in our sample to get summary distributions for Blacks and Whites at each time period.[11]

The separate graphs for each decade consist of stacked horizontal bars which depict the percentage representation of white and black men in major occupation categories.[12] The bars in each graph are "stacked" from low to high based on the socioeconomic status ranks for the occupation groupings (identified by labels on the right-hand side of the figure). The vertical "thickness" of each horizontal bar reflects the overall percentage (of the combined total of both groups) employed in the occupation category. Given this construction, the Y-axis provides the cumulative percentage distribution for workers ranked on socioeconomic status. The scale for the Y-axis runs from 0 which represents the lowest status percentile to 100 which indicates the highest status percentile.

Race differences in distribution at different status levels are depicted by shading each horizontal bar to indicate the percentage representation of Black men in the occupational category. The scale for the X-axis thus extends from 0 to 100. A thick vertical dotted line indicates the percentage representation of Black men in the combined pool of employed White and Black men. This line provides a point of reference for determining whether Black men are under-represented or over-represented in any given occupation.

In sum, these graphs depict (a) the overall occupation distribution for White and Black men, (b) whether Blacks and Whites are evenly distributed across occupations, and, if not, (c) whether the under representation of Blacks in different occupations is systematically correlated with the status ranking of the occupations.

The panels for 1940 and 1950 reveal substantial racial occupational *differentiation*. This can be seen in the fact that the shaded portions of the occupation bars do not line up on the vertical line marking the overall representation of Blacks among employed men. The panels also clearly reveal substantial racial *inequality* since the racial differences are generally patterned in such a way that blacks are systematically *under* represented in the higher ranking occupations and *over* represented in the lower ranking occupations. In both 1940 and 1950 Blacks are under represented in each of the top six occupations ranked on status and over represented in each of the bottom six occupations ranked on status.

1940

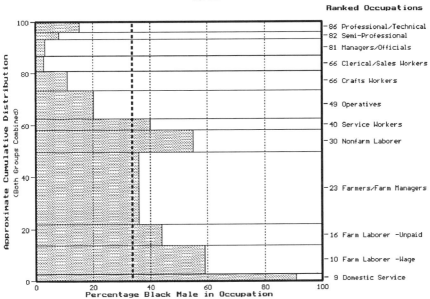

1950

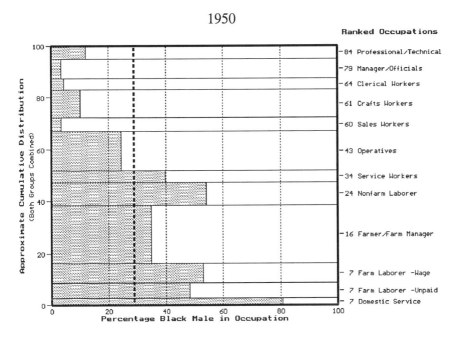

FIGURE 4.3 Percentage Distribution of White and Black Men Across Ranked Occupation Groupings by Decade.

1960

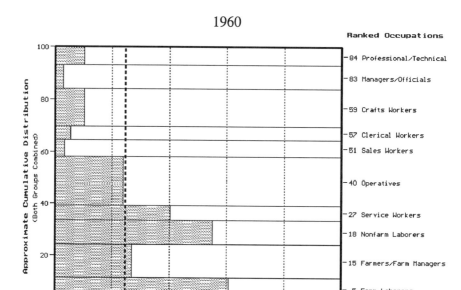

1970

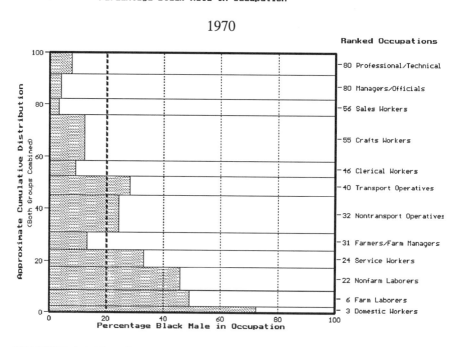

FIGURE 4.3 (Continued) Percentage Distribution of White and Black Men Across Ranked Occupation Groupings by Decade.

1980

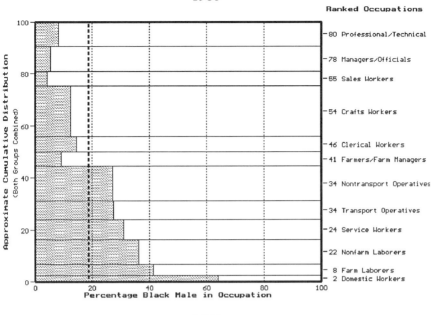

1990

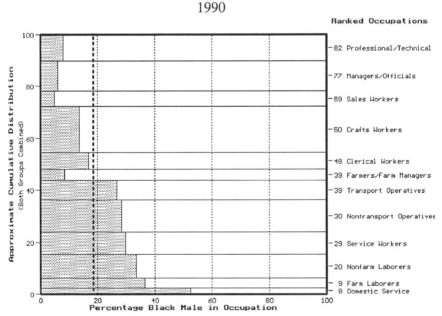

FIGURE 4.3 (Continued) Percentage Distribution of White and Black Men Across Ranked Occupation Groupings by Decade.

The panels for 1960, 1970, 1980, and 1990 reveal that these essential features of the story do not change substantially over time. In each and every decade pronounced differences are observed between the occupation distributions for White and Black men with Black men being consistently under represented in the higher status occupations and over represented in the lower status categories.

As noted above, the occupational structure of southern, nonmetropolitan counties is changing significantly over time. Between 1940 and 1990 the farm occupations declined dramatically while skilled manual (e.g., crafts workers and operatives) and white collar occupations expanded. This is readily evident in Figure 4.3 in that the vertical "thickness" of the horizontal bars for farm occupations diminishes steadily over time while the vertical "thickness" of the horizontal bars for crafts, operative, and white collar occupations, increase from one decade to another.

One consequence of these shifts in the occupational structure is that the jobs which occupy the "middle ranks" in the status structure of nonmetropolitan counties change over time. For example, in 1940 the categories of service workers, operatives, and even nonfarm laborers ranked solidly in the middle portion of the occupational hierarchies of southern nonmetropolitan areas (i.e., these occupations are at or above the fiftieth percentile mark in the cumulative status distribution). After 1960 these same occupations are found in the bottom half of the occupational hierarchy.

What remains invariant over time, however, is the fact that, regardless of which particular jobs are in the top half of the occupational hierarchy in any given decade, Black men are consistently under represented in these jobs. Similarly, regardless of what particular jobs are in the bottom half of the occupational hierarchy in any given decade, Black men are consistently over represented in these jobs. This is further evidence that White-Black differences in representation in particular occupations is not driven by cultural differences in preferences for certain jobs or occupation-specific "race codes" which are stable over time. Instead, White-Black differences in representation in particular occupations are strongly correlated with the relative standing of the occupation in the overall status structure at any given point in time. Thus, these differences change over time as the relative standing of the occupation changes.

The patterns depicted in Figure 4.3 help clarify how racial occupational inequality increased between 1940 and 1960. In 1940 a large number of both Whites and Blacks were located in the category of farmers and farm managers. This occupation group ranked very low on status and White representation in this category served to hold racial inequality down. This can be seen in the fact that the over representation of Blacks in this category is not as great as the over representation of Blacks in other low status occupations. Between 1940 and 1950, and especially between 1950 and 1960, the fraction of White men employed as farmers and farm managers fell dramatically and the moderating influence on inequality of large numbers of low-status White farmers became less important.

The patterns depicted in Figure 4.3 also provide further indication that the increase in inequality between White males and Black males observed in the 1940s and 1950s is not artifactual. In one sense, the 1940s and 1950s were decades of dramatic occupational upgrading for Black men; their representation in farm occupations declined and their representation in the categories of operatives and laborers increased. Nevertheless, two factors caused Black men to lose standing relative to White men in these decades. First, there was a considerable upgrading of the occupational mix for the entire labor force in southern nonmetropolitan areas and thus occupational standing for Black men was improving as part of a general secular trend but not necessarily in relation to the occupational standing of White men. The second is that the broad upgrading of occupations proceeded at an even faster pace for White men than it did for Black men. Thus, Black men were falling behind White men even as Black men's representation in farm occupations was declining very rapidly and their representation in white-collar occupations (professional, managerial, sales, and clerical) and skilled crafts categories was increasing rapidly.

Figure 4.4 introduces a second graphical device we use to help discuss racial inequality in occupational attainment — "inequality curves". Briefly, inequality curves provide a visual representation of the comparison of two group distributions and can be used to develop intuitive, geometric interpretation of the level of rank-order inequality registered by the index of net difference (see Appendix A for a more extended discussion of this point). In this figure, the X-axis registers the cumulative percentage distribution of White men when they are rank-ordered on occupational status and cumulated from low to high. The Y-axis registers the percentages of men who have status equal to or less than White men at any given point in the cumulative status distribution for White men. This is plotted separately for White men and Black men. The plot of these values for White men yields a diagonal line running from the lower left corner of the figure (0,0) to the upper right corner (100,100). The plot of the Y values for Black men against the X values for White men yields an "inequality

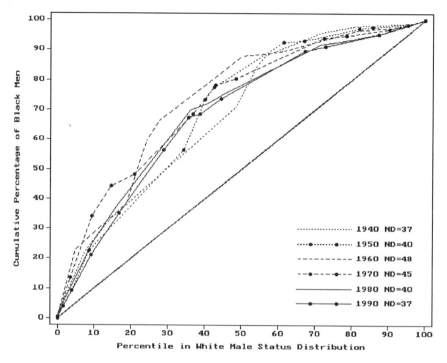

FIGURE 4.4 Cumulative Percentage of Black Men by Percentile in the White Male Status Distribution by Decade.

curve" which shows the percentage of Black men ranking at or below White men at different points in the cumulative status distribution for White men.

The inequality curve can be used to visually assess the existence, direction, and level of inequality. If the curve exactly follows the diagonal, this indicates that White men and Black men have identical status distributions (because White men and Black men cumulate at the same rate as White men are summed from low to high) and thus no inequality exists between the groups. If the curve rises above the diagonal, White men have an advantage over Black men (because Black men are cumulating more rapidly than White men as White men are summed from low to high). If the curve falls below the diagonal, Black men have an advantage over White men (because White men are cumulating more rapidly than Black men as White men are summed from low to high). The further the curve falls away from the diagonal (either above it or below it), the greater the level of inequality.

The inequality curve is particularly useful for our purposes because it has a close correspondence with the index of net difference, a measure of inequality that we use extensively in our descriptive analyses. More specifically, the value of the index of net difference is determined by the size of different areas delimited by the inequality curve and the diagonal. Thus, the value of the index of net difference can obtained by taking the area between the curve and the diagonal that falls below the diagonal (in these graphs none), subtracting from it the area between the curve and the diagonal that falls above the diagonal (in these graphs, all of it), and expressing the difference as a percentage of the total area below the diagonal. Accordingly, the index of net difference associated with the inequality curve for each decade is given in the lower, right-hand corner of the figure.

The net difference curve runs above the diagonal in every decade indicating that inequality favors Whites throughout the period of observation. Furthermore, the net difference curve shifts higher above the diagonal (indicating greater inequality) from 1940 to 1950 and then again from 1950 to 1960. It is only after 1960 that the net difference curve begins to contract back toward the diagonal line of equal status distribution. The figure shows that after some 50 years, the area between the inequality curve and the diagonal in 1990 is scarcely different from that observed in 1940.

Trends in Structural Characteristics

We use the remainder of this chapter to briefly review trends for structural characteristics of counties which our theoretical review has suggested may have implications for changes in racial occupational inequality in southern nonmetropolitan areas.

Demographic Changes

The counties in our sample were selected based on being non-metropolitan from 1940 to 1990. It is not surprising therefore that they are characterized by relatively low levels of urbanization. That said, the counties in our sample did become steadily more urbanized over time. Indeed, Table 4.6 shows that the fraction of the population residing in urban areas in the typical county in our sample more than doubled from 12.9 percent in 1940 to 30.0 percent in 1990.[13] This is an important increase in urbanization but it should be kept in perspective. Even in 1990 these counties remained largely rural.

Increasing urbanization did not generally bring increasing population size at the county level. Instead, offsetting declines in rural

TABLE 4.6 Demographic Structure, 1940-1990

Variable	N	Mean	SD	IDR	P_{10}	P_{50}	P_{90}
Percent Urban for County Population							
1940	267	15.2	17.1	38.5	0.0	12.9	38.5
1950	267	20.1	18.6	44.5	0.0	19.8	44.5
1960	267	25.3	20.5	51.4	0.0	25.6	51.4
1970	267	28.5	20.6	53.9	0.0	31.0	53.9
1980	267	29.6	19.8	54.5	0.0	31.4	54.5
1990	267	28.6	19.6	54.4	0.0	30.0	54.4
Natural Log of County Population							
1920	261	9.92	0.52	1.31	9.20	9.98	10.51
1930	267	9.94	0.58	1.46	9.15	9.98	10.61
1940	267	9.99	0.59	1.52	9.18	10.00	10.70
1950	267	9.95	0.62	1.60	9.12	9.96	10.72
1960	267	9.91	0.64	1.69	9.11	9.89	10.80
1970	267	9.90	0.66	1.70	9.11	9.87	10.81
1980	267	10.03	0.68	1.73	9.22	10.01	10.95
1990	267	10.06	0.71	1.77	9.23	10.03	10.99
Percent Black in County Population							
1920	261	40.7	19.7	52.0	15.6	41.0	67.5
1930	267	38.7	18.7	50.4	15.0	38.2	65.4
1940	267	37.5	18.7	50.3	12.9	36.4	63.2
1950	267	35.6	18.1	49.9	11.2	33.6	61.1
1960	267	34.9	17.5	48.5	10.8	33.3	59.4
1970	267	31.7	16.3	45.1	9.8	30.5	54.8
1980	267	29.4	16.4	44.7	8.3	27.8	52.9
1990	267	29.0	16.9	47.3	7.3	27.8	54.6

farm population tended to produce no, or only small, net gains in population. We measured population size by the natural log of population for substantive reasons (i.e., proportionate changes are more relevant than absolute changes) and because the distribution of population size is highly skewed. In the typical county, (the log of) population size held steady or increased slightly between 1920 and 1940 but then trended down between 1940 and 1970. The high water figure of 10.00 in 1940 represents a population of about 22,000 while the nadir of 9.87 in 1970 represents a population of about 19,340. The 1970s brought significant population growth, however, as the change in the median for (the log of) population size increased by 0.14 (this implies that the population of the median county grew by 15.0 percent between 1970 and 1980). This significant burst of growth was fol-

lowed by a decade of slow growth in the 1980s and the resulting figure of 10.03 for the sample median observed in 1990 represents a
population of about 22,700.

One clear and fundamental pattern was a strong downward
trend in the relative size of the Black population in the counties in
our sample. This is reflected in the fact that the sample median for
percent Black trended down in every decade from 1920 to 1980. It
stood at 41.0 in 1920 and only 27.8 in 1980. This 13.2 point overall
decline represented a reduction of 32.2 percent in the relative size of
the black population in the typical county in our sample. Between
1980 and 1990, the sample median for percent Black was unchanged.

Labor Force Growth and Composition

Growth in the civilian labor force is one measure of whether the
number of jobs in the local economy is expanding or contracting.
Table 4.7 shows that labor force size tended to be either stable or
declining between 1930 and 1960 and growing thereafter. In most
decades the changes in (the log of) labor force size were small to modest (usually implying percentage changes of 4 points or less).[14] The
1970s stand out as a major exception to this pattern. The median
change in (the log of) labor force size for 1980 was 0.24 which implies
that the typical county's labor force grew by about 27 percent for the
average county. In part, this decade reflects the coming of age of the
baby boom cohorts. But the implications for economic growth are not
to be taken for granted since southern, nonmetropolitan counties had
been exporting their entry-age labor cohorts through negative net
out-migration for many decades.

One potential basis for job competition and labor out migration
is a high level of "indigenous labor supply" — the balance between the
size of age cohorts entering and leaving the prime years of labor force
participation (i.e., 20-64).[15] Generally speaking, indigenous labor supply pressures were great in 1930 and continued to be significant even
in recent decades despite falling steadily over time. The median of
39.0 in 1930 indicated that the size of the entry-age cohort in the
typical county exceeded that of the exit-age cohort by an amount
equal to 39.0 percent of the labor force age population. By 1990, the
median was 12.1, less than a third of that value.

Another dramatic trend is the changing sex composition of the
labor force. Female labor force share — the percentage female for the
employed labor force — increased in each decade. It stood at 18.7
percent in the typical county in 1940 and increased to 45.6 percent in
1990. The change was so dramatic in fact that the *high* end of the

TABLE 4.7 Labor Force Growth and Composition, 1940-1990

Variable	N	Mean	SD	IDR	P_{10}	P_{50}	P_{90}
Natural Log of Civilian Labor Force							
1930	267	8.95	0.61	1.60	8.09	8.97	9.68
1940	267	8.95	0.60	1.63	8.13	8.95	9.75
1950	267	8.88	0.63	1.66	8.05	8.89	9.71
1960	267	8.82	0.66	1.71	8.01	8.80	9.71
1970	267	8.86	0.70	1.83	7.99	8.83	9.82
1980	267	9.12	0.71	1.90	8.23	9.10	10.13
1990	267	9.23	0.74	1.96	8.29	9.20	10.25
Change in Natural Log of Civilian Labor Force							
1940	267	0.00	0.14	0.34	-0.17	0.00	0.17
1950	267	-0.07	0.16	0.42	-0.30	-0.04	0.12
1960	267	-0.06	0.16	0.39	-0.25	-0.07	0.15
1970	267	0.04	0.13	0.34	-0.14	0.04	0.20
1980	267	0.26	0.14	0.28	0.12	0.24	0.40
1990	267	0.11	0.14	0.29	-0.04	0.09	0.24
Indigenous Labor Supply (Ratio of Persons 10-19 to 55-64)							
1930	267	38.5	7.3	19.5	28.1	39.0	47.6
1940	267	31.5	6.1	15.5	23.9	31.8	39.4
1950	267	24.1	7.0	19.1	13.7	25.4	32.8
1960	267	25.2	7.7	21.3	13.9	25.3	35.1
1970	267	22.4	7.5	19.5	12.8	22.4	32.2
1980	267	16.4	6.3	14.4	9.3	16.5	23.7
1990	267	12.1	6.0	13.0	5.7	12.1	18.7
Female Labor Force Share							
1940	267	19.9	6.4	17.1	12.4	18.7	29.5
1950	267	22.8	5.5	15.0	15.4	22.5	30.4
1960	267	31.1	4.4	11.8	25.2	31.1	37.0
1970	267	37.3	3.5	9.3	32.2	37.7	41.5
1980	267	41.7	3.2	8.2	37.3	42.0	45.4
1990	267	45.4	2.5	6.0	42.1	45.6	48.0

interdecile range for female labor force share in 1940 (29.5) is separated from the *low* end of the interdecile range in 1990 (42.1) by some 12.6 percentage points.

Occupation Mix

The structure of employment in southern nonmetropolitan areas changed dramatically in the post-war era. Table 4.8 shows that as

TABLE 4.8 Occupation Mix, 1940-1990

Variable	N	Mean	SD	IDR	P_{10}	P_{50}	P_{90}
Percent of Labor Force in Farm Occupations							
1940	267	52.6	18.4	47.1	26.9	56.3	73.9
1950	267	39.0	17.5	46.5	15.9	38.5	62.4
1960	267	21.0	12.7	31.9	5.7	18.5	37.6
1970	267	9.5	6.7	15.9	1.9	8.3	17.8
1980	267	5.9	4.6	10.7	1.2	4.9	11.9
1990	267	4.2	3.5	7.8	1.0	3.2	8.8
Percent of Labor Force In White-Collar Occupations							
1940	267	14.6	4.9	12.5	8.9	13.9	21.4
1950	267	20.2	5.4	13.7	13.9	19.8	27.6
1960	267	26.9	5.7	14.0	20.6	26.4	34.5
1970	267	32.3	5.7	14.0	25.9	31.6	39.8
1980	267	36.4	5.9	14.8	29.8	35.4	44.5
1990	267	41.6	6.4	15.4	34.5	40.6	49.8
Percent of Labor Force in Blue Collar Occupations							
1940	267	32.8	15.0	37.1	15.8	29.1	52.9
1950	267	40.8	13.8	36.0	23.2	39.3	59.2
1960	267	52.0	9.9	26.0	39.4	51.8	65.4
1970	267	58.2	7.1	17.2	49.6	58.2	66.9
1980	267	57.8	6.1	16.7	49.1	57.8	65.8
1990	267	54.2	6.2	15.8	45.8	54.6	61.6

recently as 1940, approximately 56.3 percent of the employed labor force was in farm occupations in the typical county in our sample. This figure fell 17.8 points to 38.5 in 1950, then fell by 20.0 points to stand at 18.5 in 1960, and fell again by 10.2 points to stand at 8.3 in 1970. Farm employment continued to fall during the 1980s and 1990s. However, by this time the levels were so low further declines could not be large. Overall then, the greatest changes occurred between 1940 and 1970 and, even though the trend is a familiar one, it is difficult to overemphasize how massive and rapid this structural change was.

As employment in southern nonmetropolitan areas shifted away from farm occupations it steadily shifted toward white collar and blue collar occupations. The percentage employed in white collar occupations (e.g., professional, managerial, sales, and clerical) in the typical county in our sample steadily increased over each decade starting at 13.9 percent in 1940 and ending at 40.6 percent in 1990. The increase in the percentage employed in blue collar occupations (e.g., crafts

TABLE 4.9 Industrial Structure, 1940-1990

Variable	N	Mean	SD	IDR	P_{10}	P_{50}	P_{90}
Percent of Labor Force in Manufacturing							
1930	267	10.6	7.7	20.3	2.7	8.0	23.0
1940	267	12.0	9.7	23.4	2.8	9.1	26.2
1950	267	16.6	10.7	26.6	4.8	14.2	31.4
1960	267	22.2	11.2	31.0	7.7	20.7	38.7
1970	267	27.8	12.1	31.5	12.8	27.0	44.4
1980	267	27.4	11.5	30.6	12.9	26.9	43.6
1990	267	25.6	10.8	28.3	11.5	25.7	39.8
Percent of Labor Force in Wholesale & Retail Trade							
1930	267	5.7	2.4	6.1	2.9	5.3	9.1
1940	267	8.4	3.2	7.9	4.8	7.9	12.7
1950	267	12.4	3.8	9.6	7.7	12.1	17.3
1960	267	15.8	3.5	8.5	11.6	16.0	20.1
1970	267	17.0	3.5	9.0	12.6	17.0	21.6
1980	267	17.2	3.3	8.8	13.0	17.1	21.8
1990	267	19.3	3.4	8.6	15.0	19.0	23.6
Percent of Labor Force in Service Industries							
1930	267	11.0	4.5	10.5	6.2	10.1	16.8
1940	267	15.0	4.9	11.8	9.4	14.2	21.2
1950	267	16.1	4.7	12.0	10.6	15.9	22.6
1960	267	22.2	5.3	12.3	16.4	21.8	28.7
1970	267	25.4	5.9	13.7	18.5	25.2	32.2
1980	267	24.1	4.9	11.5	18.5	23.4	30.0
1990	267	27.6	5.3	12.9	21.3	27.3	34.2

workers, operatives, laborers, and service workers) in the typical county was equally substantial; up from 29.1 percent in 1940 to a high-water mark of 58.2 percent in 1970 and ultimately standing at 54.6 percent in 1990.

Table 4.9 documents how the decline of southern agricultural employment was accompanied by shifts in employment toward manufacturing, trade, and service industries. The percentage employed in manufacturing in the typical county almost tripled between 1940 and 1970 increasing from 9.1 percent in 1940 to 27.0 percent in 1970. After 1970 it drifted down slightly to 25.7 in 1990. The percentage employed in trade in the typical county increased with each decade and more than doubled from 7.9 percent in 1940 to 19.0 percent in 1990. Likewise, representation in service industries expanded from 14.2 percent in the typical county in 1940 to 27.3 percent in 1990.

TABLE 4.10 Status Diversity, 1940-1990

Variable	N	Mean	SD	IDR	P_{10}	P_{50}	P_{90}
Occupational Diversity (1-Gini Index of Concentration)							
1940	267	0.52	0.10	0.27	0.38	0.52	0.65
1950	267	0.60	0.09	0.23	0.48	0.61	0.71
1960	267	0.70	0.08	0.21	0.59	0.70	0.80
1970	267	0.68	0.08	0.20	0.57	0.69	0.78
1980	267	0.63	0.06	0.14	0.55	0.63	0.69
1990	267	0.62	0.05	0.13	0.55	0.62	0.68
Mean Absolute Deviation for Occupational Status							
1940	267	17.7	3.2	8.4	13.1	18.1	21.5
1950	267	20.5	2.2	5.5	17.5	20.9	23.1
1960	267	20.7	2.1	5.5	17.6	20.9	23.1
1970	267	18.0	1.5	3.6	16.3	17.9	19.9
1980	267	16.5	1.1	2.7	15.3	16.4	18.0
1990	267	17.0	0.8	2.1	16.0	16.9	18.1

Occupational and Status Diversity

One aspect of occupational diversity is the extent to which workers are distributed evenly across major occupational roles as opposed to being concentrated in only a few categories. We measured this by one minus the gini index of concentration.[16] A score of 1 indicates completely even distribution of workers across all occupation categories (maximum diversity) and a score of 0 indicates total concentration in a single category.

As seen in Table 4.10, the typical score for this measure in 1940 was 0.52, a relatively low level of diversification which resulted because of the great concentration of workers in farm occupations in most counties. Diversification increased in the 1940s and 1950s as the labor force shifted into nonfarm occupations such as operatives and crafts workers and the median stood at 0.70 in 1960. During the 1960s diversity changed little. However, it declined in the 1970s and 1980s as employed workers began to be reconcentrated in operatives, crafts, and higher status white collar jobs (e.g., professional and managerial jobs) while representation of men in the farmer, farm laborer, and private household worker categories shrank to extremely low levels. By 1990, the diversity index for the typical county had fallen back to 0.62.

Status diversity is distinct from occupational diversity. As we use the term, occupational diversity refers to evenness of distribution across *different* occupational categories with no consideration being given to the magnitude of the status differences between the occupations. Status diversity takes this latter consideration into account and refers to the average status differences between workers. It is important for our purposes because we see it as setting logical limits for intergroup status inequality. That is, all else equal, status inequality between groups will tend to decline if occupations overall become more similar on status. We measure this aspect of the occupational mix by the mean absolute deviation of Nam-Powers socioeconomic status scores for occupations.

Status diversity increased in the 1940s. Its typical value in the counties in our sample increased from 18.1 in 1940 to 20.9 in 1950. It remained at that level through 1960 but in subsequent decades fell and by 1990 stood at 16.9, a value lower than its initial value observed in 1940. This trend is most interesting because it suggests that, all else equal, the structural "possibilities" for race inequality increased in the decades prior to 1960 and declined afterwards.

The Changing Structure of Labor Demand

Finally, we consider two variables which reflect changes in the nature of labor demand. One is the level of education "required" by the occupation mix in the local area. We measure this based on the education levels associated with occupations in 1960.[17] Trends for two measures are presented in Table 4.11. The first reflects the percentage of high school graduates "implied" by the mix of occupations in the local economy; that is, it reflects the percentage of high school graduates that would be required if occupations in the county were filled with high school graduates at the same rate observed nationally in 1960. The second reflects the average number of years of schooling completed "implied" by the occupational mix. Both measures indicate that between 1940 and 1990 the occupational mix shifted steadily from occupations with lower education requirements to occupations with higher education requirements. Overall, the median "implied" demand for high school graduates increased from 30.1 percent in 1940 to 46.7 percent in 1990.

Many occupations are strongly sex-typed such that their incumbents are either disproportionately female or disproportionately male. Since forces producing sex typing of occupations often change slowly,

TABLE 4.11 Measures of Labor Demand, 1940-1990

Variable	N	Mean	SD	IDR	P_{10}	P_{50}	P_{90}
Percent High School Graduates Implied by Occupation Mix							
1940	267	30.5	2.8	7.1	27.1	30.1	34.3
1950	267	34.2	3.1	8.1	30.3	34.0	38.5
1960	267	38.0	3.4	8.2	34.0	37.8	42.2
1970	267	42.0	3.1	7.6	38.5	41.6	46.1
1980	267	44.7	3.1	7.4	41.3	44.2	48.7
1990	267	47.3	3.2	7.7	43.7	46.7	51.3
Mean Education Implied by Occupation Mix							
1940	267	8.88	0.31	0.79	8.52	8.84	9.31
1950	267	9.25	0.32	0.82	8.85	9.25	9.67
1960	267	9.61	0.31	0.77	9.22	9.61	9.99
1970	267	10.00	0.26	0.66	9.71	9.97	10.37
1980	267	10.23	0.25	0.60	9.95	10.18	10.55
1990	267	10.43	0.26	0.59	10.15	10.40	10.74
Female Labor Force Share Implied by Occupation Mix							
1940	267	19.9	3.5	8.5	16.0	19.4	24.5
1950	267	22.5	3.6	9.1	18.0	22.4	27.1
1960	267	30.6	3.5	8.8	26.3	30.6	35.1
1970	267	36.7	2.7	6.8	33.3	36.8	40.2
1980	267	41.2	2.3	5.5	38.6	41.3	44.1
1990	267	42.7	2.0	4.8	40.1	42.6	44.9

changes in the occupational structure might be expected to affect the representation of women in the labor force. For example, rapid growth in lower-status clerical employment which is predominately female might be expected to increase the share of women in the labor force. We measured this potential aspect of occupational structure by generating "expected" levels of female labor force share by the method of indirect standardization. Specifically, we took the sex composition of occupations in 1960 (a decade near the middle of the study period) and applied them to the county-level occupation distributions in each decade to obtain the representation of women in the labor force that would be expected if the sex composition of broad occupations had remained fixed over time. As Table 4.11 shows, this measure of "expected" demand for women's labor increased steadily in each decade. Its median value stood at 19.4 in 1940 and more than doubled to 42.6 in 1990. Thus, the occupational mix shifted strongly toward female dominated occupations between 1940 and 1990.

Summary

We reviewed many different trends in this chapter. Out of all of these, one set of trends is to be emphasized above all others; declines in racial inequality in occupational attainment have not been dramatic and indeed the typical level of inequality observed in the counties in our sample was not much lower in 1990 than it had been in 1940 and 1950. Between 1940 and 1960 racial inequality in nonmetropolitan counties actually trended up and peaked in 1960. Since then it has gradually drifted down. This downward movement has been modest, however, and inequality today remains high. Indeed, it is in fact only about one-quarter to one-third off the peak values seen in 1960. We now turn in the next two chapters to the results of multivariate analyses which try to assess what factors are responsible for declines in inequality and what factors contribute to its persistence.

Notes

1. Unless otherwise noted, any reference to the "typical" county refers to the county with the median value in the distribution being described. We prefer the median over the mean (which we also report) as a summary measure of central tendency because it is less easily distorted by one or two unusual values. Similarly, we report the interdecile range (IDR) as well as the standard deviation (SD) to summarize dispersion because the interdecile range is less sensitive to extreme cases. When a variable is normally distributed, its interdecile range is about 2.5 times its standard deviation.

2. This measure is discussed in more detail in Appendix A. Substantively, scores above 10 indicate modest inequality favoring Whites, scores above 30 indicate substantial inequality, and scores above 50 indicate extensive inequality.

3. In 1950 family income data for Blacks include "unrelated individuals". In order to make an "apples-to-apples" comparison we also use income data for families and unrelated individuals for Whites. In later decades, the comparisons are based on income distributions for White families and Black families.

4. The occupation data for 1940, 1950, 1960, and 1970 are taken from published census volumes. The data for 1980 and 1990 are taken from detailed machine readable census files. The broad occupation categories used in published tabulations in 1980 and 1990 differ substantially from those used in previous censuses. To overcome this problem, we drew on detailed data and prepared tabulations for 1980 and 1990 which used major category groupings similar to those used in earlier censuses. To do this we processed the detailed occupation data for 1980 and 1990 and allocated them into 1970-equivalent categories using an allocation tables developed by Kubitschek (1986) for 1980 and the U.S. Bureau of the Census (1989) for

1990. See Stafford and Fossett (1991) for further details.

5. Nam-Powers status scores have a logical minimum of 0 which is approached when the occupation ranks lower than all other occupations on both education and income and a logical maximum of 100 which is approached when the occupation ranks higher than any other occupation on both education and income.

6. The broad categories reported in census publications for 1980 and 1990 differ from those reported in census publications for 1940 through 1970. We converted detailed occupation titles for 1980 and 1990 into detailed occupation titles used in 1970 to make the data consistent over time.

7. This measure is discussed in Appendix A.

8. To illustrate, a score of 45 would result if 65 percent of random comparisons between Whites and Blacks on occupation favored Whites while only 20 percent favored Blacks (i.e., 45 = 65 - 20). The remaining 15 percent of comparisons would be ties.

9. The standard deviation for percent Black fell from 18.7 points in 1940 to 16.9 points in 1980 and the interdecile range fell from 52.3 in 1940 to 44.7 in 1980.

10. The standard deviation for female labor force share declined by more than half from 6.4 in 1940 to 2.5 in 1990 and the interdecile range fell from 17.1 to 6.0. The standard deviation for status diversity fell by more than two thirds from 3.2 in 1940 to 0.8 in 1990 and the interdecile range fell from 8.4 to 2.1.

11. An alternative would have been to average the separate county distributions. This yields similar results.

12. Notice that the occupation categories used in this figure are more detailed than those used earlier in Table 4.3. The reason for this is that it is not necessary here to use a consistent occupational scheme over time. Thus, we use all of the occupational detail available in the tabulations for each decade.

13. We remind the reader that these comparisons are based on medians.

14. The implication of change in the natural log of labor force size for relative growth is straightforward. When the change in the natural log of size is exponentiated, it yields the multiplier which when applied to the previous decade's labor force size yields the size in the present decade. For example, the average change in the natural log of labor force size was -0.067 in 1950 and the implied multiplier is $e^{-0.067} = 0.935$.

15. In this study, we measure indigenous labor supply by expressing the difference between the 10-19 and 55-64 age cohorts relative to the population age 20-64. This captures the relative degree to which incoming cohorts will meet labor demands. We compute it for males because their labor force participation rates are uniformly high throughout the period of study.

16. The gini index indicates the extent to which the labor force is concentrated in a few of occupational categories with 0 indicating even distri-

bution across all categories and 1 indicating complete concentration in only one category. Accordingly, , one minus the gini index is a measure of occupational diversification.

17. We use the education levels for one decade to eliminate the impact of "educational inflation" which occurs when the education of persons in a given occupation increases as a consequence of broad secular trends in educational attainment.

5

Cross-Sectional Analyses

In this chapter we report the results of cross-sectional regression analyses investigating the effects of selected ecological and structural characteristics on racial inequality in southern nonmetropolitan areas. Space considerations permit us to present only a handful of the regression models we estimated in our efforts to assess the possible determinants of racial inequality. In our judgment, these are the models which best capture and summarize the key patterns of variation in our data.

The exploratory and diagnostic analyses we conducted indicated that many potential predictor variables identified in Chapter 2 could not be included in our "final" regression models for one reason or another. In some cases it was because their effects proved to be weak and inconsistent. In other cases it was because the variable proved to be conceptually and/or empirically redundant with other predictors.[1] Accordingly, the "final" models we discuss in this chapter include only a partial subset of the many predictors whose effects we examined. We crafted the specification of our "final" models based on several criteria. First, and most importantly, we emphasized substantive concerns such as the clarity of the hypothesis linking each variable in the model to racial inequality, parsimony, and the importance of each variable's effect on inequality. Secondly, we considered the consistency of the variable's effects across decades and in both cross-sectional models and longitudinal models (presented in Chapter 6).

We firmly believe that the models we present here capture important structural influences on racial inequality in nonmetropolitan stratification systems. However, we also recognize that alternative models might have been developed even using our own data set. For example, the variables percent of labor force employed in white-collar occupations and percent of labor force employed in manufacturing were highly collinear and could not both be included in the same model. We elected to include percent white collar because its theoretical motivation was attractive and because its effects were stronger and more consistent. Others may have elected to include percent manufacturing in place of percent white collar or to combine the two variables into an index of some sort. These are all defensible choices and theory in the area is not so well developed that it would rule out any of them. With this in mind, we invite others to scrutinize our results and consider possible extensions and refinements that might be pursued in future analyses.

Cross-Sectional Regressions

Table 5.1 presents the results of pooled cross-sectional regression analyses of racial inequality and mean status levels for White men and Black men. Detailed results of decade-specific, cross-sectional regressions for these dependent variables are reported in Tables 5.2-5.4.

We used ordinary least squares (OLS) regression techniques to estimate the results reported in these tables. We subjected these results to a wide range of diagnostic and sensitivity analyses to satisfy ourselves that the effects estimated were trustworthy. For example, we also estimated all models using generalized least squares (weighted) regression techniques to take account of heteroskedasticity in the regression residuals and assess its impact on OLS significance tests.[2] Similarly, we estimated all models using robust regression and bounded influence regression procedures outlined in Hamilton (1991) to guard against the impact of multivariate outliers and influential cases.[3] In addition, we performed analyses to determine whether the estimated effects of the variables were sensitive to the model specification used.[4] Space limitations do not permit us to present the results of these detailed analyses. However, unless specifically noted, they confirmed the substantive implications of the OLS results.

We present the decade-specific regressions in Tables 5.2-5.4 for the sake of completeness and because we know that some readers will want to examine the patterning of the effects across decades. However, we base our discussion of the effects of different independent variables primarily on the results of the pooled regressions presented in Table 5.1. We emphasize the pooled results for two reasons. The first is that pooling the data across decades allows parameters to be estimated more efficiently and thus provides more powerful tests of

TABLE 5.1 Pooled Cross-Sectional Regressions of Racial Occupational Inequality and Race-Specific Occupational Status on Selected Characteristics of Southern Nonmetropolitan Counties, 1940-1990

Independent Variables	SD	SES$_W$	SES$_B$
Unstandardized Regression Coefficients			
Square Root Percent Black (Level)	1.416[a]	1.034[a]	-0.383[a]
Female Labor Force Share (Level)	0.244[a]	0.376[a]	0.132[a]
Percent LF White Collar (Level)	0.117[a]	0.559[a]	0.442[a]
Status Diversity (Level)	0.569[a]	-0.306[a]	-0.875[a]
Percent Civilian LF Employed (Level)	0.161[a]	-0.215[a]	-0.376[a]
Indigenous Labor Supply (Level)	-0.084[a]	-0.088[a]	-0.004
Ln Civilian Labor Force (Level)	0.419[a]	0.309[b]	-0.109
Dummy for 1950	-1.759[a]	-2.692[a]	-0.933[a]
Dummy for 1960	-0.078	-4.105[a]	-4.027[a]
Dummy for 1970	-3.747[a]	-7.348[a]	-3.601[a]
Dummy for 1980	-7.166[a]	-11.910[a]	-4.744[a]
Dummy for 1990	-9.777[a]	-16.014[a]	-6.236[a]
Standardized Regression Coefficients[d]			
Square Root Percent Black (Level)	0.460[a]	0.255[a]	-0.095[a]
Female Labor Force Share (Level)	0.505[a]	0.591[a]	0.208[a]
Percent LF White Collar (Level)	0.253[a]	0.918[a]	0.728[a]
Status Diversity (Level)	0.292[a]	-0.119[a]	-0.342[a]
Percent Civilian LF Employed (Level)	0.089[a]	-0.091[a]	-0.159[a]
Indigenous Labor Supply (Level)	-0.154[a]	-0.123[a]	-0.006
Ln Civilian Labor Force (Level)	0.058[a]	0.032[b]	-0.011
Adjusted R Square	0.562	0.773	0.753
Number of Cases	1602	1602	1602
St. Dev. of Dep. Var.	5.022	6.609	6.593
St. Dev. of Residuals	3.324	3.148	3.276

[a,b,c] denote probability chance departure from 0 is less than 0.01, 0.05, or 0.10, respectively, using a two-tailed test.

[d] Standardized coefficients not reported for dummy variables for decade.

of statistical significance. The other is that, while the separate decade-specific regressions sometimes suggest that the effects of some independent variables may vary over time, theory provides few prior expectations regarding such patterns and we are reluctant to over-interpret the sample data in the absence of a guiding theory. In general, we concluded that the decade-specific cross-sectional results indicate that pooling observations over the six census years is justified.[5] With only a few exceptions, differences between the decade-specific models either are small and unimportant or, if statistically significant, they do not appear to follow any systematic and meaningful pattern. Given the number of parameters estimated and the lesser efficiency of estimates obtained using the smaller decade-specific samples, a certain degree of variability in the effects estimated for different decades should be expected. In light of this, we comment on the decade-specific results only when a distinct pattern with clear theoretical or substantive implications seems apparent.

Decade Effects. The pooled regression models include dummy variables which capture the additive effects of decade relative to the reference year of 1940. The effects of the dummies for decade in the model for the White-Black status difference (SD) reflect shifts in racial inequality across decades *net* of controls for other independent variables included in the model (i.e., holding constant trends in the means of the independent variables over time which might also lead to changes in inequality). These decade dummies indicate that, controlling for changes in the structural characteristics of nonmetropolitan counties, inequality changed little from 1940 to 1960 — the coefficient of -0.078 for 1960 indicates that inequality in 1960 was not appreciably lower than in 1940 — but began to drop significantly after 1960. The average level of inequality in 1970 was some 3.7 points lower than that observed in 1940; in 1980 it was 7.2 points lower, and in 1990 it was 9.8 points lower.

These decade effects may indicate broad social changes which affect southern nonmetropolitan areas *uniformly*. For example, they might reflect the impact of the Civil Rights movement and equal opportunity legislation of the 1960s. Of course, this is only speculation as direct measures of these variables are not included in the model and other interpretations of the coefficients for the dummy variables could also be offered. For example, the effects of the decade dummies could reflect the impact of changes in census procedures across time or changes in census coverage. Such alternative interpretations are not particularly compelling, but raising them serves to illustrate the "catch all" nature of the coefficients for the decade dummies. In view of this, we suggest that interpretations of decade effects should be considered tentative. Even with this caution in mind, however, it is clear that the pattern of the decade dummies suggests that, net of changes in structural characteristics, racial inequality has trended downward in recent decades.

TABLE 5.2 Decade-Specific and Pooled Cross-Sectional Regressions of Racial Inequality on Selected Structural Characteristics of Southern Nonmetropolitan Areas

Independent Variables	1940	1950	1960	1970	1980	1990	Pooled
Unstandardized Regression Coefficients[d]							
Square Root Percent Black (Level)	2.252[a]	2.437[a]	1.963[a]	0.061	0.366[b]	0.850[a]	1.416[a]
Female Labor Force Share (Level)	0.231[a]	0.210[a]	0.230[a]	0.177[a]	0.130[b]	-0.059	0.244[a]
Percent LF White Collar (Level)	-0.063	0.298[a]	0.273[a]	-0.034	-0.020	0.009	0.117[a]
Status Diversity (Level)	0.849[a]	0.137	0.182	1.670[a]	1.516[a]	1.713[a]	0.569[a]
Percent Civilian LF Employed (Level)	-0.059	0.018	0.449[a]	0.210[b]	0.203[a]	0.230[a]	0.161[a]
Indigenous Labor Supply (Level)	-0.128[a]	-0.110[a]	0.000	0.019	-0.065[b]	-0.112[a]	-0.084[a]
Ln Civilian Labor Force (Level)	1.046[a]	1.237[a]	0.112	0.189	-0.185	0.305	0.419[a]
Standardized Regression Coefficients							
Square Root Percent Black (Level)	0.643[a]	0.725[a]	0.616[a]	0.026	0.188[b]	0.442[a]	0.460[a]
Female Labor Force Share (Level)	0.261[a]	0.211[a]	0.201[a]	0.168[a]	0.135[b]	-0.045	0.505[a]
Percent LF White Collar (Level)	-0.054	0.297[a]	0.308[a]	-0.052	-0.037	0.018	0.253[a]
Status Diversity (Level)	0.480[a]	0.056	0.076	0.660[a]	0.519[a]	0.456[a]	0.292[a]
Percent Civilian LF Employed (Level)	-0.028	0.006	0.167[a]	0.118[b]	0.155[a]	0.213[a]	0.089[a]
Indigenous Labor Supply (Level)	-0.136[a]	-0.142[a]	0.000	0.039	-0.132[b]	-0.209[a]	-0.154[a]
Ln Civilian Labor Force (Level)	0.111[a]	0.144[a]	0.015	0.036	-0.042	0.071	0.058[a]
Adjusted R Square	0.737	0.620	0.466	0.415	0.333	0.406	0.562
Number of Cases	267	267	267	267	267	267	1602
St. Dev. of Dep. Var.	5.711	5.458	5.045	3.689	3.125	3.189	5.022
St. Dev. of Residuals	2.929	3.363	3.686	2.820	2.553	2.459	3.324

[a,b,c] denote probability of chance deviation from 0 is less than 0.01, 0.05, or 0.10, respectively using two-tailed test.

[d] Unstandardized regression coefficients for decade dummies in the pooled regression are -1.759 for 1950, -0.078 for 1960, -3.747 for 1970, -7.166 for 1980, and -9.777 for 1990.

TABLE 5.3 Decade-Specific and Pooled Cross-Sectional Regressions of Occupational Status for White Males on Selected Structural Characteristics of Southern Nonmetropolitan Areas

Independent Variables	1940	1950	1960	1970	1980	1990	Pooled
Unstandardized Regression Coefficients[d]							
Square Root Percent Black (Level)	1.422[a]	1.871[a]	2.272[a]	1.166[a]	0.788[a]	0.971[a]	1.034a
Female Labor Force Share (Level)	0.380[a]	0.291[a]	0.151[a]	0.136[a]	0.108[a]	0.051	0.376a
Percent LF White Collar (Level)	0.983[a]	1.065[a]	0.885[a]	0.470[a]	0.314[a]	0.341[a]	0.559a
Status Diversity (Level)	-0.245[b]	-0.946[a]	-1.274[a]	-0.516[a]	-0.163	0.167	-0.306a
Percent Civilian LF Employed (Level)	-0.350[a]	-0.172	0.146	0.146[b]	0.123[a]	0.218[a]	-0.215a
Indigenous Labor Supply (Level)	0.028	-0.073[c]	0.013	-0.037[c]	-0.040[b]	-0.044[b]	-0.088a
Ln Civilian Labor Force (Level)	1.043[b]	0.587	-0.225	0.268	0.621[a]	0.584[a]	0.309b
Standardized Regression Coefficients							
Square Root Percent Black (Level)	0.343[a]	0.426[a]	0.651[a]	0.560[a]	0.481[a]	0.527[a]	0.255[a]
Female Labor Force Share (Level)	0.362[a]	0.224[a]	0.151[a]	0.150[a]	0.133[a]	0.041	0.591[a]
Percent LF White Collar (Level)	0.712[a]	0.813[a]	0.915[a]	0.834[a]	0.706[a]	0.719[a]	0.918[a]
Status Diversity (Level)	-0.117[b]	-0.296[a]	-0.488[a]	-0.235[b]	-0.066	0.046	-0.119[a]
Percent Civilian LF Employed (Level)	-0.140[a]	-0.042	0.050	0.094[b]	0.111[a]	0.210[a]	-0.091[a]
Indigenous Labor Supply (Level)	0.025	-0.072[c]	0.018	-0.087[c]	-0.098[b]	-0.085[b]	-0.123[a]
Ln Civilian Labor Force (Level)	0.093[b]	0.052	-0.027	0.058	0.169[a]	0.141[a]	0.032[b]
Adjusted R Square	0.695	0.775	0.770	0.655	0.702	0.772	0.773
Number of Cases	267	267	267	267	267	267	1602
St. Dev. of Dep. Var.	6.757	7.130	5.519	3.206	2.626	3.053	6.609
St. Dev. of Residuals	3.730	3.384	2.647	1.884	1.434	1.459	3.148

[a,b,c] denote probability of chance deviation from 0 is less than 0.01, 0.05, or 0.10, respectively using two-tailed test.

[d] Unstandardized regression coefficients for decade dummies in the pooled regression are 2.692 for 1950, -4.105 for 1960, -7.348 for 1970, -11.910 for 1980, and -16.014 for 1990.

TABLE 5.4 Decade-Specific and Pooled Cross-Sectional Regressions of Occupational Status for Black Males on Selected Structural Characteristics of Southern Nonmetropolitan Areas

Independent Variables	1940	1950	1960	1970	1980	1990	Pooled
Unstandardized Regression Coefficients[d]							
Square Root Percent Black (Level)	-0.830[a]	-0.566[a]	0.308[c]	1.105[a]	0.421[a]	0.121	-0.383[a]
Female Labor Force Share (Level)	0.149[a]	0.081[c]	-0.079[c]	-0.041	-0.023	0.110	0.132[a]
Percent LF White Collar (Level)	1.046[a]	0.767[a]	0.612[a]	0.504[a]	0.334[a]	0.332[a]	0.442[a]
Status Diversity (Level)	-1.094[a]	-1.083[a]	-1.456[a]	-2.186[a]	-1.679[a]	-1.547[a]	-0.875[a]
Percent Civilian LF Employed (Level)	-0.292[a]	-0.190	-0.303[a]	-0.064	-0.080	-0.013	-0.376[a]
Indigenous Labor Supply (Level)	0.156[a]	0.037	0.012	-0.057[c]	0.025	0.068[b]	-0.004
Ln Civilian Labor Force (Level)	-0.004	-0.650[c]	-0.337	0.079	0.807[a]	0.279	-0.109
Standardized Regression Coefficients							
Square Root Percent Black (Level)	-0.252[a]	-0.169[a]	0.093[c]	0.440[a]	0.223[a]	0.072	-0.095[a]
Female Labor Force Share (Level)	0.178[a]	0.081[c]	-0.066[c]	-0.037	-0.024	0.097	0.208[a]
Percent LF White Collar (Level)	0.953[a]	0.767[a]	0.667[a]	0.740[a]	0.651[a]	0.766[a]	0.728[a]
Status Diversity (Level)	-0.657[a]	-0.444[a]	-0.588[a]	-0.823[a]	-0.594[a]	-0.471[a]	-0.342[a]
Percent Civilian LF Employed (Level)	-0.146[a]	-0.061	-0.109[a]	-0.034	-0.063	-0.013	-0.159[a]
Indigenous Labor Supply (Level)	0.176[a]	0.048	0.018	-0.109[c]	0.052	0.145[b]	-0.006
Ln Civilian Labor Force (Level)	-0.000	-0.076[c]	-0.043	0.014	0.191[a]	0.074	-0.011
Adjusted R Square	0.613	0.690	0.711	0.495	0.402	0.426	0.755
Number of Cases	267	267	267	267	267	267	1602
St. Dev. of Dep. Var.	5.372	5.447	5.237	3.873	3.023	2.789	6.593
St. Dev. of Residuals	3.389	3.073	2.855	2.791	2.369	2.142	3.276

[a,b,c] denote probability of chance deviation from 0 is less than 0.01, 0.05, or 0.10, respectively using two-tailed test.

[d] Unstandardized coefficients for decade dummies in pooled regression are -0.933 for 1950, -4.027 for 1960, -3.601 for 1970, -4.744 for 1980, and -6.236 for 1990.

Relative Minority Size. The first substantive variable we discuss is relative minority size. The precise nature of its effect is complicated. For the moment, we comment only on the broad pattern of its effect as revealed in the results for the pooled analysis. The effect reported here shows that percent Black has a strong and statistically significant positive effect on inequality. We found that this effect is nonlinear and could best be captured when percent Black is subjected to a square root transformation.[6] This transformation implies that a given change in percent Black (e.g., a five percentage point decline) has less dramatic consequences in areas where percent Black is already high. Stated another way, the effect of an increase in relative minority size diminishes as relative minority size becomes large.

Most counties in our sample experienced declines in percent black over the period 1940-1990. The positive regression coefficient for minority size thus implies that, all else equal, counties which experienced larger declines in percent Black would have experienced larger reductions in inequality. However, because the effect is nonlinear, the reductions would be greatest in counties where percent Black was initially moderate or small. For example, assuming a county fell by 10 points on percent Black between 1940 and 1990 — not an implausible figure since the sample median for percent black declined by 8.6 points over this period — the expected decline in the mean status difference between White men and Black men would be 2.32 points in a county where percent Black was initially 15 but only 1.12 points in a county where percent Black was initially 45.[7]

The standardized coefficient or beta for percent Black is large 0.460) and indicates that relative minority size is a strong predictor of area differences in the level of inequality. This results because the unstandardized or "metric" effect associated with minority size is large, and because minority size varies considerably across counties. The standard deviation for percent Black exceeded 16 points in each decade and this sizable variation combines with its large effect to stratify counties on inequality to a substantial degree.

Following previous examples in the literature by Brown and Fuguitt (1972) and Frisbie and Neidert (1977), we also consider the effect of minority size on White and Black status levels to gain insight into the manner in which it ultimately shapes inequality. The results from the pooled model reported in Table 5.1 suggest that relative minority size promotes racial inequality primarily by exerting positive effects on status for White men and to a lesser extent by negatively impacting status for Black men. The positive effect on status for White men is consistent with the view that a larger minority population serves to "lift up" status for White men as in the absence of a substantial minority population lower status occupations would necessarily be filled by White men. The negative effect of percent Black on status for Black men is consistent with the hypothesis that majority discrimination against minorities tends to increase when the minority population increases.

The positive effect of percent Black on White status is consistent across the decade-specific regressions though the magnitude of the effect appears to decline slightly over time. The negative effect of relative minority size on Black status is not consistent over time. While it is negative in the pooled results and negative and significant in the decade-specific regressions for 1940 and 1950, it is positive and significant in the decade-specific regressions for 1960, 1970, and 1980, and is not significant in 1990. These comments lead naturally to the question of whether the effect of percent Black on inequality is consistent over time.

Percent Black's Changing Effect Over Time. The decade-specific results presented in Table 5.2 show that the effect of relative minority size on inequality is positive in each decade. However, the magnitude of the positive effect on inequality appears to have diminished after 1960. The relationship is clearly stronger in 1940, 1950, and 1960 where the smallest effect is 1.963. It then drops off substantially in 1970 to only 0.061. The effect partially rebounds in later decades but still stands at only 0.850 in 1990 which is less than half the size of the effect observed for any decade prior to 1970.[8] The question that arises is whether this time trend is substantively meaningful.

The traditional interpretation of the effect of relative minority size has been that higher levels of minority size produce a perception on the part of the majority that their privileged position is threatened (Fossett and Kiecolt 1989; Wilcox and Roof 1978). The majority is then thought to respond with higher levels of discrimination to preserve their privileges. If this interpretation is correct, then changes in the effect of relative minority size over time suggest that the majority's ability to act effectively to conserve its advantages has weakened over time. Since the effect of relative minority size declines dramatically between 1960 and 1970 and remains reduced thereafter, one obvious possibility which comes to mind is that the Civil Rights and voting rights legislation and equal employment opportunity legislation in the 1960s may have significantly reduced the White majority's ability to protect their privileged status position as successfully as in the past. That is to say, the dismantling of Jim Crow laws, state sponsored school segregation, and other manifestations of state-enforced racial separation and inequality in the South during the 1960s may have significantly undermined and weakened the racial stratification system in the region. Furthermore, strong challenges to the morality and legitimacy of past segregationist practices may also have weakened the effectiveness of informal practices of racial discrimination.

A related possibility which complements this interpretation is that relative minority size may have increasingly become a resource for the minority under certain conditions in the post-Civil Rights era. Before 1970 relative size was undoubtedly not a significant resource for Blacks in the nonmetropolitan South. The obvious reason why it was not is that Blacks were disenfranchised and politically powerless and therefore unable to translate large relative size into political pressure. During the 1960s, successes of the Civil Rights movement, especially in the area of securing and protecting voting rights, may have fundamentally changed the structure of race relations in the South, possibly to the point that relative size became a significant resource for Blacks in some situations where previously it had primarily been only a stimulus to White discrimination.

In this view, relative minority size might still have positive effects on inequality via a positive effect on White responses to a perceived threat from the minority. But now this effect is offset in part by the emergence of relative size as a working resource for Blacks. This countervailing effect might be realized in several different ways. One obvious possibility is in the potential impact of minority voters on election results. Voting rights reform produced very significant increases in the number of Black elected officials in the South after 1965 (National Research Council 1989: 238-244) and the probability of success by Black candidates has been shown to be directly related to relative minority size (Engstrom and McDonald 1981). Undoubtedly, the emerging minority vote in the South had the impact of increasing representation of Blacks among public officials. Equally importantly, it may have lead to greater sensitivity to minority concerns on the part of majority candidates and office holders. This increased political influence by Blacks may thus have led to greater representation of minorities in government employment, appointed offices, and patronage positions and greater use of minority vendors in servicing government contracts.

This greater political influence by Blacks could well have weakened the relationship between relative minority size and racial inequality. That is, after 1960 the discrimination effect may have been offset by a resource effect which did not really exist earlier. The number of Black elected officials in the South between 1940 and 1960 was negligible (National Research Council 1989:238-244) and Black political influence in southern communities was not important during this period regardless of minority size. After 1965, the number of Black elected officials in the South began to rise rapidly. This coincides closely with the temporal decline in the effect of minority size on inequality.

Female Labor Force Share. The results of the pooled cross-sectional regression in Table 5.2 suggest that female labor force share has a strong positive effect on inequality between White and Black men. The effect is fairly consistent across the decade-specific equations between 1940 and 1980 but drops to near zero in 1990. A literal causal interpretation of the unstandardized regression coefficient of 0.244 in the pooled analysis implies that a 25 point increase in female labor force share would increase the mean status difference between White men and Black men by 6.1 points on average. Such an increase is by no means out of the question; the sample median for female labor force share increased by 26.9 points between 1940 and 1990. Thus, the substantive importance of the effect of female labor force share is clear. This conclusion is further buttressed by the variable's large standardized regression coefficient of 0.505 which signals that in this sample it is one of the more important predictors accounting for area variation in inequality.

The results for the separate regression analyses of White and Black status indicate that female labor force share affects inequality via differential positive effects on its components. Specifically, female labor force share has positive effects on mean status for both White men and Black men. However, the positive effect on status for White men is nearly three times the size of the positive effect on status for Black men. This suggests the possibility that White men are more likely than Black men to assume higher status managerial and supervisory positions when women are in the labor force in large numbers. As a consequence, the status gap between White and Black men widens when female labor force share is large.

Finally, this pattern of effects does not suggest an important pattern of direct competition between Black men and women. The hypothesis that Black men and women are competitors in the labor force would be best supported by a negative effect of female labor force share on Black status, but such an effect is not observed in Table 5.1. To the contrary, a positive effect is seen.

White-Collar Employment. We used the variable of percent employed in white-collar occupations to capture the effects of area variation in occupational structure. White-collar employment tends to be associated with prevalence of professional and business service industries which are concentrated in urban settings. White-collar jobs also tend to be higher status jobs requiring greater education and training. Thus, their presence in the local economy signals stronger demand for educated labor and greater importance of educational disparities in employment.

The results for the pooled regression for inequality shows that white-collar employment has a statistically significant positive effect on racial inequality. However, while the effect is clear and strong in the pooled model, its effects in the decade-specific models are not nearly as consistent as the effects of percent Black and female labor force share. Percent white collar has strong positive effects in 1950 and 1960, but its effects in other decades are not statistically significant. In the absence of a prior expectation of decade-to-decade differences in the effect, we give greater credibility to the more efficient pooled estimate of the effect. But it is nevertheless prudent to be cautious in interpreting an effect that is inconsistent when estimated in subsamples.

The substantive implications of the unstandardized coefficient of 0.117 in the pooled model are noteworthy. A literal causal interpretation of the effect of white collar implies that a 25 point increase in white-collar employment would produce an increase in the mean status difference between White men and Black men of over 2.9 points. This scenario is by no means out of the question since the sample median for white-collar employment shifted up by 26.7 percentage points between 1940 and 1990. The standardized effect of 0.253 for white-collar employment also indicates that the variable has substantively important implications for inequality. This standardized effect signals that in this sample percent white collar is the fourth most important predictor of area variation in inequality.

The separate regression analyses of status levels for White and Black men indicate that percent white collar has positive effects on inequality because it has differential positive effects on status for White and Black men. Greater white-collar employment is associated with higher levels of status for both groups and this pattern is clear and consistent across the decade-specific regressions for both groups. The positive effect on inequality results because the positive effect of white collar employment on status for White men tends to be greater than its positive effect on status for Black men. That is, White men tend to be better able than Black men to secure higher status employment in the context of expanding white-collar employment opportunities.

Status Diversity. Status diversity (measured by the mean absolute deviation in status) has a statistically significant positive effect on inequality in the pooled regression and in all decade-specific regressions. The effect of status diversity is not trivial. When the unstandardized regression coefficient of 0.569 in the pooled regression is given a causal interpretation it implies that an increase in status diversity of 3 points would produce an increase in the White-Black difference in mean status of approximately 1.71 points.

Shifts in status diversity of this magnitude are readily seen in our data. For example, the sample median for status diversity increased some 2.8 points from 18.1 in 1940 to 20.9 in 1960, implying a resulting increase of over 1.5 points in status inequality between White men and Black men. Between 1960 and 1980 the sample median for status diversity fell 4.5 points from 20.9 to 16.4 contributing to a decline in inequality of over 2.56 points. Of course, the net change in status diversity between 1940 and 1990 was smaller than the short run changes over one or two decades. Because it first rose and then fell, the average level of status diversity in 1980 was only 1.7 points lower than that observed in 1940 and in 1990 it rose and was only 1.2 points lower than in 1940.

The standardized coefficient of 0.292 for status diversity is the third largest among the substantively motivated independent variables. It indicates that status diversity is an important predictor of inequality in our sample. This predictive importance is particularly noteworthy in the decade-specific analyses because this variable exhibits considerably more variation in the cross-section than over time. The interdecile range is over 5.0 in three of the six decades and an area difference in status diversity of this magnitude is associated with a predicted difference in status inequality between White men and Black men of 2.98 points (based the slope of 0.596).

We have argued that status diversity affects inequality because the complexity of the status structure sets limits on the structural possibilities for inequality between groups. When occupational structure concentrates socioeconomic status in a narrow range, status inequality between groups is likely to be low. When the occupational structure yields a wider status range, status inequality between groups is likely to be high. In light of this theoretical interpretation, specific effects on status levels for White men and Black men are not substantively meaningful and do not warrant separate discussion.

Determinants of Status Diversity. It is important to note that, at least in our sample, status diversity is not a simple function of occupational or industrial structure. Some of the lowest status diversity scores are observed in predominantly agricultural communities where most of the labor force is employed in low status, farm occupations. However, low diversity scores also are observed for some communities specializing in trade and business services with predominantly high status, white-collar occupational mixes. The highest levels of status diversity are found in communities which have sizable numbers of both high and low status occupations. These tend to be communities in the middle of a transformation from a rural-agricultural economy to an urban economy organized around trade, manufacturing, and services. In both the early and late stages of this transformation status diversity tends to be low and inequality between groups is moderated by this. In the middle stages of the transformation status diversity is high as a low status farm occupations continue to be common even as higher status white-collar occupations begin to become more prevalent. It is during the middle stage of the transition that the structural possibility for group inequality is highest.

Before the transition, status inequality between groups is likely to be attenuated in part because most people in all groups are concentrated in low-status farm occupations. As the transition to an urban economy begins, the number of high-status jobs in the local economy begins to increase. These positions are first filled by members of the majority group while members of the minority remain concentrated in more traditional, low-status farm occupations. This leads to a considerable increase in inequality as the sectoral transition progresses. Then, in the final stages of the transition, the number of low-status farm positions becomes small and members of the minority come to be increasingly incorporated into the expanding higher-status urban occupations. Barring other changes, minorities are concentrated in the lower rungs of this new occupational mix. Nevertheless, intergroup inequality is again attenuated because the status structure is much compressed compared to the diversity present during the middle stages of the transition.

This scenario suggests that the traditional argument that the transformation from a rural economy to an urban economy leads to a reduction in intergroup inequality should be amended in at least one key respect. The traditional hypothesis focuses on the impact of the transition on the role of ascription in status allocation processes and ignores the impact of the transition on status diversity. When this is taken into account, we might then predict that the transition from a rural, agricultural economy will first lead to a prolonged period of elevated inequality while the transition is underway; only after the transition is complete does inequality return to its original levels and begin to decline.

There is one problem with this story; changes in status diversity are not strongly connected to urbanization in our sample. White-collar employment is moderately correlated with percent urban ($r = 0.49$), as would be expected. However, the relationships of farm and blue-collar employment to urbanization were more complex.

Farm employment has a strong negative correlation with percent urban overall (r = -0.42) in the pooled sample. However, the relationship declines over time and is much stronger in 1940 (r = -0.59) than in 1990 (r = -0.17) as farm employment was low even in rural areas. Blue-collar employment has an even more complex relationship with urbanization. Overall it has a moderate correlation with percent urban (r = 0.27) but this is misleading as the correlation is strong and positive in 1940 (r = 0.50), but weakens and reverses over time such that it is moderate and negative in 1990 (r = -0.34). Due to this complex pattern of change, the correlation between status diversity and percent urban is weak (r = 0.08) in the pooled sample, and exceeds 0.25 in the decade-specific samples only in 1940 when the correlation between status diversity and percent urban was strong and positive (r = 0.53).

Thus, while the transition to a nonfarm economy has important implications for status inequality between groups, this effect should not be interpreted as a surrogate for an effect of urbanization (at least not in any simple way). The transition to a nonfarm economy appears to first raise and then lower inequality. As discussion below will show, the same cannot be said for urbanization.

Employment Rate. The employment rate had a significant effect in the pooled regression, however, the effect was positive rather than negative as predicted by conventional theory. That is, full employment was associated with greater rather than lesser inequality. All significant effects in the decade-specific regressions were also positive. Applying a causal interpretation to the regression coefficient of 0.161 in the pooled analysis, a five point increase in the employment rate produces a 0.80 increase in inequality. This is not a large effect. The standardized regression coefficient of only 0.089 also indicates that it is not an important predictor. Nevertheless, the effect is statistically significant and is somewhat puzzling.

The overall positive effect on inequality in the pooled analysis results because the employment rate has negative effects on status levels for both White men and Black men and the magnitude of the negative effect is larger for Black men. This suggests that high status employment may be less sensitive to employment rates and that it is low status employment opportunities which expand most rapidly during full employment. Thus, full employment appears to disproportionately bring in marginal workers in lower status occupations. As these workers are more commonly Black rather than White, it leads to an increase in status inequality among *employed* workers.

There are two reasons for being cautious in accepting this interpretation uncritically. One is that it is not entirely supported by the decade-specific results. A negative effect of full employment on status for Black men is observed in most decades and thus the coefficient from the pooled analysis is a reasonable summary (although the negative effects are not statistically significant in more recent decades). The situation for White men is more complicated. The coefficient for employment level has a negative effect on status in the pooled analysis but in the decade-specific results a statistically significant negative effect is observed only in 1940 whereas statistically significant positive effects are observed in 1970, 1980, and 1990. The estimated effect of full employment on status for White men in the pooled analysis is thus somewhat questionable. If we emphasize the results for more recent decades, we would conclude that full employment leads to greater inequality because it has neutral effects on status for Black men and positive effects on status for White men.

The second reason for being cautious in interpreting the pattern of effects seen here is that status and inequality are measured for employed workers only.[9] Perhaps full employment would have a positive effect on mean status for Black men if the mean for status were somehow computed for the labor-force-eligible population (e.g., able-bodied persons ages 25-64) rather than only employed persons. The problem of course is that status scores for non-employed persons are not available. To get around this, we conducted additionally analyses (not reported here) which examined the effects of full employment on labor force participation rates for White and Black men. Results from these analyses indicated that full employment had positive effects on labor force participation rates for White men and Black men. Labor force participation, however, is not equivalent to socioeconomic status and presumably participants who move in and out during cyclical expansions and contractions are more likely to be in marginal positions. Still, the idea of measuring mean status from a broader population than the employed should be considered in future research.

We also investigated the question of whether employment rates for White males might be a better predictor of inequality and group-specific status levels than employment rates for the total labor force. Our reasoning for considering this hypothesis is that conservative actions on the part of majority group members may be more likely when the effects of recession begin to affect the majority group. Furthermore, the employment rate for the majority group should be measured directly because its correlation with the total employment rate is by no means perfect because the total employment rate is a weighted average of the rates for different demographic groups (e.g., White men, Black men, White women, etc.) and these may vary considerably.

Findings from additional regression analyses (not reported here) showed that substituting the employment rate for White men for the total employment rate affected the substantive conclusions of the analysis only slightly. The employment rate for White men did have a negative effect on inequality in the pooled model as predicted by theory. However, the effect was weak; it was not statistically significant; and it was not consistent across the decade-specific regressions. Finally, the employment rate for White men had negative effects on mean status levels for White men and Black men similar to those observed for the total employment rate. The only difference was that the effect on Whites was larger than before and thus the effect on inequality tended toward zero.

Indigenous Labor Supply. Indigenous labor supply had significant effects on inequality but they were negative rather than positive as predicted by ecological theory. The imbalance between cohorts just entering prime labor force ages and cohorts exiting these ages declined steadily over time (the sample median fell from 31.8 in 1940 to 12.1 in 1990). We expected that this would tend to moderate labor force competition and lead to reductions in inequality. Instead, we found inequality tended to be higher in areas where indigenous labor supply was low. Whether the pattern is substantively important or not is a matter of judgment. On the one hand, a decline in the indigenous labor supply of 15 points (quite plausible over the full time period) would imply an increase in inequality of 1.26 points if the regression coefficient from the pooled model is given a literal causal interpretation. On the other hand, the standardized regression coefficient for the pooled model is only -0.154 and suggests that indigenous labor supply is not an important predictor of area variation in inequality.

Examination of the results of the effects of indigenous labor supply on White and Black status means suggests that the negative effect on inequality derives from the combination of a negative effect on White status and a neutral effect on Black status. These patterns are evident in the pooled analyses and are largely consistent from decade to decade. The negative effect of indigenous labor supply on mean status for Whites was expected. It suggests that "malthusian" pressure on employment opportunities leads to marginalized status outcomes. The surprising result is that there is not a corresponding negative effect on mean status for Blacks (and consequently no positive effect on inequality). Perhaps, demographic pressures are relieved by out-migration (which is common in nonmetropolitan areas where indigenous labor supply is high) and as a result competition effects on inequality are not great.

Another possibility is that the effect of indigenous labor supply is difficult to estimate due to collinearities with other variables in the model. For example, indigenous labor supply is moderately collinear with relative minority size ($r = 0.44$), possibly due to higher fertility in the minority population. It is interesting to note that, when this powerful predictor is removed from the model the effect of indigenous labor supply turns positive and is statistically significant. Thus, it is possible that the effect of competition pressures resulting from large entry cohorts is confounded in this sample with intergroup competition associated with relative minority size. Historically Black net out-migration from southern nonmetropolitan counties has significantly exceeded White net out migration. If this pattern has been especially pronounced in counties where job competition resulting from indigenous labor supply is high, it may produce a complicated feedback relationship between demographic pressure and minority composition.

Labor Force Size. We use the natural logarithm of total labor force size to measure labor market scale.[10] We use the natural log transformation in our model specification to take account of the fact that differences in size of any particular magnitude become less important as labor force size becomes large. We should also note that size may also be considered a surrogate for urbanization since urbanization was not included in the final models but is positively correlated with labor force size.

Labor force size has a positive and statistically significant effect on inequality in the pooled analysis. However, the regression coefficient of 0.419 does not suggest that the effects of size are very important. The difference between the highest and lowest sample medians for size observed in different decades is only about 0.40 and the largest decade-specific sample standard deviation is only 0.75. Shifts in labor force size of this magnitude would imply changes in inequality of only 0.17 and 0.31 points, respectively, based on the unstandardized regression coefficient for labor force size. In addition, the standardized regression coefficient of 0.058 is the smallest of the effects estimated and indicates that labor force size is not a strong predictor of inequality despite the fact that its effect is statistically significant.

While the effect of labor force size is not important, it is nevertheless interesting because its positive sign is inconsistent with conventional expectations which predict that larger, and presumably more efficient and rational labor markets will provide better relative opportunities for minority workers. The analyses focusing on separate status levels for White men and Black men show that the overall positive effect of labor force size on inequality results because size has a net positive effect on status levels for White men (as predicted by ecological theory), but no significant effect on mean status levels for Black men (in contrast to expectations). We investigated the possibility that this pattern may have resulted because size is correlated with other variables in the model. Thus, we looked to see if the prediction of a negative effect might be confirmed in an alternative model specification. However, we could find no evidence to support this speculation. It would appear then that notions that increasing labor market scale does not necessarily promote reductions in inequality.

Selected Comments on Other Independent Variables

Several variables we discussed in our theoretical review were not included in our final regression models. As we noted earlier, we excluded some of them because they were conceptually or empirically redundant with other variables included in the model. Others were excluded because we found they did not have significant and consistent effects. This section briefly summarizes the results of unreported analyses exploring the effects of these variables.

Urbanization. We did not include urbanization as a predictor in the final regression models. The primary reason for this is that it is collinear with other variables in the final model, especially white-collar employment, labor market size, and status diversity (in that order) and did not have a significant effect on inequality when added to the final model. One way to interpret this result is to argue that these three variables represent some of the key aspects of urban economies — large size, diversity, and concentration of administrative and bureaucratic activity— and thus urbanization should not be expected to exert a separate effect when these variables are included in the model. This is fine as far as it goes. However, we found that when we used alternative specifications where urbanization was substituted for one more of these collinear predictors (i.e., percent white collar, size, and status diversity), it had a positive effect on inequality rather than the negative effect predicted by theory. The reason for this is that urbanization had positive effects on White status which either equaled or exceeded its positive effects on Black status.

These findings provide additional evidence that conventional hypotheses predicting that urbanization tends to reduce inequality must be reconsidered. Additional unreported analyses discussed earlier suggested urbanization brings with it a more diversified occupational structure that permits greater status inequality to emerge. As the status structure becomes more complex, White men tend to fill the highest status positions and Black men improve their status only by moving into lower and middle status occupations "vacated" as Whites move into higher status positions. Thus, rather than undermining the racial stratification order, urbanization appears to accommodate it and bring about structural changes that create the possibility of even greater inequality.

The conventional prediction that urbanization sets in motion forces of social change that have negative effects on stratification based on ascription is apparently invalid in the short run. At the very least, it is not supported with our sample data. Possibly a negative effect is observed in the very long run. That is, perhaps it has a curvilinear effect of the type Lenski has postulated for the impact of economic growth on inequality in the *intra*group size distribution of income; positive initially but negative in the long run. If so, its negative impact does not take hold for several decades because we failed to detect a negative effect even when we used specifications with two- and three-decade lags.

We also investigated the possible long run effects of urbanization in another set of analyses (not reported here) but found only slender evidence of any negative effect. Specifically, we coded counties as being in the early, middle, or late stages of transition to a nonfarm economy.[11] For counties having completed the transition, we coded the number of decades since completing the transition. We then entered these variables in our cross-sectional models.[12] Based on this reformulation of traditional ecological theory, we expected counties in the middle stage of the transition would have higher levels of inequality and that inequality would tend to be lower for counties in the final stage and lower still for those which had been in the final stage of the transition for several decades.

The results from these analyses showed that inequality was higher for counties in the middle stage of the transition, but only when status diversity was dropped from the model. This was not surprising as the middle stage of the transition promotes racial inequality by increasing the amount of status diversity. However, results for the pooled analysis showed counties in the final stage transition did not have lower inequality as predicted and that length of time in the final stage also did not have a negative effect.

Decade-specific analysis provided the only evidence consistent with the reformulated urbanization hypothesis. As in the pooled model, number of decades in the final stage was either zero or positive (not negative) in the decade-specific regressions for 1940, 1950, and 1960. However, its effects in the decade-specific regressions for later decades were negative as predicted. These results were interesting because few of the counties had entered the final stage of the transition to a nonfarm economy prior to 1950. Thus, the effect of time since completion of transition is difficult to estimate in decade specific analyses before 1960. Still, even in the equations for later decades, the effect of time since completion of the transition is weak and evidence to support a revised version of the urbanization hypothesis is slender at best.

Manufacturing Concentration. We could find no evidence in our analyses to confirm predictions that manufacturing concentration has negative effects on racial inequality. This was true regardless of whether its effect was assessed by adding it to the final models, or by including it and dropping mildly collinear variables (e.g., female labor force share). In the former case manufacturing concentration did not have any consistent significant effects. In the latter it had weak and inconsistent positive effects.

This finding runs counter to at least some cross-sectional studies which have found manufacturing to have negative effects on racial inequality in metropolitan areas. One potential explanation of this is that manufacturing concentration may be a surrogate for unionization. The correlation between manufacturing concentration and unionization is relatively close in national-level samples of metropolitan areas. This is not the case in the nonmetropolitan South where manufacturing establishments typically are in mature industries and are attracted to their location by the availability of docile, low-wage labor. Thus, unionization is weak throughout the nonmetropolitan South and the correlation between unionization and manufacturing also is weak. This could lead manufacturing concentration to have significant effects in national samples of metropolitan areas but not in the present sample of southern, nonmetropolitan counties.

Fossett (1983) reported evidence consistent with this interpretation. In an analysis of racial income inequality using data for a national sample of metropolitan areas in 1970 he found that (a) manufacturing concentration and unionization were highly correlated, (b) both had negative effects on inequality, and (c) the effect of unionization was stronger even though the reliability of this measure probably much worse than the reliability of the measure of manufacturing. He thus argued on theoretical grounds that unionization was probably the key effect and that manufacturing concentration's effect on inequality resulted from its relationship with unionization and was reduced to zero when unionization was controlled.

Manufacturing concentration might still be considered to have a reduced form causal effect on inequality on the assumption that it is a primary cause of unionization. However, the results here undermine that view; manufacturing concentration varies considerably across counties and over time in the nonmetropolitan South, but unionization is essentially invariant at low levels.[13]

Education Demand. In Chapter 2 we considered perspectives which argued that increasing demand for educated labor may lead to greater racial inequality in labor market outcomes. Ultimately, we did not include specific measures of demand for education in our final models. The reason for this decision is that the measures we developed were highly collinear with percent employed in white-collar occupations (r = 0.97) which was included. When we substituted measures of education demand in the model in place of percent white collar, the substantive implications of their effects were essentially identical to those associated with the for percent white collar. Thus, if percent white collar is interpreted as a surrogate measure of education demand, we can conclude that education demand has a strong positive effect on inequality.

We decided to include percent employed in white-collar occupations in the model in place of measures of education demand because we view demand for education as flowing from changes in the occupational structure. Thus, we see changes in the occupational structure as the main engine driving education demand and through it inequality. However, some may prefer to think of demand for education as the proximate cause in a more complex causal chain wherein increased white-collar employment increases the demand for educated labor which in turn promotes inequality. In our view, the data are consistent with either interpretation.

Changes Over Time in Model Fit

Another aspect of the cross-sectional analyses we consider is the pattern of steady decline over time in the explained variation in the decade-specific regression analyses (e.g., the multiple squared correlation coefficients). Close inspection shows that this occurred because the variance of the independent variables with the strongest standardized effects (betas) on inequality declined over time (i.e., percent Black, female labor force share, and status diversity). Thus, their capacity to "explain" inequality diminished even though their metric effects (unstandardized regression coefficients) were fairly consistent over time.[14] This interpretation is consistent with the fact that the standard deviations of the residuals for the decade-specific equations were all quite similar. This suggests that, relative to the model used, the systematic variation in inequality generated by differences in ecological structure declined while the unpredicted residual variation in inequality remained constant. This pattern then produced declining multiple R squares for the equations over time. One implication of this interpretation is that the parameter estimates of the cross-sectional effects are more efficient for the earlier decades because the cross-sectional variation for many of the independent variables is greater in those decades and provides better opportunities for establishing metric effects.

Decade-to-Decade Changes in Inequality

The dummy variables for decade in the pooled regression give some insight into changes in racial stratification that occur system wide and are not associated with the structural characteristics of communities. However, as we noted earlier, inferences about decade effects on inequality should be considered tentative at best since the dummy variables are "ignorance" terms which pick up all manner of effects associated with decade. With this caveat in mind, we nevertheless note that the coefficients for 1950 and 1960 in the pooled regression in Table 5.1 appear to suggest that inequality was not changing in any obviously important way between 1940 and 1960 for the counties in our sample. The larger negative coefficients for decades after 1960 and especially for 1980 and 1990 are more suggestive of real and even substantial changes in inequality. The coefficient for 1990 of -9.77 indicates that inequality in 1990 is appreciably lower across-the-board when compared with its average level in 1940 (the reference decade for the coefficient). In our view, it is difficult to attribute an effect of this magnitude to changes in census methodology or other alternative explanations.

The overall pattern of the decade effects thus indicates that significant systemic reductions in average inequality occurred in the 1960s and especially the 1970s, but not before. This pattern is consistent with findings reported in studies of national and regional trends (Fossett, Galle, and Kelly 1986) and suggests that there is little evidence to indicate that inequality was systematically declining before the Civil Rights era.

A further question we can try to address is the extent to which changes in the average level of inequality in southern, nonmetropolitan counties since 1940 reflects changing county distributions on structural characteristics which affect inequality on the one hand and system-wide changes in average levels of inequality on the other. We investigate this question by examining the gross changes in average inequality and comparing them to the decade-to-decade changes implied by the dummy variables for decade in the pooled model. The difference represents the combined effects of changes in the means for the structural characteristics of counties. We then break this portion of the change in inequality into components which reflect the impact of changes in the means for each independent variable. These components are obtained for each variable by taking the change in the mean for the independent variable and then multiplying it by the coefficient for that variable in the pooled regression model in Table 5.1.

Results summarizing these calculations are presented in Table 5.5. This table shows that between 1940 and 1950, the average for the mean difference in socioeconomic status between White men and Black men increased by 1.90 points from 13.42 to 15.32. The effect of "decade," that is the average change in inequality controlling for structural characteristics, was -1.76. Changes in the structural characteristics of the counties accounted for a combined total increase of 3.63 points. Thus, changes in structural characteristics were responsible for the increase in average inequality during the 1940s; their combined impacts overwhelmed a smaller "system-wide" decade decline in inequality of -1.76 and produced an overall increase in inequality.

The most important shifts in structural characteristics were an increase in status diversity (contributing 1.59 points to inequality), an increase in female labor force share (contributing 0.71 points to inequality), an increase in white-collar employment (contributing 0.65 points to inequality), and a decline in indigenous labor supply (contributing 0.62 points to inequality). The only structural shift producing a decline in inequality was the decline in percent Black and its contribution was relatively small (-0.21 points).

Inequality increased by an average of 4.03 points between 1950 and 1960, rising from 15.32 to 19.35. The decade-to-decade change implied by the dummy variables for decade was 1.68 points, a modest increase in inequality across the counties net of changes in structural characteristics that was similar in magnitude to the decline observed for the previous decade.[15] Shifts in structural characteristics accounted for an increase in inequality of 2.35 points. The most important shifts in structural characteristics were increases in female labor force share (contributing 2.02 points to inequality) and white-collar employment (contributing 0.78 points to inequality).

Between 1960 and 1970 average inequality fell about 3.06 points from 19.35 to 16.29. Decade-to-decade change in inequality implied by the dummy variables for decade was -3.67 and thus accounts for all of the observed reduction in inequality. The total impact of shifts in structural characteristics was a relatively small increase of 0.61

TABLE 5.5 Sources of Decade-to-Decade Changes in Racial Inequality Implied by Pooled Cross-Sectional Regression Analysis and Changes Over Time in Means of Independent Variables

Independent Variables	1940-1950	1950-1960	1960-1970	1970-1980	1980-1990
Sample Mean for Inequality at Beginning of Decade	13.42	15.32	19.35	16.29	13.48
Sample Mean for Inequality at End of Decade	15.32	19.35	16.29	13.48	12.81
Change in Mean Inequality over Decade	1.90	4.03	-3.06	-2.81	-0.67
Impact of Mean Change in Independent Variable on Mean Inequality[a]					
Square Root of Percent Black	-0.21	-0.09	-0.40	-0.31	-0.10
Female Labor Force Share	0.71	2.02	1.51	1.07	0.90
Percent LF White Collar	0.65	0.78	0.63	0.48	0.61
Status Diversity	1.59	0.11	-1.54	-0.85	0.28
Percent Civilian LF Employed	0.29	-0.37	0.16	-0.39	-0.13
Indigenous Labor Supply	0.62	-0.09	0.23	0.50	0.36
Ln Civilian Labor Force	-0.03	-0.02	0.02	0.11	0.05
Total Impact of Changes in Independent Variables[b]	3.63	2.35	0.61	0.62	1.98
Decade Effect[b]	-1.76	1.68	-3.67	-3.42	-2.61

[a] Based on regression coefficient for variable in the "pooled" model in Table 5.1 and the change in the mean for the variable over the past decade

[b] The sum of the total impact of changes in the independent variables and the decade effects does not always equal the total change in inequality due to rounding error.

points. This net impact was the result of several offsetting patterns in the shifts in structural characteristics. As in the 1940s and 1950s, increases in female labor force share and white-collar employment promoted increases in inequality, adding 1.51 and 0.63 points, respectively. Unlike previous decades, however, these effects were partially offset by significant reductions in inequality produced by declines in status diversity and relative minority size which reduced average inequality by 1.54 and 0.40 points, respectively.

Average inequality fell by 2.81 points in the 1970s dropping from 16.29 in 1970 to 13.48 in 1980. As in the 1960s, the major factor producing this decline was a system-wide decline in average inequality net of changes in structural characteristics. This decade-to-decade change in inequality implied by the dummy variables for decade was -3.42. Shifts in structural characteristics affected inequality in the manner observed for the 1960s. Increases in female labor force share and white-collar employment contributed to increases in inequality (adding 1.07 and 0.48 points to inequality, respectively) and declines in status diversity relative minority size contributed to reductions in inequality (reducing inequality by 0.85 and 0.31 points, respectively). The net impact of all shifts in noncyclical structural characteristics was an increase in inequality of 0.62 points.[16] On balance, this was overwhelmed by systemic reductions in inequality affecting all counties.

Average inequality fell by 0.67 points in the 1980s dropping from 13.48 in 1980 to 12.81 in 1990. Again, the major factor producing this decline was a system-wide decline in average inequality net of changes in structural characteristics. This decade-to-decade change in inequality implied by the dummy variables for decade was -2.61 points which was substantial if slightly smaller than that observed for the previous two decades. Increases in female labor force share and white-collar employment contributed to increases in inequality (adding 0.90 and 0.61 points to inequality, respectively). Increasing status diversity and declining indigenous labor supply led to smaller increases in inequality (producing increases of 0.28 and 0.36 points, respectively). The net impact of all shifts in noncyclical structural characteristics was an increase in inequality of 1.98 points. On balance, this was overwhelmed by systemic reductions in inequality affecting all counties.

The effects of changes in the structural characteristics of counties for the entire period 1940-1990 can be summarized as follows. *Combined shifts in structural characteristics fostered increases in inequality in every decade.* The impact of these effects were greatest in the 1940s and 1950s, but they continued at a lower level in the 1960s and 1970s and were again large in the 1980s. Between 1940 and 1990, changes in the structural characteristics of counties promoted increases in inequality averaging a total of 9.19 points. That is, the transition from rural communities with farm economies, little occupational diversification, and low female labor force representation to more urbanized communities with more diversified occupational mixes, greater white collar employment, and increased female labor force participation promoted significant increases in inequality.

These relative large increases in inequality traceable to changes in structural characteristics were generally offset by systemic declines in racial inequality associated with decade-to-decade changes in inequality net of structural characteristics. These most important of these changes were large reductions in average inequality concentrated in the 1960s and 1970s with another significant decline observed in the 1980s. Over the entire period 1940-1990, they contributed to a total reduction in inequality of 9.78 points.

This pattern strongly suggests that declines in inequality after 1960 reflected a systemic shift that affected the entire regional system of racial stratification. The obvious factors that come to mind are socio-political change resulting from the Civil Rights movement and related legislation, judicial action, and executive policy initiatives (e.g., affirmative action). The overall temporal pattern contradicts arguments that declines in inequality were steady and ongoing before the political successes of the Civil Rights movement in the 1960s.

Summary

The cross-sectional regression analyses presented in this chapter provide evidence that structural characteristics of nonmetropolitan areas have important consequences for racial inequality. In particular, relative minority size, female labor force share, white-collar employment, and status diversity are shown to have strong to moderate positive effects on inequality. Female labor force share and white-collar employment have been increasing steadily decade by decade and this pattern of structural change has tended to promote increases in inequality over time. Status diversity first increased and then later decrease and thus has not generated a clear trend in inequality over time. Relative minority size has declined steadily over time and constitutes the only pattern of structural change that has promoted reductions in inequality. Analysis later in the chapter showed that, when all structural changes are considered together, their net effect has been to promote greater inequality in every decade since 1940.

The regression analyses reported here also indicated that, when the inequality-promoting impact of these structural changes is taken into account, inequality declines in the 1960s, 1970s, and 1980s are larger than gross changes in average inequality would suggest. That is to say, estimates of reductions in inequality occurring after 1960 are greater when structural characteristics are statistically controlled. The inequality reductions associated with these negative "decade effects" were largest in the 1960s and diminished in magnitude in subsequent decades. The overall trend thus suggests that changes in the socio-political sphere after 1960 promoted systemic reductions in inequality which, while declining in magnitude over time, more than offset the increases in inequality that can be traced to changes in the structural characteristics of southern, nonmetropolitan communities.

One question that obviously has important implications for many of the interpretations we have offered here is that of whether it is reasonable to assume that the effects of the structural characteristics estimated in the cross-sectional regressions can serve as a basis for developing causal explanations of changes in inequality over time. In previous research an affirmative answer to this question has routinely been taken for granted, in part because the data used typically did not permit investigators to go beyond cross-sectional analysis. We assembled longitudinal data for the expressed purpose of going one step further. We now turn in the next chapter to present the results of that investigation.

Notes

1. Conceptual and empirical collinearities among predictors are endemic in comparative research and must be dealt with carefully since they can render estimates of model parameters untrustworthy (Gordon 1968; Hanushek and Jackson 1977). Following Gordon (1968), we narrowed the final set of predictors by choosing single measures from among sets of conceptually similar predictors on the basis of desirable measurement properties (i.e., reliability, well-behaved distributions, etc.) and choosing single measures from among sets of empirically collinear but *conceptually distinct* predictors on the basis of theory and prior research.

2. Not unexpectedly, the OLS residuals show greater variance for counties with (a) smaller population size, (b) smaller percentage Black in the population, and (c) smaller decade-specific census sampling rates for census tabulations. These patterns of heteroskedasticity violate OLS assumptions and raises questions about the appropriateness of OLS standard error estimates and associated significance tests. Following Hanushek and

Jackson (1977) and other standard treatments, we addressed this problem by performing weighted least squares regressions in which we weighted individual cases in inverse proportion to the expected sampling variance of the dependent variable. These analyses consistently confirmed the significance tests reported for the OLS analyses.

3. Specifically, we computed Tukey's biweight estimates of regression parameters via the method of iteratively reweighted least squares (IRLS) described in Hamilton (1992:190-195). We used the tuning parameter of 4.685 which yields good protection against outliers when data do not meet classical distributional assumptions yet has 95 percent of the efficiency of OLS estimates when classical assumptions are met. We implemented the "bounded-influence" version of this procedure which downweights high "leverage" cases as well as outliers (Hamilton 1992: 207-211). We obtained standard errors for performing significance tests by using asymptotic estimators adapted from Street, Carrol, and Ruppert (1988) as described in Hamilton (1991:198-200).

4. That is, we took each equation then systematically dropped each independent variable in turn and reestimated the equation. This strategy indicates whether or not the effects estimated for a given independent variable are sensitive to the presence or absence of other predictors in the model. Obviously, it is comforting if this is not the case.

5. We used decade interactions in the pooled data set to explore this assumption, but did not rely solely on statistical significance in our evaluation. Instead, we gave considerable weight to the question of whether the decade-to-decade variation was substantively meaningful and could be interpreted in terms of existing theory.

6. The square root transformation does not perfectly capture the non-linearity in the effect of percent Black, but it performs well and serves the purpose better than any other commonly used monotonic transformation.

7. This is calculated according to $2.32 = 1.416(\sqrt{15} - \sqrt{5})$ and $1.12 = 1.416(\sqrt{45} - \sqrt{35})$.

8. Unreported analyses we examined showed that the nonlinearity in the relationship is also changing over time. Specifically, when the effect of percent Black is estimated using a second-degree polynomial, the effect is approximately linear in 1940 and 1950 and becomes increasingly nonlinear over time. By 1970 and 1980, the nonlinearity is such that inequality actually begins to fall after percent Black reaches 50-60 points. We do not pursue this finding in more detail in the present analysis because the nonlinearity just described is estimated from only a handful of cases where values of percent Black significantly exceed 50. A larger sample of such cases is needed to establish this pattern with greater confidence.

9. Conventional usage of the concept of status does not readily accommodate the unemployed and especially persons not in the labor force. For example, status scores for the unemployed or for persons not in the labor force are not routinely published.

10. We considered using the natural log of population instead because the labor force was revised considerably in 1940 compared to the gainful worker concept used in 1930, and because the minimum age for the labor force changed from 10 to 14 to 16 to 18 between 1930 and 1980. However, we found that the correlation between the population measure and the labor force measure exceeded 0.97 in each decade so we elected to use the more direct measure of labor force size.

11. The early stage was 50 percent or more employed in farm occupations. The middle stage was 10-49 percent employed in farm occupations. The late stage was less than 10 percent employed in farm occupations.

12. Specifically, we entered a dummy variable for middle stage, a dummy variable for late stage, and a variable measuring number of decades in final stage. The early stage (or farm economy category) served as the reference point for interpreting the dummy variables.

13. Unionization efforts in the South may be undercut by racial divisions among workers. If so, that implies that the potential impact of manufacturing on worker unionization is weak in the presence of powerful racial cleavages.

14. One important exception is the declining effect of percent Black over time.

15. The decade-to-decade change implied by the effects of the dummy variables is distinct from their normal interpretation as deviations from the reference year of 1940 in the pooled equation.

16. Percent of civilian labor force employed is a relatively transitory, cyclical variable and we do not see it as reflecting long-term trends in community characteristics.

6

Longitudinal Analyses

The problems associated with inferring the magnitude and even the direction of causal effects from cross-sectional data are increasingly recognized. A recent discussion by Lieberson (1985) stressed this point. He noted that causal parameters estimated from cross-sectional data may be misleading under a wide range of commonly occurring circumstances such as: (a) when causal effects are not reversible and symmetric, (b) when the systems under observation are not in or near equilibrium (i.e., when the causal impacts of past changes in independent variables have not had sufficient time to be realized), and (c) when causal relations among variables involve reciprocal effects and/or feedback loops. Since these and other potentially troubling problems often cannot be ruled out in cross-sectional analyses, Lieberson (1985) argues that great caution should be exercised when applying causal interpretations to parameter estimates obtained from cross-sectional data. In particular, he cautions that literal causal interpretations that *changes* in an independent variable will in fact be followed by subsequent *changes* in a dependent variable should be viewed skeptically until such interpretations are supported with evidence from direct analysis of longitudinal data.

We take these cautionary statements seriously. Thus, our goal in this chapter is to present analyses of longitudinal data which will provide further evidence regarding whether the causal interpretations of the cross-sectional effects reviewed in the previous chapter are justified. Before discussing these analyses, however, it is important to stress that we do not believe the examination of longitudinal data is a panacea. The estimation of longitudinal models, like the estimation of cross-sectional models, requires that important theoretical assumptions be made *prior* to estimating equations (Finkel

1995; Kessler and Greenberg 1981). These assumptions are by no means trivial and, as in cross-sectional work, they must be correct or almost so to justify causal interpretations of model-based parameter estimates.

Furthermore, we also note that, while longitudinal data are *in principle* more attractive than cross-sectional data, certain practical problems may neutralize the advantages that analyses of longitudinal data have over analyses of cross-sectional data. One potentially important problem relevant in our situation is that structural variables often change slowly. As a result changes in the independent variables from one time period to the next may be small compared to the cross-sectional variation in the independent variables (which reflects the cumulative results of changes over many time periods). In the present study, for example, the standard deviation for decade-to-decade changes in percent Black is about 3 percentage points. In contrast, the smallest standard deviation for cross-area variation in percent Black in any decade is over 16 percentage points.[1] Since the reliability of regression coefficients is closely tied to the amount of variance in the independent variables, cross-sectional data would, other things being equal, provide the better basis for estimating the effects of percent Black.

This problem can be further exacerbated by the impact of measurement error. The amount of measurement error in the dependent and independent variables is the same in both cross-sectional and longitudinal analyses since the data points are the same. However, measurement error that is inconsequential in a cross sectional analysis might prove more troublesome in a longitudinal analysis. The reason for this is that the focus in the longitudinal analysis is on changes in variables across time and the ratio of signal to noise is inherently lower for change scores than for level scores since change scores are derived from two level scores each of which is subject to error (Kessler and Greenberg 1981). Coupled with the fact that change scores often have less variance in the first place, undesirable consequences of measurement error may be especially worrisome in longitudinal analyses.

Finally, we should point out the common practical problem that structural variables often change in unison. This is not an uncommon problem in nonexperimental data generally and it historically has been a particular problem in research which examines changes in inequality over time using national-level time-series data. Our longitudinal models follow a panel design rather than a time series design, still it is not hard to anticipate that, in southern nonmetropolitan counties, shifts in the occupation mix toward white-collar occupations have tended to occur simultaneously with increasing representation of women in the labor force and shifts toward urban, nonagriculaturally based economies. The fact that none of this is surprising does not negate the difficulties it presents to analysts who seek to assess the separate effects of these various trends.

These remarks are not intended to undermine confidence in the longitudinal analyses we are about to present. Rather we offer them to make the point that unquestioning faith in any type of data or mode of analysis is misplaced. Thus, the results we present in this chapter should not necessarily be seen as superior to the results of cross-sectional analyses we presented in the preceding chapter just because the longitudinal aspects of our data are exploited more fully. What we hoped for was for the two sets of analyses to be completely consistent since this would permit us to say that our conclusions were supported by two different modes of analysis, each of which has its own strengths.

In fact we find there are some differences between the longitudinal results in this chapter and the cross-sectional results in the previous chapter. In our view most of the differences are minor and, all in all, the consistency of effects across analyses is the single most compelling finding. However, to the extent that there are differences between the results of the longitudinal analyses and the cross-sectional analyses, we are not prepared to argue that one set of results should be presumptively adopted over the other. Our panel analysis of inequality is the first of its kind (at least to our knowledge) and we have undertaken it because we believe it can provide important evidence to inform our understanding of the structural determinants of racial inequality. However, we also recognize that these results have not been replicated and confirmed by others. In contrast, cross-sectional analyses of racial inequality have a long history of replication and incremental extension. Consequently, we have a broader base of prior evidence to provide a context for assess the "reasonableness" of the cross-sectional results we obtained earlier in Chapter 5. It would be unwise to set those results aside for the results of longitudinal analyses which have yet to stand the test of time.

This said, we now review evidence from four sets of models which investigate the effects of changes in structural characteristics on racial inequality in nonmetropolitan counties of the South. We first consider regression models which predict the level of the dependent variable with the lagged level of each independent variable and the changes of each independent variable over the last time period. Next we consider models which include the lagged value of the dependent variable as a predictor along with measures of changes in the independent variables. The inclusion of the lagged value of the dependent variable focuses attention on change in the dependent variable since other predictors are predicting variation in the dependent variable that exists net of controls for the initial value of the dependent variable. In the third set of models we predict the dependent variable with its lagged value and with both change scores for the independent variables and lagged level scores for the independent variables. We then conclude our longitudinal analyses by presenting exploratory covariance structure models (i.e., LISREL models) which we use to assess certain assumptions which bear on the interpretation of the OLS results presented in the first three sets of models.

Models Including Changes in Independent Variables

Table 6.1 presents results for models that predict the *level* of the dependent variable using *lagged values* of the independent variables and their *change scores* for the past decade.[2] In the case of percent Black the twice lagged value and the once lagged change score are used. We adopt this specification because there is reason to expect negative feedback between change in percent Black and change in inequality since previous research has suggested that percent Black tends to decline as inequality increases (Stinner and DeJong 1969; Burr, Galle, Potter, and Fossett 1991). Turning to the longer lags helps minimize unwanted complications associated with this feedback without resorting to a more complicated model which allows for reciprocal effects.

A decade-specific analysis for 1940 is not possible since data for 1930 are not available for the dependent variable. Thus, compared to the cross-sectional results we previously reported, we present one less decade-specific regression and we lose one wave of observations from the pooled model.

Our interest in this model focuses on the comparison of the coefficients of each independent variable's lagged score and change score. If causal interpretations of the cross-sectional effects discussed in the previous chapter are valid, the change score will tend to take the same sign as the lagged effect and be similar in magnitude. One caveat to this general rule of thumb is that estimates of the change effect will tend to be less efficient (i.e., less reliable) than estimates of the level effect because the independent variables' variation over time tends to be small compared to their cross-sectional variation. Furthermore, as we noted earlier, coefficients for change scores tend to be attenuated in this situation because measurement error is likely

TABLE 6.1 Decade-Specific and Pooled Cross-Sectional Regressions of Racial Inequality on Level and Change Scores for Selected Structural Characteristics of Southern Nonmetropolitan Areas, 1940-1990.

Independent Variables	1950	1960	1970	1980	1990	Pooled[d]
Square Root Percent Black (Level Lag 2)	2.236[a]	2.081[a]	0.121	0.198	0.738[a]	1.229[a]
Square Root Percent Black (Change Lag 1)	3.384[a]	0.254	-0.616	-1.746[c]	2.189[b]	1.128[a]
Female Labor Force Share (Level Lag 1)	0.151[a]	0.202[a]	0.148[b]	0.162[a]	-0.028	0.202[a]
Female Labor Force Share (Change)	0.056	-0.060	0.008	0.154	-0.223[c]	-0.034
Percent LF White Collar (Level Lag 1)	0.043	0.098	-0.085[c]	-0.049	-0.023	0.050[b]
Percent LF White Collar (Change)	0.658[a]	0.126	0.085	0.073	0.121[c]	0.217[a]
Status Diversity (Level Lag 1)	0.328[a]	0.223	1.664[a]	1.574[a]	1.787[a]	0.612[a]
Status Diversity (Change)	-0.223[c]	0.333[c]	1.599[a]	0.925[a]	1.668[a]	0.494[a]
Indigenous Labor Supply (Level Lag 1)	-0.073	-0.008	-0.014	-0.101[a]	-0.132[a]	-0.075[a]
Indigenous Labor Supply (Change)	-0.102	-0.184[b]	-0.059	-0.083[b]	-0.084	-0.028
Ln Civilian Labor Force (Level Lag 1)	0.859[b]	-0.117	0.141	0.101	0.147	0.262
Ln Civilian Labor Force (Change)	-0.322	7.422[a]	4.415[a]	-1.528	3.178[b]	2.218[a]
Adjusted R Square	0.684	0.518	0.426	0.350	0.402	0.556
Number of Cases	267	267	267	267	267	1335
St. Dev. of Dep. Var.	5.458	5.045	3.689	3.125	3.189	4.804
St. Dev. of Residuals	3.069	3.505	2.794	2.519	2.467	3.200

[a,b,c] Denote a probability of chance deviation from 0 of less than 0.01, 0.05, or 0.10, respectively, using a two-tailed test.

[d] Rows displaying coefficients for dummy variables for decade are omitted to conserve space; the coefficients are 2.551[a] for 1960, -1.164[b] for 1970, -3.679[a] for 1980, and -6.630[a] for 1990.

to represent a larger component of the total variation in the change scores than in the total variation in the level scores.

The results from the pooled regression in Table 6.1 are generally consistent with the results of the pooled, cross-sectional regressions reported in Tables 5.1 and 5.2 of the previous chapter. Not surprisingly, the greatest consistency was observed for the effects of the lagged levels of the independent variables. All lagged level scores had the same sign as in the previously reported cross-sectional regressions. Additionally, these effects are generally similar in size and statistical significance.

The effects of the change scores for the independent variables are consistent with the effects of the lagged level scores in most but not all cases. Change effects for relative minority size, white-collar employment, and status diversity are statistically significant and in the same direction as the cross-sectional level effects. These are among the most important variables in the cross-sectional results reviewed earlier and the analyses here confirm the results seen in the cross-sectional analyses where they all have positive effects on inequality.

Among the variables which had important effects in the cross-sectional results, only female labor force share has mixed results in the change analysis. The lagged level score effect was positive and significant as predicted and as previously observed in the cross-sectional results, but the change score effect is not statistically significant. One possible explanation of this anomaly is that the parameter estimate for the change score effect is less reliable than the level effect because the temporal variation in female labor force share is smaller than the cross-area variation.[3] On the other hand, it may simply be that the change effect is not as strong as the cross-sectional results would suggest.

The level effect of indigenous labor supply is negative and statistically significant as previously observed in the cross-sectional results. However, the effect of change in indigenous labor supply is not statistically significant. The negative level effect of indigenous labor supply was not predicted. The fact that the change effect is not consistent with the cross-sectional effect raises further questions about our understanding of the role of indigenous labor supply.

Finally, the effect of (the natural logarithm of) labor force size also bears mention. The level effect in the cross-sectional analysis is positive and significant. In this change analysis, the lagged level effect is not significant, but the effect of the change score for labor force size is positive and significant. We cannot trace the discrepancy between the effect for the level score and change score for labor force size to problems in the data. In view of this, we should probably reconsider the interpretations we attach to the level and change scores for labor force size.

Under conventional ecological theory, labor force size can be considered a surrogate for market scale and intensity of labor market competition. Changes in labor force size reflect changes in market scale, but they also might be considered a surrogate for economic growth. If so, the discrepancy between the effects of the level and change scores is a problem of theory and interpretation until empirically distinct measures of change in market scale and economic growth can be obtained.

The decade-specific results for the analyses using change scores for the independent variables are less consistent than the results for cross-sectional models. This is not unexpected. As we noted earlier, change scores are less reliable than level scores. In addition, the change scores here exhibit less variation than the level scores. Both of these factors make the estimates of the change effects less reliable. In our view, this provides good justification for focusing on the results for the pooled analysis rather than the decade-specific analyses since pooling improves the efficiency of the parameter estimates.

Model Predicting Changes in Dependent Variables

Table 6.2 presents results for regressions of *changes* in the dependent variable on *changes* in the independent variables. This description may not seem accurate on first consideration because the named dependent variable is the *level score* for the dependent variable. A change interpretation is entirely appropriate, however, because the lagged value of the dependent variable is included as a predictor in the equation and variation in the level of inequality that remains after taking account of its prior level represents change.

This specification is desirable on at least two counts. One is that including the lagged level of inequality is a means for controlling for regression to the mean since counties at the extremes on inequality often have a tendency to move back toward the mean (and are less likely to move further toward the extreme). In addition, this specification may also reduce serial autocorrelation by controlling for unmeasured causes of inequality in each area that are relatively stable over time (Finkel 1995; Kessler and Greenberg 1981).[4]

We focus our attention on the results of the pooled analysis. The effects seen here can be easily and briefly summarized. All change effects have the same sign, same level of statistical significance, and approximately similar magnitude previously observed in Table 6.1.

TABLE 6.2 Decade-Specific and Pooled Cross-Sectional Regressions of Racial Inequality on Lagged Dependent Variable and Change Scores for Selected Structural Characteristics of Southern Nonmetropolitan Areas, 1940-1990.

Independent Variables	1950	1960	1970	1980	1990	Pooled
White-Black SES Difference (Level Lag 1)	0.824[a]	0.763[a]	0.414[a]	0.498[a]	0.664[a]	0.677[a]
Square Root Percent Black (Change Lag 1)	1.354[b]	2.622[a]	1.069	-0.895	2.530[a]	2.115[a]
Female Labor Force Share (Change)	-0.020	0.025	-0.019	0.035	-0.032	-0.030
Percent LF White Collar (Change)	0.492[a]	0.196[b]	0.271[a]	0.032	0.216[a]	0.219[a]
Status Diversity (Change)	0.257[a]	0.549[a]	-0.157	0.177	0.356	0.221[a]
Indigenous Labor Supply (Change)	-0.005	0.004	0.041	-0.054	-0.056	-0.020
Ln Civilian Labor Force (Change)	0.786	4.428[a]	1.652	-1.327	2.295[c]	1.313[b]
Dummy for 1960						3.536[a]
Dummy for 1970	-----	-----	-----	-----	-----	-1.827[a]
Dummy for 1980	-----	-----	-----	-----	-----	-2.473[a]
Dummy for 1990	-----	-----	-----	-----	-----	-1.832[a]
Adjusted R Square	0.857	0.656	0.409	0.360	0.461	0.682
Number of Cases	267	267	267	267	267	1335
St. Dev. of Dep. Var.	5.458	5.045	3.689	3.125	3.189	4.804
St. Dev. of Residuals	2.062	2.961	2.835	2.499	2.341	2.710

[a,b,c] Denote probability is less than 0.01, 0.05, or 0.10, respectively (two-tailed test).

Thus, changes in minority size, white-collar employment, status diversity, and labor force growth all have positive and significant effects on changes in inequality. Change in female labor force share and indigenous labor supply do not have statistically significant effects on changes in inequality.

Table 6.3 presents results from a set of regressions using a third specification for investigating change in inequality. It is similar to the previous specification in that it predicts changes in inequality with the lagged level of inequality and changes in the independent variables. It extends the previous specification, however, in that it also includes the *lagged levels* of the independent variables. Thus, the effects of changes in the independent variables are estimated controlling for the prior level of inequality and the prior levels of the structural characteristics.

The change effects observed in the previous two analyses are confirmed again with the results obtained using this specification for investigating change in inequality. That is to say, increases in minority size, white-collar employment, status diversity, and labor force size have positive and significant effects on change in inequality. Changes in female labor force share and indigenous labor supply do not have statistically significant effects on inequality.[5]

Interestingly, the lagged levels of minority size, female labor force share, and status diversity all have significant positive effects on change in inequality. These results indicate that even net of the prior level of inequality and recent changes in these variables, inequality tends to increase in counties that have higher level scores for minority size, female labor force share, and status diversity. The lagged level of indigenous labor supply has a significant negative effect on inequality. The lagged level of labor force size does not have a statistically significant effect.

The last effect we discuss is that of the lagged level of inequality. The coefficient for this variable indicates the tendency of inequality to carry forward over time net of the levels of and changes in structural characteristics. A small effect for this variable indicates that inequality is not stable; that is, it has low "inertia" and does not tend to persist over time. Instead, it must be "recreated" anew each decade. A coefficient near 1.0 indicates that inequality has high inertia and, once created, does not dissipate rapidly but rather tends to carry forward over time. It is important to remember, however, that this interpretation is net of the effects of other variables. That is to say, inequality may persist in an area due to the levels of and changes in structural characteristics such as minority size. The question here is, net of such effects, does inequality tend to persist?

TABLE 6.3 Decade-Specific and Pooled Regressions of Racial Inequality on its Lagged Level and on the Lagged Levels and Changes in Structural Characteristics of Southern Nonmetropolitan Areas, 1940-1990.

Independent Variables	1950	1960	1970	1980	1990	Pooled[d]
White-Black SES Difference (Level Lag 1)	0.813[a]	0.697[a]	0.317[a]	0.346[a]	0.470[a]	0.551[a]
Square Root Percent Black (Level Lag 2)	0.237	0.014	-0.365[c]	0.194	0.514[a]	0.362[a]
Square Root Percent Black (Change Lag 1)	1.483[b]	1.589[c]	0.308	-0.952	3.104[a]	2.099[a]
Female Labor Force Share (Level Lag 1)	-0.017	0.147[a]	0.078	0.090[c]	-0.062	0.080[a]
Female Labor Force Share (Change)	0.005	0.063	-0.002	0.134	-0.124	0.003
Percent LF White Collar (Level Lag 1)	0.135[a]	-0.056	-0.092[b]	-0.035	0.008	0.001
Percent LF White Collar (Change)	0.504[a]	0.139[c]	0.106[c]	0.048	0.159[a]	0.182[a]
Status Diversity (Level Lag 1)	-0.127	0.294[a]	1.318[a]	1.000[a]	0.886[a]	0.303[a]
Status Diversity (Change)	0.175[b]	0.576[a]	1.202[a]	0.892[a]	1.192[a]	0.453[a]
Indigenous Labor Supply (Level Lag 1)	0.059[c]	0.084[b]	-0.006	-0.103[a]	-0.111[a]	-0.032[b]
Indigenous Labor Supply (Change)	-0.004	-0.010	-0.061	-0.086[b]	-0.083[c]	-0.032
Ln Civilian Labor Force (Level Lag 1)	0.098	-0.941[a]	-0.018	0.066	-0.005	-0.082
Ln Civilian Labor Force (Change)	0.025	4.413[a]	3.142[b]	-1.598	2.737[b]	1.814a
Adjusted R Square	0.862	0.696	0.517	0.446	0.535	0.702
Number of Cases	267	267	267	267	267	1335
St. Dev. of Dep. Var.	5.458	5.045	3.689	3.125	3.189	4.804
St. Dev. of Residuals	2.029	2.782	2.564	2.326	2.174	2.623

a,b,c Denote probability is less than 0.01, 0.05, or 0.10, respectively (two-tailed test).

d Rows displaying coefficients for dummy variables for decade are omitted to conserve space; the coefficients are 3.039[a] for 1960, -1.870[a] for 1970, -3.070[a] for 1980, and -3.047[a] for 1990.

The pooled analysis indicates that inequality is less than perfectly stable. The coefficient of 0.551 indicates that, all else equal, slightly more than half of the initial level of inequality will carry forward to the next decade. Alternatively, this means that an initial level of inequality will fall by almost half with each successive decade. Again, however, this is net of the effects of structural characteristics which may well serve to recreate and maintain inequality.

The decade-specific results indicate that the effect of the lagged value of inequality diminishes over time. This means that the "stability" of inequality is declining over time. Between 1940 and 1960 inequality tended to be carried forward to the next decade almost in full. Net of changes in other variables, counties retained an average of approximately 80 to 70 percent of their initial level of inequality (i.e., the coefficients of 0.813 and 0.697 indicate that on average counties retained 81.3 and 69.7 percent, respectively, of their initial values on inequality). Stability effects were much smaller after 1960. For every decade after 1960, counties on average retained less than 50 percent of their initial level of inequality, net of the effects of the independent variables.

The decade-specific results indicate that the persistence of inequality over time, its "inertia" if you will, fell substantially between 1960 and 1970. This suggests that the racial stratification system in the South changed in some important and fundamental way between 1960 and 1970. One obvious possibility is that Civil and Voting Rights legislation and other public policy initiatives introduced in the 1960's, reduced the ability of White majority populations to maintain racial advantage over time.

Time effects are also seen in the coefficients of the dummy variables for decade in the pooled model. The coefficients for the decade dummies (reported in the notes of Table 6.3) are 3.039 for 1960, -1.870 for 1970, -3.070 for 1980, and -3.047 for 1990. These represent the average change in inequality over the past decade (relative to 1950) net of the effects of the levels and changes in the structural characteristics and the prior level of inequality. They indicate that during the 1950s inequality increased by an average of just over 3 points (relative to its level in 1950), then declined by almost 5 points during the 1960s (erasing the increase of 3.039 which accrued in the 1950s and dropping an additional 1.870 points), then declined by an additional 1.2 points during the 1970s (falling from 1.870 to 3.070 below the 1950 average), and did not change appreciably in the 1980s. This pattern is very similar to the pattern seen for the "decade effects" in the cross-sectional regressions analyses reported in the previous chapter. That is to say, inequality increased in the 1950s, fell substantially in the 1960s and then fell again but by a smaller amount in the 1970s. The only major difference between the two sets of results is that, in the cross-sectional regressions, inequality fell by a small amount in the 1980s whereas the longitudinal regressions show inequality to be stable rather than falling in the 1980s.

Exploratory Covariance Structure Models

In this section we present the results of covariance structure analyses investigating changes over time in racial inequality. We perform these analyses in order to evaluate one of the central assumptions required to justify causal interpretations to the OLS regression results presented earlier in this chapter. Specifically, we examine the assumption that errors of prediction in inequality are uncorrelated across time (i.e., no serial autocorrelation). To our knowledge, this represents the first time this assumption has been assessed in a comparative analysis of racial inequality.

Using Level-Score Specifications to Investigate Change

Before we can introduce the results of the covariance structure analyses, we first need to introduce the model specification we will use. Three closely related specifications examining change in inequality are shown in Table 6.4. The results for these three models are reported for illustrative purposes only. Thus, we use a very simple model which includes only one structural variable — relative minority size — and dummies for decade as independent variables. The coefficients for the models were estimated using the pooled sample and OLS methods.

The first specification regresses a change score for the dependent variable on a level score for the dependent variable, a change score for the independent variable, and a lagged level score for the independent variable. The second specification is similar but substitutes the level score for inequality as the dependent variable. (This is the kind of specification used previously in Table 6.3.) The third specification presented investigates change in inequality by regressing the level score for inequality on its lagged level score and on the current and lagged level scores for the independent variable. While this last specification is less intuitive, it is mathematically equivalent

TABLE 6.4 Pooled Regressions of Change and Level of Racial Inequality on Lagged Level and Change Scores for Percent Black for Southern Nonmetropolitan Areas, 1940-1990.

Independent Variables	(1) Change	(2) Level	(3) Level
Inequality (Lagged Level)	-0.375[a]	0.625[a]	0.625[a]
Percent Black[d] (Lagged Level)	0.326[a]	0.326[a]	-1.576[a]
Percent Black[d] (Change)	1.902[a]	1.902[a]	-----
Percent Black[d] (Level)	-----	-----	1.902[a]
Dummy for 1960	2.986[a]	2.986[a]	2.986[a]
Dummy for 1970	-2.743[a]	-2.743[a]	-2.743[a]
Dummy for 1980	-3.197[a]	-3.197[a]	-3.197[a]
Dummy for 1990	-2.127[a]	-2.127[a]	-2.127[a]
Adjusted R Square	0.577	0.669	0.669
Number of Cases	1335	1335	1335
St. Dev. of Dep. Var.	4.247	4.804	4.804
St. Dev. of Residuals	2.763	2.763	2.763

[a,b,c] denote probability is less than 0.01, 0.05, or 0.10, respectively (two-tailed test).

[d] Percent Black is measured by the square root.

to the second specification, yields identical substantive information about changes in inequality, and, as will be made clear later, has key advantages which will be important in later analyses.

In Equation 1 change in inequality is regressed on the lagged level of inequality, the lagged level of (the square root of) percent Black, change in (the square root of) percent Black, and dummy variables for decade effects.[6] The change score for minority size captures the effect of change in minority size on change in inequality. The lagged level of inequality allows for the possibility that change in inequality depends on the initial level of inequality. The lagged level of (the square root of) percent Black allows for the possibility that change in inequality depends on the initial level of the independent variable. Finally, the decade dummies capture average changes in inequality associated with different decades (not associated with changes in percent Black).

The coefficient of -0.375 for the lagged level of inequality in Equation 1 indicates regression to the mean wherein areas which initially have high levels of inequality tend to experience higher declines in inequality. It also indicates that inequality's persistence is not perfect and it must be partially recreated each decade if the initially observed levels are to be maintained. The coefficient of 0.326 for the lagged level of (the square root of) percent Black indicates that inequality tends to increase in areas that initially have large minority populations. Finally, and of primary interest here, the coefficient of 1.902 for the change in percent Black indicates that increases in (the square root of) percent Black are associated with increases in inequality.

Equation 2 contains all of this substantive information even though the specification is slightly different. In this equation, the level of inequality, not change, is the dependent variable. However, the model also includes the lagged level of inequality. Since the level and the lagged level scores define the change score for inequality, no information about change in inequality is lost; it is merely represented in a slightly different way. (This is the specification used in Table 6.3). This can be seen in the fact that the standard deviation of the residuals (i.e., the average errors of prediction) is the same for both equations while the explained variance (i.e., R^2) for the equations is different.

Inspection of the results showed that the regression coefficients obtained using this specification are exactly the same as those obtained using Equation 1 with one exception. The lone difference between the two sets of results is that the coefficient for the lagged level of inequality in Equation 2 is 0.625 compared to -0.375 in Equation 1. Inspection reveals that the coefficient for lagged inequality in Equation 2 is equal to 1.0 plus the coefficient for this same variable in Equation 1 (i.e., 0.625 = 1.0 + -0.375). The substantive meaning of the coefficient for lagged inequality in Equation 2, however, is exactly the same as that implied by the coefficient for lagged inequality in Equation 1. The coefficient of 0.625 indicates that only a portion of any initial deviation from the average level of inequality is carried forward to the next decade. All else equal, inequality does not persist indefinitely. If it did, the coefficient for lagged inequality would be 1.0 which would indicate that, once created, area differences on inequality tend to persist indefinitely. Since the coefficient for the lagged level of inequality is less than 1.0, we see that inequality tends to dissipate or decay over time. This is the same meaning conveyed by the coefficient for lagged inequality in Equation 1 which is that extreme levels of inequality tend to fall back toward the mean over time.

Equation 3 differs from Equation 2 in that it includes the level score for (the square root of) percent Black instead of the change score. The two level scores define change in (the square root of) percent Black so no information about change in relative minority size is lost; but it is represented in a different way. Three things should be noted about the results obtained using this specification. One is that this specification is mathematically equivalent to the specification used in Equation 2 and this can be seen in the fact that the model fit statistics (i.e., adjusted R-Square and standard deviation of residuals) are identical for both equations. A second thing to note is that the coefficient attaching to change in minority size in Equations 1 and 2 attaches to the level of minority size in Equation 3. Third, the coefficient attaching to the initial level of minority size in Equation 3 reflects the difference between the coefficients for the change score and level score for minority size in Equation 2 (i.e., -1.576 = 0.326 – 1.902).

The key point to be taken from this discussion is that Equation 3, which at first glance does not appear to be a specification for investigating change in inequality, can in fact be used to obtain the coefficients of either Equation 1 or Equation 2, specifications which are more obviously relevant for investigating change in inequality.[7]

More generally, the "level or static score" specification used in Equation 3 has the form

$$Y_t = b_1 Y_{t-1} + b_2 X_{t-1} + b_3 X_t$$

and can be used to obtain the parameters of the "change score" specification used in Equation 1 which has the form

$$y = b_4 Y_{t-1} + b_5 X_{t-1} + b_6 x$$

where $b_1 - b_6$ are unstandardized regression coefficients, Y and Y_{t-1} are the contemporaneous and lagged values of the dependent variable, respectively, X_t and X_{t-1} are the contemporaneous and lagged values of the independent variable, respectively, and x and y represent change scores for X and Y, respectively (given by $X_t - X_{t-1}$ and $Y_t - Y_{t-1}$).[8]

The implications of the coefficients from the level score specification for change in the dependent variable can be summarized as follows.[9] The coefficient for the lagged value of the dependent variable, b_1, indicates the persistence or stability of the dependent variable over time. Alternatively, since change in the dependent variable is defined by $Y_t - Y_{t-1}$, the expression $b_1 - 1.0$ defines the effect of the initial level of the dependent variable on its change. This can be interpreted as the tendency for the dependent variable to regress to the mean over time. This is the same meaning this coefficient has in the specification used in Equation 2.

The coefficient for the contemporaneous value of the independent variable, b_3, can be interpreted as the effect of change in the independent variable on change in the dependent variable. Thus, it has the same meaning as the coefficients attaching to the change scores for the independent variable in Equations 1 and 2.

Finally, while the coefficient for the lagged level of the independent variable does not have a convenient substantive interpretation, it can be combined with the coefficient for the more recent level of the independent variable to obtain the effect of the lagged level of the independent variable on change in Y (i.e., b_5 in the change score specification is given by $b_2 + b_3$ in the level score specification)

Thus, we can use parameters from the level score specification to obtain the parameters of the change score specification as follows:

$$y = (b_1 - 1) Y_{t-1} + (b_2 + b_3)X_{t-1} + b_3 x.$$

That is, $b_4 = (b_1 - 1)$, $b_5 = (b_2 + b_3)$, and $b_6 = b_3$. These relationships can be illustrated using the coefficients for (the square root of) percent Black reported in Table 6.4. Ignoring the effects of decade, the level score equation is

$$Y_t = 0.625 Y_{t-1} + -1.576 X_{t-1} + 1.902 X_t$$

and it implies the following change score equation

$$y = -0.375 Y_{t-1} + 0.326 X_{t-1} + 1.902 x_t$$

obtained according to

$$y = (0.625 - 1.0)Y_{t-1} + (-1.576 + 1.902)X_{t-1} + 1.902 x_t.$$

These results perfectly reproduce the coefficients estimated directly using the change score specification (Equation 1 in Table 6.4).

The point to take from this discussion is that the level score specification and the change score specification are mathematically equivalent. Thus, they can be used interchangeably to investigate change in inequality.[10] We establish this point because, while the level score specification is less intuitive for investigating change, it has important advantages which can be exploited when we estimate the model parameters using the methods of covariance structure analysis. Less cryptically, the level score specification can be used to test certain key assumptions underlying the OLS models of change reported earlier in this chapter.

Moving Beyond OLS Specifications

The possibilities for using the level-score specification to directly test assumptions which go unexamined in OLS analyses are illustrated in Figure 6.1. This figure depicts a multi-wave, panel model for investigating change in inequality.[11] The model is organized around a level score specification which, as we have just demonstrated, can be used to investigate change in the dependent variable. The model shown goes beyond an OLS specification, however, in that it allows for associations among the error terms for the dependent variable.

In OLS specifications (such as those used to obtain the results presented in Tables 6.1-6.3 presented earlier in this chapter), these associations among error terms are *assumed* to be zero. Such assumptions are necessary to estimate the model by the method of ordinary least squares (OLS). While assumptions about error correlations should never be taken for granted, this is an especially important concern in panel models (i.e., change models) because correlations among the errors for the dependent variable are not uncommon in such analyses. Indeed, serial correlation among errors for the dependent variable can arise in many different ways (e.g., misspecification of the functional form of the effect of one of the independent variables). This possibility is troubling because parameter estimates obtained by OLS regression may be seriously flawed when these error correlations are not zero (Tuma and Hannan 1984: 430-431; Kessler and Greenberg 1981:87-89).

Our goal here is to use the method of covariance structure analysis to obtain empirical estimates of the correlations among the error terms for the dependent variable. This will then permit us to assess whether our OLS estimates of the effects of the changes in

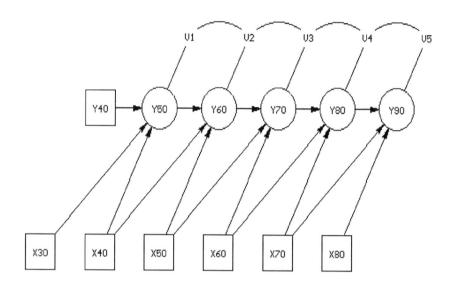

FIGURE 6.1 Simplified Representation of Model Investigating Serial Autocorrelation in Disturbances for Inequality.

and levels of structural independent variables on inequality are confirmed or called into question when serial autocorrelation is taken into account.

Estimating the model depicted in Figure 6.1 is easier said than done. The reason for this is that the formulation shown in the figure is "underidentified" and cannot be estimated because the number of unique parameters (i.e., the coefficients associated with each of the straight and curved lines connecting variables and error terms) to be estimated from the data exceeds the number of independent pieces of information available in the covariance matrix which can be used to estimate the model. Consequently, the causal effects and error correlations can only be estimated if the model is simplified so as to achieve identification; that is, so as to establish a model where the number of parameters to be estimated does not exceed the number of unique elements in the covariance matrix for the variables.

In OLS regression, identification is achieved by simplifying the model by presumptively setting the error correlations to zero. As we have noted, the assumption that these correlations are zero is questionable and should not be taken for granted. In view of this, we take a different approach here and achieve identification by imposing equality constraints on selected parameters of the model. This approach is made feasible by the fact that we are drawing on panel data and estimating particular effects at multiple points in time. Thus, for example, we impose the constraint that all effects of lagged inequality be equal (i.e., we assume that the effect of the lagged value of inequality on the level of inequality is consistent over time). As a result of this equality constraint, we need estimate only one coefficient instead of a separate one for each time period. Similarly, we impose equality constraints on the effects of each independent variable in essence hypothesizing that their effects are consistent over time and thus can be represented by a single coefficient rather than a series of separate coefficients for each time period.

The approach of using equality constraints to achieve model identification is attractive because the hypothesis of consistent effects is highly plausible in the present case and the adequacy of equality constraints can be directly assessed by empirical tests. Kessler and Greenberg (1981) and Finkel (1995) argue that equality constraints represent relatively weak assumptions about the pattern of effects (especially when contrasted with assumptions that error correlations are zero) which can be reasonably entertained in most analyses. Indeed we have already implicitly invoked equality constraints when we focused our primary attention on the pooled cross-sectional models presented in Chapter 5 and the pooled change analyses presented earlier in this chapter.

When it is reasonable to assume consistency of effects over time several advantages accrue. For example, the model to be estimated is more parsimonious and the parameters of the model are estimated more reliably (i.e., pooling yields more efficient estimates of the regression coefficients). An additional benefit which is important in the present context is that assuming effects to be consistent over time greatly reduces the number of unique coefficients to be estimated from the data and thus generates an overidentified model. We can then use the resulting "extra" degrees of freedom to specify a model where correlations among error terms are estimated from the data instead of being assumed to be zero (as would be the case in an OLS analysis). Significantly, we are not simply substituting one "arbitrary" identifying assumption for another. The model we are investigating is highly overidentified. Thus, hypotheses that particular effects are consistent over time can be directly tested at the same time the error correlations are estimated.

Covariance structure analyses estimating models formulated along the lines of the model depicted in Figure 6.1 are presented in Table 6.5. Two key differences distinguish the models presented in the table from the model in the figure; namely, the table presents estimated effects for all independent variables used in our earlier change analyses (not just minority size as in the figure) and, unless otherwise noted, the table presents a single estimate of each effect which applies to all waves. The parameter estimates for the covariance structure models presented in the table are maximum likelihood estimates obtained using the LISREL 8 program (Jöreskog and Sörbom 1993).

Model A is a "baseline" model which closely corresponds to the pooled OLS regression model reported in Table 6.3. Like the pooled OLS model, this model estimates only a single value for the coefficient for each independent variable (i.e., it constrains the effects of the independent variables to be the same in all time periods). In addition, it is similar to the OLS specification in that all correlations among error terms are not estimated and instead are constrained to be zero. Not surprisingly, the coefficients reported for Model A are very close to those reported for the pooled model in Table 6.3. Indeed, the substantive implications of the two models are essentially identical.

Two minor differences between this model and the decade-specific equations reported in Table 6.3 should be noted. One is that the parameter estimates are obtained by the method of maximum likelihood rather than the method of least squares. This is really not of major consequence here, but it can lead to minor differences in the numerical values estimated for some coefficients.

The second difference is that the results reported in Table 6.5 are not directly estimated (as they are in Table 6.3) but are instead obtained indirectly from the results of a "level score" specification. As we noted earlier in this chapter, change score specification and level score specification are mathematically equivalent and thus the impact of the level and changes in the independent variables on changes in the dependent variable can be derived from the coefficients estimated using a level-score specification. Modeling requirements dictate that we use the level-score specification. However, our substantive interest is focused on change and we report the results from the level-score analyses in a format that parallels the OLS change-score regressions reported in Table 6.3. This simplifies the comparison of results of the two sets of analyses and facilitates discussion of change effects.

Specifically, Table 6.5 reports coefficients for the initial levels of the independent variables and coefficients for their change over time. Based on strategies outlined earlier in this chapter, these are obtained from the level score specification as follows. Coefficients for the initial level of the independent variable are obtained by summing the coefficients for the earlier and the more recent levels of the independent variable in the level score specification. The coefficients for the change in each independent variables are obtained from the coefficients for the more recent level score in the level score specification.

Assessing the goodness of fit of covariance structure models involves judgment on the part of the investigator; there are no hard and fast rules for establishing when a model is adequate. One indicator of fit for Model A is the model χ^2 of 527.6 with 182 degrees of freedom. The probability value for this statistic is less than 0.001 indicating that the differences between the observed covariance matrix and the covariance matrix implied by the model results cannot be plausibly attributed to chance.

Unfortunately, this is a global statistic which is not very informative when considered in isolation. One reason for this is that χ^2 registers lack of fit arising from overall model misspecification without indicating the source of model misspecification. There are many different ways in which the model may be misspecified (e.g., nonlinear relationships, variation in causal effects over time, correlations among disturbances, unreliable indicators, violations of distributional assumptions, and causal feedback resulting from inequality's effects on the independent variables) and some will be of greater concern than others in any particular analysis. Given this, some have argued that χ^2 is best examined in relation to model complexity. Thus, for example, Hayduk (1987:168) notes the suggestion that model fit may be considered "acceptable" if the ratio of χ^2 to model degrees of freedom does not exceed 3.

This is the case in the present analysis, but even with this refinement, a strict mechanical application of χ^2 as a measure of model fit is not wholly appropriate (Mueller 1996; Bollen 1989; Jöreskog and Sörbum 1993). Instead, it is best to view model χ^2 as

TABLE 6.5 Exploratory Covariance Structure Analyses of Changes in Racial Inequality in Southern Nonmetropolitan Areas, 1940-1990[a]

Independent Variables	A	B	C
White-Black SES Difference (Lag 1)	0.57	0.71	0.73
1970-1990 Value	-----	0.42	0.50
SqRt Percent Black (Lag 2)	0.40	0.36	0.28
SqRt Percent Black (Change Lag 1)	2.09	1.86	1.90
Female Labor Force Share (Lag 1)	0.08	0.04	0.03
Female Labor Force Share (Change)	0.00	-0.01	-0.01
Percent LF White Collar (Lag 1)	0.01	0.03	0.02
Percent LF White Collar (Change)	0.20	0.21	0.20
Status Diversity (Lag 1)	0.26	0.25	0.20
Status Diversity (Change)	0.42	0.43	0.40
Indigenous Labor Supply (Lag 1)	-0.04	-0.01	-0.02
Indigenous Labor Supply (Change)	-0.04	-0.03	-0.03
Ln Civilian Labor Force (Lag 1)	-0.02	0.13	-0.11
Ln Civilian Labor Force (Change)	1.48	1.42	1.42
Serial Error Covariances[b]	-----	-----	-0.72
Model DF	182	181	180
$\chi 2$	527.6	449.7	445.0
RMSE of Fitted Residuals	0.81	0.60	0.61
Goodness of Fit Index (GFI)	0.93	0.94	0.94
Comparative Fit Index (CFI)	0.98	0.99	0.91

[a] Coefficients are derived from results for level-score specifications using procedures outlined in the text.

[b] Error covariance term is significant at 0.05 and implies decade-specific first-order serial correlations of between -0.03 and -0.07.

just one among several benchmarks for evaluating model fit and guiding revisions to the model. It is most valuable when it is used to compare competing models and is less helpful when it used as a global indicator for evaluating a single model.

We emphasize the view that assessment of model fit should give great weight to considerations of parsimony and substantive implications of the models. Bentler (1989), Bollen (1989), Hayduk (1987), Mueller (1996); Bollen (1989); Jöreskog and Sörbum (1993), and others have argued that model fit should be evaluated based on the theory guiding the model formulation and based on comparisons with other substantively meaningful models. They also argue that parsimony is an important consideration and that, given the sensitivity of the χ^2 test, care should be taken to avoid "overfitting" the sample data since the resulting model may fit the sample data very well without necessarily reflecting patterns in the population from which the sample was drawn.

When these considerations are emphasized, alternative goodness of fit indices suggested by Jöreskog and Sörbum (1993) and others and the root mean square error of the residuals from the fitted covariance matrix should be examined as supplements to χ^2 to help assess differences between models. More importantly, the investigator must exercise judgment and weigh the trade-offs between parsimony, theoretical relevance, and statistical fit.

Goodness of fit indices reported by the LISREL program suggest the model fit is adequate. The ratio of chi-square to degrees of freedom is not excessive (i.e., it is below 3). Analysis of the residuals also indicates that there are no obvious major problems with the model. The residuals suggested the possible presence of feedback due to effects of inequality on some of the independent variables. This was most apparent in the case of relative minority size. We were able to minimize this problem by using the twice lagged level and the once lagged change for minority size. The residuals also suggested that some assumptions regarding equality constraints and error correlations should be reconsidered. We dealt with these possibilities by relaxing some equality constraints in Model B and making further allowances for certain error correlations in Model C.

Inspection of partial regression leverage plots for OLS regressions comparable to Model A did not reveal important nonlinearities except in the case of minority size where mild nonlinearity was evident even when the square root transformation of minority size is used. We did not address this problem since we could find no evidence to suggest it had important consequences for substantive implications of the model and because techniques for dealing with nonlinearity in covariance structure analyses are cumbersome to say the least. Finally, graphical analysis of the dependent and independent variables suggested that distributional assumptions were questionable.[12]

Model B addresses problems associated with the assumption that causal effects are constant over time. Detailed analysis indicated that improvements in model fit generated by relaxing equality constraints are not generally compelling with one exception to be noted below. The major reason for this is that decade-to-decade variation in the coefficients usually does not manifest a clear trend or pattern (this can be seen by examining the decade-specific effects reported earlier in Table 6.3) and cannot be readily linked with a guiding theoretical interpretation. Furthermore, even when model fit is marginally improved in the strict mechanical sense indicated by a χ^2 test, the substantive implications of the model are rarely altered in any important way whereas the "costs" in terms of parsimony and ease of interpretation are often considerable. Thus, we conclude that, in general, the assumption of consistency of causal effects is quite reasonable and should not be abandoned.

We deviate from this general conclusion in one instance. This is reflected in the specification shown in Model B which relaxes the consistency constraint for the coefficient for the lagged value of inequality. Specifically, we represented the effect of the "stability" coefficient (i.e., the coefficient for the lagged value of the dependent variable) with two coefficients; one which applies to the 1950 and 1960 waves and another which applies to the 1970, 1980, and 1990 waves. This produces a substantial reduction in error χ^2 which in our view justified the slight loss of parsimony.[13] We used this specification because the "stability" of inequality is substantially higher in the 1950 and 1960 panels and lower afterwards. As we noted previously, this pattern may suggest that institutional forces perpetuating inequality were weakened when Civil Rights legislation, Voting Rights legislation, and various anti-discrimination initiatives were implemented during the 1960's. Of course, while this interpretation is consistent with the observed change in the stability coefficient over time, this specific hypothesis is not tested by the model since direct measures of the causal mechanisms are not represented in the model.

Additionally analyses (not reported here) indicated that Model B was a good compromise between parsimony and model fit relative to assumptions about the consistency of causal effects over time. Model fit indices did not improve substantially when we relaxed consistency constraints for other independent variables. For example, we considered whether the effect of minority size might have weakened after 1960 based on the hypothesis that the potential resource aspects of relative minority size might have become more important after the passage of voting rights legislation in the 1960s. However, when we estimated an alternative version of Model B which allowed a shift in the effect of minority size after 1960, the reduction in χ^2 was not statistically significant even though the 1950-1960 effects of minority size were estimated to be slightly larger than the 1970-1990 effects.[14]

The coefficients estimated using Model B are fundamentally similar to those for obtained using Model A with the obvious exception that in Model B the stability of inequality diminishes over time (i.e., the regression to the mean effect is stronger after 1960). The results for both models are essentially similar to those suggested by the pooled OLS regression reported in Table 6.3. The important causal effects are the positive effects on inequality associated with increases in relative minority size, white collar employment, status diversity, and labor force growth. The weak effects of female labor force share and indigenous labor supply observed in Model A and in the pooled analysis reported in Table 6.3 diminish even further under the specification used to estimate Model B.

Model C is the final model we report in our review of covariance structure analyses. It implements a model in which the standard OLS assumption of uncorrelated errors is partially relaxed. Specifically, this model allows for first-order serial correlations in the errors for inequality subject to the constraint that these error correlations are equal across waves. This specification addresses the possibility that inequality is spuriously correlated over time, possibly due to omitted variables that were stable over time, or due to misspecifications of the functional forms of the effects of the independent variables. The relatively simple structure of the error correlations we use in this specification reflects the fact that previous theory and research do not provide much guidance in this area.[15]

The results for Model C indicate that the errors of prediction for inequality at different points in time are negatively associated. The metric value for the error covariances reported in the table is significantly different from zero ($p < 0.05$), but it is not readily interpretable. Its substantive implications are more easily assessed when it is expressed in standardized form as a serial correlation coefficient. The first-order serial autocorrelations implied by the error covariance term are small, varying from -0.07 to -0.03. These autocorrelation terms do not appear to be substantively important as their inclusion does not appreciably improve the model fit indices.

The key question, of course, is whether these error correlations have an important impact on the causal effects estimated for the independent variables. That is, do they alter causal interpretations derived from the model. We could find no evidence that this is the case. Inspection of the results for Model C shows that the coefficients for this model are quite close to those reported for Model B. In no instance does the observed difference affect the substantive interpretation of the model in any important way.

Thus, while serial correlation is found in the data, as is often the case in longitudinal analyses, there is no evidence that it plays an important role in shaping estimates of the effects the independent variables and thus there is no basis for discounting the OLS change models reported earlier in this chapter. We must hasten to add, however, that the model specification we used to investigate error correlations is guided by relatively weak theory. It is for this reason that we describe our analyses as exploratory in nature and stress that the results we report must be viewed as being highly tentative. Future studies should build on these models and consider a broader range of substantively motivated structural models of racial inequality.

Summary

In this chapter we reviewed evidence which suggests that cross-sectional analyses and longitudinal analyses yield largely similar findings regarding the impact of structural variables on racial inequality. This is particularly true for three variables which have the strongest overall effects on inequality; namely relative minority size, percent employed in white collar occupations, and status diversity. These variables have clear and consistent positive effects on inequality in all modes of analysis we considered. Female labor force share has strong, positive effects on inequality in cross-sectional analyses, but this effect is not confirmed in the longitudinal models.

The longitudinal models are also interesting in that they suggest that the "stability" of inequality diminished after 1960. This implies that "inertial" and institutional forces perpetuating inequality became less effective. Such an interpretation rounds out our understanding of the appreciable declines in inequality that occurred after 1960 (as reflected in the decade effects presented in Table 6.3).

In principle, analyses based on longitudinal data are superior to analyses based on cross-sectional data. However, as we cautioned at the beginning of the chapter, in practice, longitudinal data are rarely free of limitations and problems. For that reason, readers should not casually assume that the longitudinal analyses presented here render cross-sectional analyses irrelevant. Of course, we firmly believe that our longitudinal analyses do provide valuable information which should be taken into account when structural theories of inequality are evaluated. But we are careful to stress that our longitudinal analyses must be seen as exploratory in nature. There are no prior examples of longitudinal analysis comparable to ours in the literature. On the one hand, that means that our analyses provide an important new contribution to the study of racial inequality in nonmetropolitan areas. On the other hand, it also means that findings developed from longitudinal analyses have yet to be replicated and refined by others. Until this is done and until longitudinal analyses of inequality are more common in the literature, it would be unwise to abandon the much greater body of literature that is based on analyses of cross-sectional data.

Notes

1. The same comparison holds for the square root of percent Black, the variable used in the regression analyses. The standard deviation for decade-to-decade changes is 0.3 while the standard deviation for level scores is 1.7. Thus, the cross-sectional variation is more than 5 times greater than the temporal variation.

2. Note that for percent Black the twice lagged level score and the once lagged change score are used instead of the once-lagged level score and the change score. This is because there is reason to expect negative feedback between change in percent Black and change in inequality, that is, percent Black declines as inequality increases (Stinner and DeJong 1969). Turning to the longer lags helps minimize the effect of this feedback. Future research should consider models which allow for reciprocal effects.

3. The mean for female labor force share does change substantially over time. However, changes within decades are more uniform than level scores within decades as the standard deviation for the change scores is less than one third that observed for the level scores.

4. This is more readily apparent when noting that this specification is mathematically identical to a specification where the level of inequality is regressed on the lagged level of inequality and changes in the other independent variables.

5. As note earlier, an alternative specification using the lagged change in female labor force share (and the twice lagged level) showed a significant positive effect suggesting that the specification used here is not optimal for assessing the effect of female labor force share.

6. For reasons outlined earlier, level and change scores for percent Black is measured one decade prior to similar measures for inequality. Thus, the "level" score for percent Black is one decade prior to the level score for inequality; the "lagged" level score for percent Black is one decade prior to

the lagged level score for inequality, and the "change" score for percent Black is measured one decade prior to the change score for inequality. In view of this, it would be more precise to label the measures of percent Black as twice-lagged level, lagged change, and lagged level. Here, however, we label the measures "lagged level", "change", and "level" because it simplifies exposition without altering any substantive implications of the analysis.

7. This point is made in some detail in Finkel (1995) and Kessler and Greenberg (1981). Our discussion summarizes many of the points they make in their lengthier statements.

8. Following standard notation, t denotes the current time period and t-1 denotes the prior period. In this study these would represent decades.

9. An extended discussion of the interpretation of these parameters and a comparison of this model to other models is presented in Kessler and Greenberg (1981: Chapter 2).

10. To complete the symmetry, coefficients from the change score specification yield coefficients from the level score specification as follows: $b_1 = (1 + b_4)$, $b_2 = (b_5-b_6)$, and $b_3 = b_6$.

11. For simplicity, the figure depicts only one independent variable.

12. As the distributional assumptions of the maximum likelihood method were not met, and since the analyses were exploratory in nature, we did not report significance levels for the effects reported in Table 6.5. In addition, significance levels were reported for the "level-score" specification estimated and not for the change-score specification reported.

13. Model B has one less degree of freedom than Model A but χ^2 decreases by 77.9. Thus, error χ^2 is reduced by about 15 percent when the effect of the lagged level of inequality is allowed to vary over time and χ^2 per degree of freedom is reduced from 2.90 to 2.48. By comparison, the next most promising candidate for relaxing a consistency constraint is the effect of relative minority size. However, relaxing equality constraints on this effect to allow for a pre- and post-1960 effect reduced χ^2 by only about 5 points.

14. The improvement in model fit when equality constraints were relaxed to permit a pre- and post-1960 effect was slight as χ^2 was reduced by only about 5 points.

15. We also investigated second and third order serial autocorrelations subject to the constraint that they were equal across waves. These effects were not statistically significant.

7

Overview and Discussion

Our study builds on the longstanding tradition of ecological research which documents substantial variation in racial occupational inequality across local areas and attempts to explain it in terms of the structural characteristics of the different areas. Our main contributions to this literature have been to extend previous cross-sectional methodologies by drawing on data which span several decades. This allowed us to evaluate the consistency of cross-sectional results across time and to directly investigate models of change in inequality over time. Additionally, we focused on nonmetropolitan counties of the South, a type of local community which has been somewhat neglected in previous research.

Building on previous empirical and theoretical work, we developed an ecological model of inequality and tested it using both cross-sectional and longitudinal specifications. The results indicated that the relative size of the minority population, female labor force share, white-collar employment (or alternatively demand for educated labor), and status diversity all have significant, positive effects on status inequality between White men and Black men as predicted by theory. However, contrary to traditional expectations, labor force size, labor force growth, employment rates, and urbanization either did not have consistent effects on inequality or had positive rather than expected negative effects on inequality.

These results were largely consistent across methodology (cross-sectional vs. longitudinal) suggesting that results from earlier studies using cross-sectional methods may be relatively robust. This might also suggest that the conditions necessary to apply causal interpretations of cross-sectional results — reversible, symmetric causal relationships with systems in equilibrium — approximately hold in this research context. One important result in this regard was the finding from the covariance structure analyses that serial autocorrelation was minimal. Nevertheless, the cross-sectional and longitudinal results did vary sufficiently that cross-sectional analyses should be viewed as tentative until confirmed with longitudinal data.

This should not be taken to imply that we view the results of our longitudinal analyses as definitive. As we noted earlier, longitudinal data are not a panacea and that, at least in this research context, results from longitudinal analyses were not unquestionably superior to results from cross-sectional analyses. In principle, longitudinal data are attractive and even when conditions justify the use of cross-sectional methods it is desirable to see consistency across cross-sectional and longitudinal results. In practice, however, the estimates of effects for many independent variables were less efficient in the longitudinal analyses because the temporal variance in the independent variables often was considerably smaller than their variation across areas at any given point in time. Consequently, the effect estimates from longitudinal analyses varied more from decade to decade and were generally less clear in pattern than those obtained from cross-sectional analyses. This methodological problem was serious enough that cross-sectional results might justifiably be given greater weight in situations where cross-sectional and longitudinal results conflict and the assumptions needed for drawing causal inferences from cross-sectional data are plausible.

One practical implication to be taken from this is that large samples are highly desirable when investigating longitudinal models of racial inequality. This is especially true when estimating the effects of independent variables that change slowly over time (e.g., percent Black, occupational structure, etc.). Our sample was much larger than the typical sample used in ecological studies of racial inequality but investigators contemplating future longitudinal should consider using even larger samples to obtain more efficient parameter estimates of the effects of changes in structural characteristics on inequality. Larger samples may be especially important if future studies are to move toward estimation of more complicated and subtle effects.

The use of longitudinal data did lead to one notable finding not reported in previous research — the changing relationship between percent Black and racial inequality over time. Blalock (1967) predicted a nonlinear relationship but it had not been consistently reported in the literature and it had never been examined over time. Our results from cross-sectional analyses show that the relationship changed from strong and positive in 1940, 1950, and 1960 to only weakly positive in 1970, 1980, and 1990. The results from the longitudinal analyses were consistent with this but did not strongly confirm the pattern (i.e., the chi-square test for changing effects of percent black over time was marginal).

We suggest the possibility that this pattern reflects a fundamental change in the effect of percent Black on inequality over time. The explanation we offer is that successes of the Civil and Voting Rights movements of the 1960s and 1970s may have increased chances for Black advantages in relative population size to be translated into political power. This in turn may have given Blacks access to middle and higher status level occupations tied to hiring and appointment decisions by elected officials, or possibly through other indirect influences. In other words, a Black political power base that previously did not exist in predominantly Black nonmetropolitan counties may have emerged in the 1960s and 1970s with important implications for status inequality. While this is an after the fact interpretation, we hope it will be explored more rigorously in subsequent research.

A related pattern revealed in the longitudinal analyses is the weakening in the persistence of inequality over time and the apparent systemic decline in inequality, both especially pronounced after 1960. The reduced persistence of inequality was seen in that regression toward the mean on inequality observed in the longitudinal analyses was much greater in 1970-1990 than in 1950-1960. The systemic decline in inequality was seen in that dummy variables for decade in the pooled cross-sectional analyses showed average inequality in 1970-1990 to be considerably lower than in 1940-1960.

Another finding that is new to the literature is the potential negative consequences for minority men resulting from the movement of women into the labor force. The cross-sectional results were quite consistent in showing large negative effects, but the longitudinal results failed to confirm this pattern. Causal interpretation of the strong cross-sectional results should not be ruled out (nor accepted) until theory is refined to the point that a more definitive interpretation of the discrepant findings can be offered.

The cross-sectional analyses indicated White-Black inequality among men increased with increasing female labor force share because female labor force share has a positive effect on the status of White men and a negative effect on the status of Black men. This suggests that women and Black men are in competition either directly or indirectly and that Black men apparently compete at a disadvantage with respect to occupational status. In contrast, White men benefit from the presence of all minority groups in the labor force and rise up to higher status position in the occupational hierarchy when either the female labor force share or the Black male labor force share increases. Given the dramatic increase in the female labor force participation rate over the last fifty years (Abel-Kemp 1994; Waite 1981), future research should examine this relationship in more detail to clarify its possible causal impacts on race inequality.

Also new to the literature, we found that white-collar employment and status diversity had strong positive effects on racial inequality. These effects were confirmed in both cross-sectional and longitudinal analyses and were very robust. The effect of status diversity represents a relatively "pure" structural effect; the extent of status diversity sets a structural "ceiling" on the potential for racial inequality. The effect of white-collar employment needs to be clarified in future research. Three major interpretations are plausible at this time. One is that it is a surrogate for increasing demand for formally educated labor which renders minority men less competitive in the labor market. Another is that it represents a shift toward jobs emphasizing face-to-face interaction with co-workers and customers where minority status is particularly problematic. Yet a third is that it indicates a shift toward occupations where women are particularly strong competitors to minority men and may be preferred by employers over minority men.

Another important set of findings from our analyses were that we find no support for arguments that labor force growth and full employment leads to reductions in racial inequality; at least not in any simple, straightforward way. Neither cross-sectional nor longitudinal results gave any evidence that fast growing, full employment economies were characterized by lower inequality. If anything, inequality tended to be greater in these areas. We interpret this as support for Heistand (1964) who argues that economic growth does not reduce relative inequality because Whites are as likely to benefit from growth as Blacks. Alternatively, it might be that the conventional presumption of the effect of economic growth is too simplistic. Perhaps economic growth and full employment facilitate reductions in inequality in some circumstances (as yet not sufficiently well-specified by theory or identified in empirical research), but have no effect in other circumstances. The failure of the data to confirm the effect of economic growth strongly indicates that the theory underlying this relationship must be refined and better specified or it should be abandoned.

We also find little support for the universalism thesis which predicts market scale (indexed by labor force size) and urbanization will have negative effects on racial inequality. To the contrary, we found size had a positive effect on inequality (and we observed a similar positive effect for urbanization in unreported analyses where it was used in place of size). As with the effects of economic growth and full employment, we interpret this finding as indicating that extant theory is too simplistic. For example, size and urbanization are associated with white-collar employment, status diversity, and greater female labor force participation, all of which appear to promote inequality. Thus, the "reduced form" effects of size and urbanization should be seen as ambiguous. Even when these factors are controlled, our analyses showed size and urbanization to be compatible with inequality in the short-run.

Perhaps the hypothesized effects of size and urbanization are realized only in the very long run and the short run effects should be discounted. Unfortunately, very long-run influences of size and urbanization cannot be tested with our data. Thus, while it is possible to keep the universalism thesis alive by arguing that the short- and long-term effects of urbanization are different, this is yet to be demonstrated with empirical research.

In sum, the analysis of longitudinal data for nonmetropolitan counties strongly confirms the ecological thesis that structural characteristics of communities play an important role in determining the level and changes in racial inequality. The results from this initial foray into models of change in inequality are important because they solidify many extant hypotheses, support several newly developed hypotheses, and call some widely accepted hypotheses into question. They are also important because they point to the potential value of further research using longitudinal designs since many of our findings could not have been obtained with cross-sectional data for a single decade. No doubt additional findings will be generated by future studies building on this study. Indeed, at this point we have only scratched the surface in testing models of change in racial inequality and even further refinement in theory and techniques of analysis will be required before the possibilities are fully exploited. We look forward to future developments in this area and the contributions it will bring and hope to participate in the process.

Long Time Coming

In closing, what can we say about the future of inequality in southern nonmetropolitan areas? If the past is any guide to the future, equality between Whites and Blacks will not be soon upon us. Even if we optimistically extrapolated from recent trends of declining inequality in the 1970s and 1980s and projected similar reductions into the future, it would be many decades before approximate equality between Whites and Blacks would occur. At a minimum, then, the time table for forecasting the demise of racial stratification in the nonmetropolitan South should be calibrated in generations, not decades; certainly not in years.

Unfortunately, there is no realistic basis for assuming that even the modest declines in racial inequality between White and Black men observed in recent decades will be repeated in the immediate future. As we documented in our analysis in Chapter 5, shifts in occupational mix toward white-collar jobs with higher educational requirements and movement of women into the labor force have been associated with increasing inequality between White and Black men. These structural trends are likely to continue and may work against future reductions in inequality. In addition, the steady declines in the relative size of the Black population in nonmetropolitan areas of the South, declines which promoted reductions inequality between White and Black men for several decades, have apparently stalled and thus this possible source of change in inequality is not likely to be an important factor in the near future.

In short, changes in the structural characteristics of southern, rural areas are not likely to promote significant reductions in racial inequality in the future. To the contrary, based on the analysis we presented in Table 5.5, changes in structural characteristics of southern, nonmetropolitan counties have tended on balance to promote increases in inequality in recent decades and more of the same can be anticipated for the future.

Our analysis in Chapter 5 also indicated that declines in inequality were seen in recent decades only because negative "decade effects" were large enough to overcome increases in inequality that were promoted by changes in community structure. Can we anticipate a continuation of these negative "decade effects"? While our data do not provide a firm basis for establishing the causal factors which account for these effects, their timing and pattern suggest that they are at least partly linked to social and political changes that were initiated during the 1960s, expanded and consolidated during the 1970s, and maintained during the 1980s. We have in mind here changes in law and policy governing civil and voting rights and implementation of programs aimed at curbing discrimination in employment, education, and other venues of socioeconomic competition and attainment and redressing the effects of past discrimination. If we are correct in this assessment, we do not see a basis for forecasting a continuation of large negative decade effects in the future. The reductions we estimated were larger in decades proximate to these social changes and somewhat smaller in the 1980s.

From any vantage point, the 1990s have been a decade in which law and policy promoting reductions in racial inequality have not only *not* been expanded, but have instead often been scaled back or dismantled. Equal opportunity enforcement activity fell to very low levels in the late 1980s in response to evolving legal opinions as well as changes in political climate and administrations and it is not likely to return again to the levels observed in the mid-1970s (Rose 1994). Affirmative action programs have similarly been under attack and are in retrenchment if not full retreat. While the consequences of these equality-promoting policies remain a subject of debate, the trends we have just noted can hardly be viewed in any way as strengthening efforts to promote equality of opportunity and outcome in socioeconomic attainments. Furthermore, no new programs or policy initiatives which have similar goals of fostering large-scale, systematic reductions in inequality are likely to be offered in the near future.

This suggests that sociologists and other social scientists should redouble efforts to identify the various factors that affect movements toward or away from racial integration and equality. If such knowledge can be established and refined, policy makers may have additional options at their disposal for addressing the problem of racial inequality. If viable policy options are not identified, we raise the concern that strides toward equality which were observed in the 1960s and 1970s, but which have been shortening decade-by-decade since, may falter altogether and race relations in the United States may backslide into a protracted cycle of repolarization and heightened potential for renewed political conflict. It is regrettable that we end on such a pessimistic note, but racial equality has been a long time coming to the rural South and any realistic appraisal of the near future must acknowledge that fact and its implications.

APPENDIX A

Measuring Inequality

The notion of inequality is one of the most important concepts in the social sciences but few methodological studies have advanced a general conceptual framework for measuring inequality between groups.[1] As a result, researchers have little to guide them and often select measures of *inter*group inequality based on convenience and custom rather than knowledge of the conceptual properties of available measures. This is unfortunate because different measures embody different conceptualizations of inequality (usually left implicit rather than made explicit) and do not necessarily correlate strongly with each other. Indeed, studies by Fossett, Galle, and Kelly (1986) and Stafford and Fossett (1989; 1992) have reported that the results of some analyses varied significantly depending on which measure of occupational inequality was used.

We believe investigators should use measures which have been shown to faithfully register the aspects of inequality that are central to their research concerns. In view of this, we adopt both a narrow goal and a broad goal in this chapter. Our narrow goal is to make the methodological case for the measures of inequality we use in this monograph. Our broader goal is to provide a review of general issues regarding the measurement of intergroup inequality with the hope that it will help other investigators make more informed choices about the measures they adopt.

Measurement Theory

An accepted framework for evaluating and choosing among different measures of intergroup occupational inequality has yet to be established. In this respect, the literature on *inter*group inequality is less well developed than the literature on *intra*group income inequal-

195

ity where many highly regarded studies have compared the strengths and weaknesses of different measures (e.g., Allison 1978; Atkinson 1970; Blau 1977; Dalton 1920; Schwartz and Winship 1979; Kolm 1976a; 1976b). The literature examining measures of intragroup income inequality is notable for its cumulative nature; criteria for measures have been suggested, debated, and refined, and the merits of choosing one measure over another have been explored in considerable depth and detail.

We seek to establish a similar line of inquiry focusing on the measurement of intergroup occupational inequality.[2] We work toward that goal in this section by first identifying the different aspects of inequality that a summary measure can register. We then introduce five formal guidelines which measures must conform to if they are to reflect these aspects of inequality. These guidelines establish minimum criteria for acceptable measures of inequality and thus provide a basis for discussing the advantages and disadvantages of different measures. Finally we close this section by noting two practical concerns which may also be considered when selecting a measure of inequality.

Aspects of Inequality

An index score summarizing inequality between two group distributions on a comparison variable can register several different things. The most fundamental things it can indicate are the *existence* and *direction* of inequality. If it indicates existence, it will convey whether or not the differences observed between the two distributions reflect an advantage for one group over the other. If it indicates direction, it will additionally convey *which* of the two groups has the advantage.

Next, depending on whether the comparison variable has ordinal, interval, or ratio properties, a measure can indicate the *extent*, *absolute magnitude*, or *relative magnitude* of group advantage. The *extent* of inequality may be examined when the comparison variable has ordinal-level properties. It refers to how consistently (i.e., with what relative frequency) members of one group are advantaged or disadvantaged in their comparisons with members of another group. If the comparison variable has interval-level properties, the *absolute magnitude* of inequality may be examined; it pertains to how "big" advantages are when members of two groups are compared. The *relative magnitude* of inequality may be examined when the comparison variable has ratio-level properties. It pertains to how "big" advantages are in proportional (i.e., percentage) terms when members of two groups are being compared. We now offer guidelines which help insure that measures register the aspects of inequality we have just identified. Our guidelines focus on requirements for measures summarizing group comparisons on variables with ordinal- and interval-level properties. Thus, they insure that measures register information regarding the existence, direction, extent, and absolute magnitude of inequality. They do not require measures to register information regarding the relative magnitude of inequality. The reason for this is that we are not aware of any accepted scaling of occupation that has ratio-level properties. Thus, we do not give attention to questions concerning the proportional magnitude of group differences on a ratio-level variable.[3]

Guidelines for Measures of Occupational Inequality

The Principle of Existence. The notion of inequality implies that differences between two group distributions on an ordered variable involve a pattern of systematic advantage favoring one or the other of the two groups. It is crucial, then, that measures register only systematic patterns of advantage. Stated another way, measures must be capable of registering the absence of inequality under circumstances where group distributions are *different* but where the differences do not constitute a pattern of systematic advantage for either group. Indices which fail to satisfy this requirement conflate *differentiation* with *inequality* and should not be accepted as measures of inequality.

The Principle of Directionality. The notion of inequality implies that one group is systematically advantaged relative to another group. Therefore, it is crucial that measures of inequality exhibit directionality. That is, measures should possess a score which indicates equality between the two groups, a range of scores which reflect advantage to one group, and a range of scores which reflect advantage to the other group. Measures that do not satisfy this requirement are fundamentally flawed since they cannot indicate which group, if either, enjoys an advantage over the other.

These first two principles identify characteristics that measures of inequality should have, but they do not specifically identify how measures should respond to particular comparisons of distributions or how they should respond to changes in group distributions. The next three principles address these issues.

The Principle of Distribution Dominance. If one group's ascending cumulative percentage distribution on a variable is nowhere above and is somewhere below the comparable distribution for another group, measures must show an advantage to the first group.[4] Additionally, if two groups have identical cumulative percentage distributions, measures must register zero inequality.

This principle is weak in two respects. First, while it specifies that inequality exists and what its direction is when one cumulative percentage distribution completely "dominates" another, it does not specify the *extent or magnitude* of inequality to be registered. Thus, different measures may conform to this principle yet yield different outcomes regarding the extent or magnitude of inequality between the groups.

Second, the principle is weak because it does not specify that inequality exists (and, if so, which group is favored) when cumulative percentage distributions cross. For example, while the principles specifies that inequality favors group A over groups B and C in Figure A.1, it is silent on the question of whether inequality exists between Groups B and C and, if it does exist, which group should be favored. Measures which conform to the principle of distribution dominance can differ with regard to the extent, magnitude, and even direction of inequality they register between groups B and C. The outcome such measures will register will depend on the specific assumptions embodied in their particular rules of computation.

Given the relatively weak requirements imposed by this principle, a measure which does not conform to it should be seen as flawed.

The Principle of Transitivity. Measures should generate scores that are transitive across pairwise comparisons among three or more groups. This guideline may be posed in weak and strong versions.

The strong version requires that, given three groups, A, B, and C, a measure that indicates Group A to have an advantage over Group B and Group B to have an advantage over Group C should also indicate Group A to have an advantage over Group C. Furthermore, the measure should indicate that Group A's advantage over Group C is greater than both Group A's advantage over Group B and Group B's advantage over Group C.

The weak version of this principle requires that, given three groups, A, B, and C, a measure that indicates Group A to have an advantage over Group B and Group B to have an advantage over Group C should never indicate Group C to have an advantage over Group A. Furthermore, the measure also should never indicate that Group A's comparison with Group C is worse than either Group A's comparison with Group B or Group B's comparison Group C.

Both the strong and weak versions of this principle imply that a measure which indicates equality between two groups should also

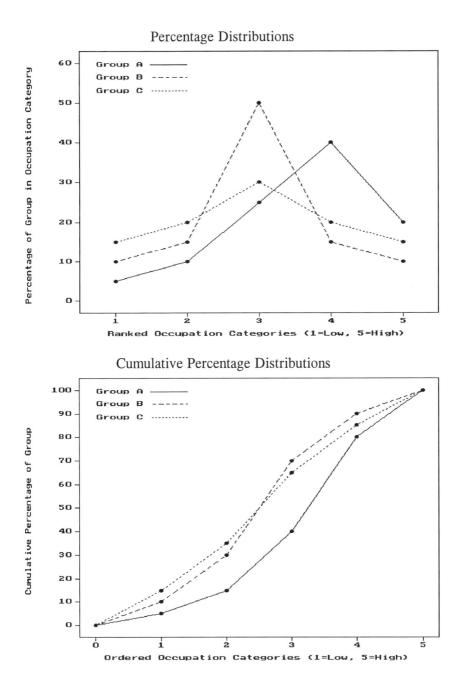

FIGURE A.1 Percentage and Cumulative Percentage Distributions for Three Hypothetical Groups Across Ordered Occupation Categories.

indicate identical outcomes for both groups when they are compared with any third group. Measures that fail to satisfy these requirements will not yield an unambiguous ordering of pairwise inequality comparisons among three or more groups.

The Principle of Altered Ranks. This principle consists of two stipulations regarding how measures of inequality on *ordinal* variables should respond to a change in status for any member of one group if it alters that individual's *rank-order position* relative to one or more members of a second group. First, measures should respond by indicating either greater advantage (or lesser disadvantage) if the change in the ordinal comparison was favorable to the individual or greater disadvantage (or lesser advantage) if it was unfavorable. Second, the greater the number of comparisons affected, the more dramatic should be the measure's response. When both groups are represented by at least one member at all ranks, these stipulations imply that changes in inequality will be more dramatic as the number of ranks "crossed" increases since any multiple-rank move can be divided into multiple single-rank moves which individually must all produce changes in inequality.

Measures that do not satisfy these requirements are insensitive to changes in ordinal inequality that result when members in one group improve their rank position relative to members of another group. Specifically, such measures fail to register changes in the *extent* of inequality, the relative frequency with which members of one group are advantaged over members of another group.

The Principle of Altered Differences. This principle consists of two stipulations regarding how measures of inequality on *interval-*level variables should respond to a change in status for any member of one group that alters the *differences* observed when that individual is compared with members of a second group. First, measures should respond by indicating either greater advantage (or lesser disadvantage) if the change in the difference was favorable to the individual or greater disadvantage (or lesser advantage) if it was unfavorable. Second, the greater the change in the difference, the more dramatic should be the measure's response.[5]

Measures that do not satisfy these requirements are insensitive to changes in *interval-*level inequality that occur when members in one group reduce the size of their status disadvantage (increase the size of their advantage) in comparisons with members of another group. Such measures fail to register changes in the *absolute magnitude* of inequality.

The five principles just introduced define a partial measurement theory for intergroup inequality on ordinal and interval variables.

The measurement theory is incomplete in that different measures satisfying these principles may not necessarily order inequality comparisons in exactly the same manner. This is because the guidelines offered do not specify how measures should behave when cumulative percentage distributions for two groups cross. This imprecision reflects ambiguities in the concept of intergroup inequality in the social sciences. *The adoption of any particular measure which satisfies the guidelines we have suggested will thus imply endorsement of additional specific assumptions about how measures should behave when cumulative percentage distributions cross.* Researchers should be aware of this fact and consider the implications for their substantive research interests.

Additional Practical Concerns

Choosing a measure of inequality involves practical as well as conceptual considerations. We note two practical issues that will be relevant to the choice of an inequality measure in most situations.

Symmetrical Distribution Around Zero. It is desirable that measures have a theoretical range that is symmetrically distributed around the point of equality. It is also desirable for the point of equality for measures to be zero. Given these two characteristics, the sign of a measure will indicate which group is advantaged and which is disadvantaged and different situations of group advantage and disadvantage can be readily compared.[6] The theoretical distribution of a measure is symmetrical when its value simply changes sign when the two groups being compared exchange distributions.

This practical requirement has no implications for how measures will order a series of inequality comparisons and thus is does not speak to the conceptualization of inequality. However, measures whose theoretical range is symmetrically distributed around zero are more easily interpreted.

Amenability to Hypothesis Testing. It is desirable that measures have known sampling distributions which will permit the calculation of confidence intervals around "point estimates" of inequality. This also will permit formal hypothesis tests to establish the statistical significance of measured inequality. The importance of this characteristic is obvious when measures are computed using sample data since it is desirable to have a basis for assessing whether measured advantage is "real" or simply an inconsequential "accident" of sampling. This characteristic also is important when measures are computed using population data. The reason for this is that micro-level processes generating status outcomes usually involve random components and are unlikely to produce *exactly* identical status distributions for different groups even when the underlying social process does not intrinsically favor one group over the other. Thus, it is reasonable to ask whether inequality observed at the population level could have occurred by chance when compared against a null model of no group advantage.

Selected Measures of Ordinal Inequality

In this section we examine selected indices which have previously been used to measure inequality between group distributions on ordinal variables. Our goal is to determine whether they conform to, or fail to conform to, the guidelines offered above. And thus, their adequacy (or inadequacy as the case may be) to serve as measures of intergroup inequality.

Index of Dissimilarity. The index of dissimilarity (D) is widely used to measure intergroup inequality. This is interesting in light of the fact that the measure was first popularized in sociology as an index of residential segregation (Duncan and Duncan 1955).[7] The computing formula when it is applied as measure of inequality is given by:

$$D = 100 \cdot \Sigma \mid w_i - b_i \mid / 2$$

where i denotes the i'th category of a distribution, and w_i and b_i denote the proportions of Whites and Blacks, respectively, in the category.

The value of the measure indicates the minimum percentage of one group (either one) that must change categories to make its relative frequency distributions identical to that for the other group. This convenient interpretation and the simplicity of D's computing formula account for much of the measure's popularity. Unfortunately, while the index of dissimilarity has been widely used to measure inequality (e.g., Abrahamson and Sigelman 1987; Hare 1965; Siegel 1965; Bahr and Gibbs 1967; Gibbs 1965; Jiobu and Marshall 1971; Roof 1972; Johnson and Sell 1976; Beck 1980; Elgie 1980; LaGory and Magnani 1979), and has been promoted for this purpose (Fox and Faine 1973; Palmore and Whittington 1970; US Bureau of the Census 1970), it is not an attractive measure.[8] Indeed, it fails to satisfy even one of the five guidelines for measures of inequality introduced above.

The major problem with D is that it registers all differences between group distributions and does not distinguish in any way between differences that confer systematic group advantage and differences that are random with respect to rank position. This can be seen in the fact that D can take a value of 0 only when group distributions are *exactly* identical. This violates the principle of existence which allows for the possibility that group distributions may be equal even when they are not identical.

D also violates the principle of directionality since it does not register the direction of group advantage. Since the principles of distribution dominance, transitivity, and altered ranks all incorporate the notion of directionality, it follows that D also violates these principles. These are basic and profound limitations that invalidate D as a measure of inequality.

Regarding practical concerns, D is not symmetrically distributed around the point of equality and is thus wanting in that respect. However, conclusions regarding confidence intervals and tests of statistical significance for the measure are mixed. The statistical significance of distributional differences summarized by D can be established by performing a chi-square test of the difference between group distributions. But confidence intervals for point estimates of inequality cannot be easily computed because formulas for the standard error of D are not available.[9]

Recent studies have shown that D's logical problems can have significant practical consequences because the measure sometimes suggests patterns of inequality that are quite different from those suggested by alternative measures with more attractive properties (Fossett, Galle, and Kelly 1986; Stafford and Fossett 1989). Figure A.2 illustrates how this can occur. It presents occupational comparisons between White men and Black men and between White men and White women based on data for southern, nonmetropolitan counties in 1970.[10] The first panel of the figure shows the differences between the percentages of White men and Black men in rank-ordered occupation categories. In this panel, negative differences (greater Black representation) are observed for lower-ranked categories and positive differences (greater White representation) are observed for higher ranked categories.[11] The value of D for this comparison is 37.7.

The second panel of the figure shows the differences between the percentages of White men and White women in rank-ordered occupation categories. Here the differences observed are only weakly correlated with status. Positive differences (greater male representation) are sometimes observed when status is high, but positive differences also are observed when status is low. Nevertheless, the value of D for this comparison is 47.2 and thus suggests that inequality between White men and White women is greater than inequality between White men and Black men.

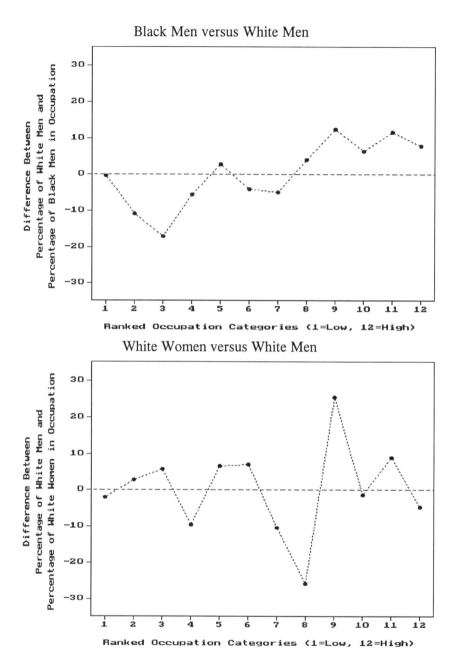

FIGURE A.2 Differences Between Percentages of White Men, Black Men, and White Women by Ranked Occupation Categories.

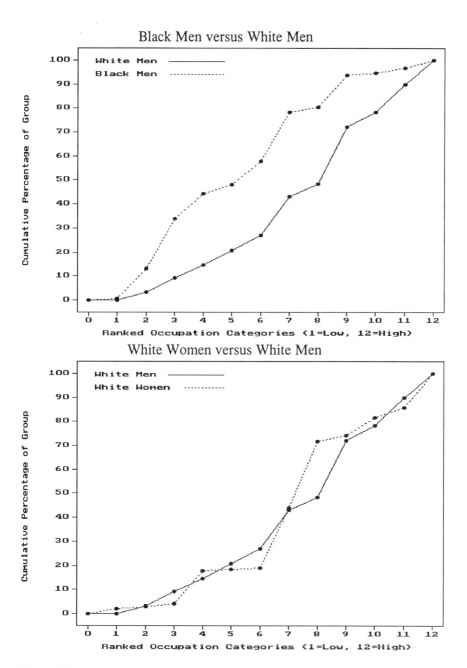

FIGURE A.3 Comparing Cumulative Occupation Distributions for Black Men and White Women to the Cumulative Occupation Distribution for White Men.

Figure A.3 shows that this conclusion is quite misleading. The first panel presents the ascending cumulative percentage distributions for White men and Black men. At no point is the distribution for White men above the distribution for Black men, and throughout most of the distribution the cumulative distribution for White men is far below that for Black men indicating that White men have a considerable advantage over Black men. According to the principle of distribution dominance, then, this is a clear case of inequality favoring White men.

The second panel presents the ascending cumulative percentage distributions for White men and White women. The two distributions cross at least five times, indicating that at some points White men have an advantage over White women while at other points the reverse is true. Thus, while D indicates a high level of inequality, the graphical analysis is much more ambiguous. Indeed, the principle of distribution dominance gives no clear guidance as to which group is favored, since the cumulative percentage distributions for White men and White women cross.

The serious flaws with D are not surprising since it has been widely used to measure segregation — group differences in distribution across nominal categories. Its wide use as a measure of inequality would appear to be explained primarily by its ease of computation and interpretation. At one time, the absence of attractive alternative measures of ordinal inequality based on comparisons of full group distributions was also a consideration. This last justification is no longer defensible, however, as several more attractive alternative measures are now available.

Index of Net Difference. The index of net difference (ND) is a measure of ordinal inequality introduced by Lieberson (1975) which has seen increasing use in recent years (e.g., Riedesel 1979; Villemez 1978; Villemez and Wiswell 1978; Fossett, Galle, and Kelly 1986; Fossett, Galle, and Burr 1989; Burr, Fossett, and Galle 1990). An efficient computing formula adapted from Lieberson (1975) is given by:

$$ND = 100 \cdot \Sigma \, w_{i+1}B_i - \Sigma \, b_{i+1}W_i$$

where i denotes the i'th category in a ranked distribution, , and w_{i+1} and b_{i+1} are the proportions of Whites and Blacks, respectively, in category i+1, and W_i and B_i are the cumulative proportions of Whites and Blacks, respectively, in categories of *below* rank i+1.

A less practical but informative computing formula is given by Fossett and South (1983):

$$ND = \Sigma \Sigma (X_{ij}w_ib_j)$$

where i, w_i, and b_i are as given before, and X equals +1 if i > j, 0 if i = j, and -1 if i < j. This second formula reveals ND to be the average of an index of ordinal advantage, X, assigned to all pairwise comparisons between Blacks and Whites. It takes a value of +1.0 when Whites in the comparison are of higher status than Blacks, a value of 0.0 when they are of equal status, and -1.0 when Whites are of lower status than Blacks. In light of this, ND can be interpreted as the difference between (a) the proportion of pairwise comparisons between Blacks and Whites where Whites are of higher rank, and (b) the proportion of comparisons where Blacks are of higher rank.

ND requires only ordinal level measurement for the comparison variable. It also can be applied when the comparison variable is measured on either an interval or a ratio scale, but it will draw on only the rank-order information in the scales and thus will register the extensiveness of inequality but not the absolute or relative magnitude of the inequality. For example, the maximum positive score of 100 will obtain when all members of Group A are in higher-status white collar occupations (e.g., professionals and managers) and all members of Group B are in unskilled manual occupations (e.g., laborers and service workers). But this maximum score would not be changed if *all* members of Group B are promoted to skilled manual occupations (i.e., crafts workers). The reason for this is that ND registers only the ordinality of differences between members of Groups A and B and is insensitive to the fact that the difference between a manager and a laborer might be considered greater than the difference between a manager and an electrician.

The index of net difference satisfies all of the guidelines introduced above with two qualifications. The first is that, as we have just seen, ND is a measure of ordinal inequality only and thus satisfies the principle of altered ranks but not the principle of altered differences. This limitation is a potential concern only if the comparison variable is measured on an interval or ratio scale *and* the investigator is interested in measuring not only the extensiveness but also the absolute or relative magnitude of inequality.

The second qualification is that the index of net difference satisfies only the weak version of the principle of transitivity. (This is the case for all measures of ordinal inequality.) It does not satisfy the strong version of this principle because there are certain conditions under which Group A can have an advantage over Group B and B can have an advantage over Group C, yet A's advantage over C will not be larger than *either* A's advantage over B or B's advantage over C (to meet the strong version of the principle it should be larger than both of them).

This is possible is when *all* members of A rank above *all* members of B and *all* members of B rank above *all* members of C. In this situation, $ND_{AC} = ND_{AB} = ND_{BC} = 1.0$. Obviously, this is a an unusual circumstance and its practical relevance may be limited. It is very rare to have no overlap at all in three empirical distributions and, if there is even one tie among the comparisons between members of A and B or among the comparisons of members of B and C, then ND will conform to the strong version of the principle of transitivity.

On the whole, then, ND grades out well against our guidelines (with the qualification that it measures ordinal inequality only) and as a bonus has an appealing substantive interpretation.

The sampling distribution for ND has not previously been presented, but Lieberson notes it has a close relationship with the Mann-Whitney U statistic and recommends the use of this test to establish the statistical significance of the difference in ranks between two samples. Below we show that ND is equivalent to Somers' d_{yx} and that standard errors for this statistic can be used to establish confidence intervals for ND as well as providing a basis for testing its statistical significance.

In sum, ND is an attractive measure of intergroup inequality on ordinal variables. Its advantage over D can be readily seen by considering the results it yields for the occupation comparisons presented in Figures A.2 and A.3 above. The value of ND for the occupation comparison between White men and Black men is 45.1 and indicates considerable advantage for White men. For the occupation comparison between White men and White women, its value is 5.1 and indicates a modest advantage favoring White men. These results are consistent with the graphical analysis in Figure A.3.

Differences in Mean Percentile Scores. It is often useful to describe location in an ordered distribution in terms of percentile scores. These indicate the fraction of the population ranking above or below the case in question (e.g., an individual scoring at the 90th percentile on education ranks above 90 percent of the population and below 10 percent of the population). When distributions for two groups are combined, the percentile scores for the joint distribution will by definition range between 0 and 100 and have a mean of 50. The group difference in mean percentile scores (DMPS) for this combined distribution can be used to measure intergroup inequality. Its value can be obtained using the following computing formula:

$$DMPS = \Sigma \, w_i PS_i - \Sigma \, b_i PS_i,$$

where i, w_i, and b_i are as described above and PS_i is the percentile score for category i obtained for the *combined* distribution of Whites and Blacks.[12]

The maximum difference in mean percentile scores between groups will result when all members of one group rank higher than all members of the other group. In this case, the mean percentile score for the lower group will be one half their population percentage and the mean percentile score for the higher group will be 100 minus one half their population percentage. The theoretical range for the difference between the mean percentile scores for the two groups will thus be -50 to 50.[13]

The measure just described meets all of our guidelines and is closely related to ND. In fact it is equal to one half the value of ND.[14] The proof is straightforward and need not be presented as it follows directly from the fact that the probabilities of members of one group ranking above or below members of another group are an exact function of their percentile locations in the combined distribution. This finding provides another interpretation of ND — it is the difference in mean percentile scores between groups rescaled to a logical range of -100 to 100. It also provides an alternative computing approach. More importantly, standard errors for confidence intervals and tests of statistical significance for the mean difference in percentile scores, and hence ND, can be computed using time honored formulas for differences of means.

A further comment on the difference of means in percentile scores is that, while it may appear on first glance to be an interval level measure of inequality, it is not quite that. The process of assigning percentile scores amounts to scaling occupation on a continuum from 0 to 100 and gives the appearance of interval-level information. However, since the scores are determined by rank-order location in the combined distribution of both groups they do not have true interval-level properties. This can be seen in several ways. One is that it is not possible to improve an individual's percentile score relative to members of another group without also changing the percentile score for at least one individual in the other group (since at least two individual's must change ranks). In contrast, it would be possible to improve an individual's score on a true interval-level variable such as education measured in years of schooling completed without affecting any other individual's score.

Another way the less-than-interval-level properties of percentile scores can be seen is that the difference of mean percentiles scores conforms to the weak version of the principle of transitivity, but not the strong version. Like the index of net difference (which it is equivalent to), it cannot distinguish between inequality comparisons among three distributions that do not overlap. A true interval-level inequality measure can.

Gini Index. The Gini index (G) is most commonly known for its application to the measurement of *intra*group income inequality. In that application, the Gini summarizes the comparison of cumulative income shares to cumulative population shares for members of a single population ranked on income. The plot of income shares against population shares defines the familiar Lorenz curve and the value of the Gini reflects the ratio of the area between the diagonal line of complete equality, which obtains when all persons have identical incomes, and the Lorenz curve. Its application to *inter*group inequality is somewhat different and involves the comparison of cumulative population shares for one group to cumulative population shares for another group when both are ordered on values of an ordinal variable. The computing formula given here is adapted from Shryock and Siegel (1976:98):

$$G = \Sigma \, B_i W_{i+1} - \Sigma \, B_{i+1} W_i$$

where i, B_i, and W_i are as given above.

In this application, the Gini index is equivalent to the index of net difference. We can demonstrate this by performing some simple manipulations of the formula as follows:

$$
\begin{aligned}
G &= \Sigma \, B_i W_{i+1} - \Sigma \, B_{i+1} W_i \\
&= \Sigma \, (w_{i+1} + W_i)B_i - \Sigma \, (b_{i+1} + B_i)W_i \\
&= \Sigma \, (w_{i+1}B_i + W_iB_i) - \Sigma \, (b_{i+1}W_i + B_iW_i) \\
&= (\Sigma w_{i+1}B_i + \Sigma \, W_iB_i) - (\Sigma b_{i+1}W_i + \Sigma \, B_iW_i) \\
&= \Sigma \, w_{i+1}B_i - \Sigma b_{i+1}W_i + (\Sigma W_iB_i) - \Sigma \, B_iW_i) \\
ND &= \Sigma \, w_{i+1}B_i - \Sigma b_{i+1}W_i,
\end{aligned}
$$

where w_i, b_i, W_i, and B_i are as given above. The equivalence of G and ND was first noted by Neidert (1980), but the demonstration given here is more general.[15] Based on this equivalence, the Gini's properties as a measure of intergroup inequality are identical to those noted for the index of net difference and thus need not be discussed at length. It is an attractive measure, all the more so because it is an established and familiar one.

A final point regarding G is that a graphical interpretation can be developed that helps clarify the particular way it and ND resolve inequality comparisons when cumulative percentage distributions for groups cross. Figure A.4 presents data previously examined in Figure A.3. Here, however, the data are presented using a graphical device we term an *inequality curve*. In the inequality curve, the X axis gives percentile locations in the ascending cumulative occupation distribution of the reference group and the Y axis gives the percentage of members in the comparison group that have similarly accumulated. The resulting curve thus indicates the percentage of members in the comparison group that are of equal or lower status than members of the reference group at any point in the percentile status distribution for the reference group.

A second curve is also plotted. This is the curve that results when the ascending cumulative percentage of the reference group is plotted against itself. This forms an ascending diagonal line with a slope of 1.0. This line indicates the percentage of the reference group that is of equal or lower status than members of the reference group at different points in the percentile status distribution for the reference group. This diagonal line represents more than just equality between groups; it represents *exact equivalence*. When the cumulative distribution for the reference group on the X axis dominates that of the comparison group on the Y axis (as in the first panel of Figure A.4), the inequality curve will be nowhere below and somewhere above the diagonal and thus indicates that differences between the distributions favor the reference group (i.e., the group on the X axis).[16] When the cumulative distribution for the comparison group dominates that of the reference group, the inequality curve will be nowhere above and somewhere below the diagonal and thus indicates that differences between the distributions favor the comparison group (i.e., the group on the Y axis).

The area above the diagonal indicates the maximum possible advantage favoring the reference group on the X axis. The ratio of the area between the inequality curve and the diagonal to the total area above the diagonal indicates the proportion of the maximum possible inequality favoring the reference group that is realized. The area below the diagonal indicates the maximum possible advantage favoring the comparison group on the Y axis. The ratio of the area between the inequality curve and the diagonal to the total area below the diagonal indicates the proportion of the maximum possible inequality favoring the comparison group that is realized. The value of G and ND are given by the difference between these two components. That is, G and ND can be obtained by subtracting the second component — that is, the ratio of the area between the diagonal and the

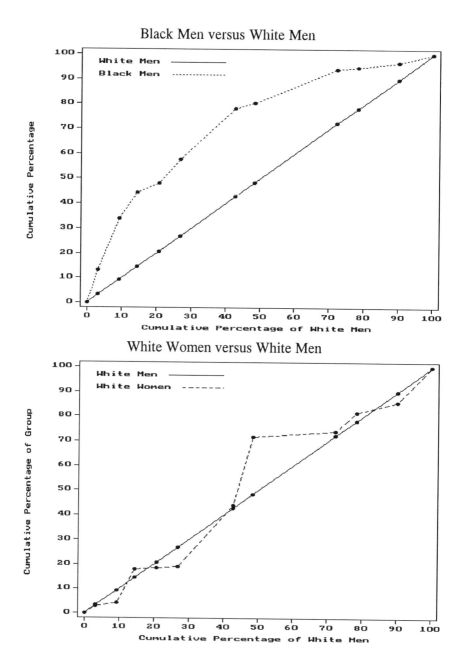

FIGURE A.4 Inequality Curves Comparing the Cumulative Distributions for Black Men and White Women to the Cumulative Distribution for White Men.

inequality curve that is *below* the diagonal to the total area below the diagonal — from the first component — that is, the ratio of the area between the diagonal and the inequality curve that is *above* the diagonal to the total area above the diagonal.

If the cumulative distribution for the reference group dominates that for the comparison group, the inequality curve will be above the diagonal and will not cross it and the resulting value of G which will be positive (indicating the reference group is advantaged). If the cumulative distribution for the reference group is dominated by that for the comparison group, the inequality curve fall below the diagonal but will not cross it and the resulting value of G will be negative (indicating the reference group is disadvantaged).

When the cumulative distributions for the groups cross, the inequality curve will cross the diagonal line of exact equivalence. An example of this is shown in the second panel of Figure A.4. In this situation, G and ND may be either positive, negative, or zero, depending on the sizes of the two components; that is, depending on whether differences favoring the reference group are smaller, larger, or no different from differences favoring the comparison group.

This graphical analysis of G and ND reveals the important characteristic that most values of these measures can be produced by inequality curves with different shapes. Thus, for example, the value of 0 can be produced by an infinite variety of inequality curves so long as the areas between the diagonal and the inequality curve are equal in size above and below the diagonal. The diagonal line representing exact equivalence is only one of these possible curves. *Thus, equality may result even when distributions are highly dissimilar.*[17]

Additionally, this graphical analysis reveals that G and ND weight advantages at different points in the cumulative distributions the same whether they occur at lower ranks, middle ranks, or higher ranks of the group on the X axis. This characteristic is consistent with the principles of measurement outlined above, but it is not required by them. A measure might instead be constructed so it will give greater weight to differences between distributions that occur at higher (or lower) ranks if this fits the conceptualization of inequality advanced by the investigator.[18]

Differences in Cumulative Percentages. Differences between groups at selected points in their cumulative distribution on an ordinal or interval variable have often been used to measure inequality. For example, many studies measure racial occupational inequality by the difference between the White and Black percentages above selected locations in a ranked occupation distribution such as the White-Black difference in percent employed in white-collar jobs

(Brown and Fuguitt 1972; Frisbie and Neidert 1977; Wilcox and Roof 1978). These measures conform to the principles of existence, directionality, transitivity, and symmetry, and have the advantages of being simple in construction and interpretation. Additionally, significance tests and standard errors can be computed using standard formulas for differences of proportions.

Interestingly, it can be easily shown that the difference in cumulative percentages and the index of net difference are equivalent when the ordinal variable in the comparison is a dichotomy. Thus, it might be argued that the difference in cumulative percentages satisfies *all* of the suggested guidelines for measures of occupational inequality. But, this is only true when the variable in question is legitimately conceived as a ranked dichotomy. Otherwise, the measure does not conform to either the principle of altered ranks or the principle of distribution dominance.

The principle of altered ranks is violated because changes in ranks will not be registered unless they cause individuals to cross the particular rank at which the group distributions are divided. The principle of distribution dominance is violated because the cumulative percentage distributions are compared only at one point, not at all points, and will fail to detect situations where cumulative percentage distributions for groups are equal at the point of comparison but unequal at some other point. Consequently, the measure may be quite misleading when cumulative distributions cross, as in the second panel of Figure A.3, since different "cut points" in the cumulative distribution could yield markedly different results.

Another concern with these measures is that it is often difficult to justify the chosen point of comparison and thus the choice may be criticized as being arbitrary or based on convenience rather than theoretical relevance. One way to guard against this possibility is to replicate analyses using several points of comparison to show that the results obtained do not depend on the choice of any single point of comparison. Unfortunately, this cannot eliminate the closely related concern that differences in percentages above or below arbitrarily selected cut points are insensitive to the social meaning of the category that may be tied to the marginal distribution for the variable.

For example, when used to measure occupational inequality, differences in cumulative percentages ranking above a certain category do not take account of the "hierarchical" meaning that attaches to these jobs based on their location in the occupational structure for the particular community or the particular historical period. The risk is that the point of comparison selected, say the percentages with White-collar jobs, may not have similar hierarchical meaning in different communities or at different times. It is not likely, for example, that group differences in percentages with White-collar jobs have the same meaning in 1890 and 1990 because White-collar jobs were fewer in number and higher in the status hierarchy in the earlier year.[19] Measures based on comparisons of full distributions avoid this problem because they do not arbitrarily focus on selected portions of the occupation distribution.

Odds Ratios for Cumulative Percentages. Relative odds ratios comparing percentages above and below a given value of an ordinal or interval variable have also been used with some frequency in the study of racial occupational inequality (Turner 1951; Spilerman and Miller 1976; Fossett and Swicegood 1982). These kinds of relative odds ratios have the same characteristics as differences in cumulative percentages with the exception that their theoretical distribution is not symmetrically distributed around zero. This problem can be easily corrected, however, by taking the logarithm of the relative odds ratio to create a log-odds ratio or "logit". This form of the variable has the advantage of fitting comfortably in the frameworks of log-linear and logistic regression analysis (e.g., Fossett and Swicegood 1982; Fossett 1986) where confidence intervals and tests of statistical significance are readily available.

One controversial characteristic of odds ratios is that they are insensitive to the marginal distribution of occupations. That is, changes in the total number of individuals in each occupation category do not affect the measure so long as the relative odds of group membership in the category are not affected. This characteristic has been championed by some as a virtue that prevents variations in occupational structure from distorting the measurement of inequality (Stolzenberg and D'Amico 1977; Semyonov, Hoyt, and Scott 1984). Others have criticized the characteristic as a defect because it leads the measures to be insensitive to the hierarchical "meaning" of being in a particular occupation in a particular community or historical setting (Fossett 1986).

In terms of the dimensions of inequality considered here, relative odds ratios do not conform to the principle of altered ranks or the principle of distribution dominance for the same reasons that differences of proportions above or below selected "cut points" do not conform to these principles. In addition, relative odds ratios can be misleading when used to answer questions about extent — the relative frequency with which members of one group actually have higher rank when compared with members of another group.

The desirability of this characteristic of relative odds ratios has been debated elsewhere (Stolzenberg and D'Amico 1977; Spilerman

1977; Fossett and Swicegood 1982; Fossett 1986; Semyonov, Scott, and Hoyt 1984) and need not be discussed at length here. The key issue is whether access to the categories in question has social meaning independent of the overall opportunity structure. For example, in 1940 clerical jobs are in the top third of the status hierarchy in southern nonmetroplitan areas and in 1990 they are in the middle third. Access to these jobs in 1940 means something quite different than it does in 1990. Odds ratios are insensitive to this fact. By comparison a measure such as the index of net difference compares the full distributions for each group and indicates the extent to which Whites have an advantage relative to Blacks in terms of holding higher ranked positions in the local status hierarchy. It is sensitive to the fact that the status of holding a clerical job is different in 1940 and 1990.

Measures of Ordinal Association. Two familiar measures of ordinal association — Goodman and Kruskall's (1954) gamma and Somers' (1962) d_{yx} — summarize the outcomes of pairwise comparisons between members of a population on ordinal variables X and Y (Wilson 1974) and can be adapted to the measurement of intergroup inequality when X is taken to be an arbitrarily ranked dichotomy indicating group membership. Applied to the investigation of racial occupational inequality, for example, X would be an arbitrarily ranked race dichotomy (e.g., White = 1, Black = 0) and Y would be occupation. Following standard conventions for computing gamma and d_{yx}, pairwise comparisons between members of a population on these variables are grouped into: concordant pairs (C) where one individual is either higher or lower on both X and Y; discordant pairs (D) where one individual is higher on X but lower on Y, or the reverse; and pairs tied on Y (T_y).[20] Thus, in this example, concordant pairs are pairings where Whites have higher occupational standing than Blacks, discordant pairs are pairings where Blacks have higher occupational standing than Whites, and ties are pairings where Whites and Blacks have equal occupational rank.

Hypotheses of ordinal association involve predictions regarding the relative prevalence of concordant and discordant pairs. Wilson (1974) notes two closely related forms of ordinal association of interest here. The hypothesis of a "no reversals" ordinal relationship predicts that, when race is different *and* occupation is different, occupational differences will tend to favor one group. The hypothesis of an "asymmetric" ordinal relationship predicts that, when race is different, occupation differences will tend to favor one group. With race coded as described above, positive relations imply occupational advantages favoring Whites and negative relationships imply occupational advantages favoring Blacks.

TABLE A.1 Nonfarm Occupation Distribution for White and Black Men in Allen Parish, Louisiana, in 1960.

Occupation	White	Black
Highest Status Rank		
5. Upper White Collar	564	39
4. Lower White Collar	294	9
3. Skilled Manual	789	44
2. Semi-Skilled Manual	925	273
1. Unskilled Manual	262	338
Lowest Status Rank		
Total	2834	703

Note: Occupations are ranked on status as follows: (5) professionals and managers, (4) sales and clerical workers, (3) craftsmen, (2) operatives and service workers, and (1) domestic service workers and laborers.

The general form of the measures of association corresponding to these hypotheses is given by (P–Q)/R, where P is the number of pairings conforming to the positive form of the hypothesis, Q is the number of pairings conforming to the negative form of the hypothesis, and R is the number of pairings relevant for testing the hypothesis (Wilson 1974).[21] For tests of a no reversals relationship, P is equal to the number of concordant pairings, Q is equal to the number of discordant pairings, and R is equal to the sum of concordant and discordant pairings. Pairings involving ties on Y are excluded because they are consistent with both the positive and negative forms of the hypothesis. The test statistic is thus equal to (C–D)/(C+D) which is Goodman and Kruskall's (1954) gamma. For tests of an asymmetric ordinal relationship, P is equal to the sum of the concordant pairings, Q is equal to the number of discordant pairings, and R is equal to the sum of concordant pairings, discordant pairings, and ties on Y. The test statistic is thus equal to $(C–D)/(C+D+T_y)$ which is Somers' (1962) d_{yx}. The logical range for both measures is -1.0 to 1.0 with 0.0 indicating no inequality.

To illustrate the application of gamma and d_{yx} to the measurement of inequality, data on the distribution of Black and White males across five ranked occupation categories for Allen parish, Louisiana in 1970 are presented in Table A.1. The values of gamma and d_{yx} computed using these data are 0.711 and 0.632, respectively. Gamma's value of 0.711 indicates a strong ordinal relationship between race and occupation wherein occupation comparisons consistently favor

Whites. Specifically, for pairwise comparisons between Blacks and Whites where an occupation difference exists, the difference between the proportion of cases showing White advantage (0.855) and the proportion showing Black advantage (.144) is 0.711.

The lower value of d_{yx} compared to gamma is to be expected since gamma excludes ties from the denominator. Still d_{yx} indicates a strong ordinal relationship between race and occupation wherein occupation comparisons between Whites and Blacks consistently favor Whites. Specifically, the difference between the proportion of comparisons favoring Whites (0.760) and the proportion favoring Blacks (0.128) is 0.632. Ties on occupation account for the remaining comparisons.

One of the advantages of using gamma and d_{yx} as measures of inequality is that their sampling distributions are known. Thus, standard errors and confidence intervals can be computed and hypothesis tests can be readily performed. The standard error for gamma (σ_γ) is conservatively approximated by:

$$\sigma_\gamma = 1 / \sqrt{((P - Q) / N(1 - \gamma^2))}$$

when the sample size (N) is 50 or larger (Bohrnstedt and Knoke 1982:295). In the present example, the standard error of gamma is 0.080 and the ratio of gamma to its standard error is 8.887. Thus, gamma is significant at the 0.01 level using a two-tailed test.

Somers (1980) provides the following formula for calculating the approximate standard error of d_{yx} (σ_d):

$$\sigma_d = 2/3K \cdot \sqrt{((K^2 - 1)(C + 1) / [N(C - 1)])},$$

where K is the number of categories in the dependent variable, occupation, and C is the number of categories in the independent variable, race, and N is the sample size. The standard error for d_{yx} in the present example is 0.046 and the ratio of d_{yx} to its standard error is 13.74. Thus, d_{yx} is also significant at the .01 level using a two-tailed significance test.

Gamma and d_{yx} have many desirable properties to recommend them as measures of inequality. First, they meet the guidelines for measures of inequality suggested in this chapter. Second, they are well known and widely used measures. Third, they have known standard errors and which permit calculation of confidence intervals for point estimates of inequality and which provide a basis for statistical tests about the existence of inequality. The difference between gamma and d_{yx} is found in their denominators which register the number of pairwise comparisons considered when computing the measures. The denominator for gamma includes only comparisons where Blacks and Whites differ on occupational rank; it excludes comparisons involving ties. The denominator for d_{yx} includes all pairwise comparisons between Blacks and Whites. Given this, it would appear that d_{yx} is more attractive on theoretical grounds since few conceptions of inequality argue that ties are irrelevant.

Gamma may have a certain appeal when the dependent variable is crudely measured and the number of ties is "exaggerated". This kind of measurement error will bias d_{yx} downward because its the maximum inequality it can register falls directly as the number of ties increases. Gamma may be less sensitive to this problem since its calculation does not include comparisons involving ties. It might then be viewed as an "upper-bound" estimate of the value d_{yx} would approach if ties resulting from measurement error were eliminated. This interpretation of gamma depends on two assumptions. The first is that inequality *within* broad categories is an important component of the "true" level of total inequality. The second is that most ties are products of measurement error.

We explored this issue by examining occupation data for White men and Black men in 196 metropolitan areas in 1970. Two occupational ranking schemes were considered. The first used nine categories while the second used five categories obtained by collapsing several adjacent categories in the first scheme.[22] Gamma and d_{yx} were calculated for each metropolitan area using both coding schemes. The mean for d_{yx} was 0.385 using the nine-category scheme and 0.379 using the five-category scheme. The corresponding means for gamma were 0.456 and 0.484.

Under both schemes gamma was considerably higher than d_{yx}. As noted earlier, this is to be expected because d_{yx} is diminished by the presence of ties and ties are abundant in both situations. What is surprising, however, is that gamma under the five-category scheme was higher than d_{yx} under the nine-category scheme. This calls into question the assumption that ties are primarily the result of measurement error. The mean for d_{yx} declined when the five-category scheme was used, but the magnitude of the decline was relatively small. This calls into question the assumption that inequality within categories is a large component of overall inequality.

The fact that the mean for gamma increased when the five-category scheme was used is significant because it indicates that, while the impact of collapsing categories always has a conservative effect on d_{yx}, its effect on gamma cannot be predicted in advance. If inequality *within* collapsed categories is greater than inequality across the remaining categories, then collapsing categories will cause inequality to be underestimated. If inequality within broad categories is not as great as inequality across the remaining broad categories, collapsing categories will cause inequality to be overestimated. Otherwise, collapsing categories should have no systematic effect on inequality. As a rule, it is probably the case that inequality in distribution across adjacent categories is likely to be less severe than inequality in distribution across more distant categories. Thus, collapsing adjacent categories may tend to *increase* the value of gamma.

Equivalence of ND and Somers' d_{yx}

Lieberson's (1975) index of net difference and Somers' d_{yx} are equivalent measures. This can be shown by reexamining one of the computing formulas for ND provided earlier:

$$ND = \Sigma \Sigma (X_{ij}w_i b_j)$$

where i, w_i, and b_j are as described earlier, and X is a measure of ordinal advantage coded +1.0 if i > j, 0.0 if i = j, and -1.0 if i < j. In pairwise comparisons between Whites and Blacks, the three conditions for evaluating X directly correspond with concordant pairs, ties on Y, and discordant pairs. Thus, ND is the difference between the number of comparisons where Whites have higher occupational standing than Blacks and the number of comparisons where Blacks have higher occupational standing than Whites divided by the total number of comparisons. That is, ND is equal to $(C-D)/(C+D+T_y)$, the formula for d_{yx}. This finding further expands the logical underpinnings of ND and identifies another set of procedures for calculating standard errors to place confidence intervals around the measure and test the statistical significance of point estimates of inequality. Unlike, standard errors and significance tests for ND derived from its equivalence with the mean difference in percentile scores, these standard errors and significance tests do not require assumptions of normality which may be inappropriate when applied to ordinal data.

Measures of Interval-Level Inequality

To this point, all of the measures we have reviewed require only that the comparison variable have ordinal-level properties. All of these measures may be applied to comparison variables measured on either interval- or ratio-level scales, but since they do not draw on the properties of these scales, they should be described as measures of ordinal-level inequality only. This can be seen in the fact that measures such as ND and gamma satisfy the principle of altered ranks (which is critical to the measurement of ordinal-level inequality) but they do not satisfy the principle of altered differences (which is critical to the measurement of interval-level inequality).

Surprisingly, only a few of the commonly used measures of intergroup inequality require that the comparison variable be measured on a scale with interval- or ratio-level properties. The difference of means and the difference of medians are two measures which require interval-level measurement. The ratio of means, the ratio of medians, the difference of mean logs, and the index of average relative advantage require ratio-level measurement (Fossett and South 1983). Here our interest is limited to a review of strategies for measuring occupational inequality so we conclude by examining measures of interval-level inequality. We forego a review of measures of ratio-level inequality because scales of occupational status do not have ratio-level properties.

The obvious but nevertheless critical requirement for using a measure of interval-level inequality is that the comparison variable must be measured on a scale which has interval-level properties. A variety of strategies for scaling occupation have been proposed in the literature (e.g., Reiss, Duncan, Hatt, and North 1961; Siegel 1965; Treiman 1975; Nam and Powers 1983) and refined over the years. The most popular of them have in common the fact that occupations are conceived as varying along an underlying continuous metric such as prestige or socioeconomic status and then scored accordingly based on analysis of the attributes of occupations such as the income and education attainments of the incumbents of the occupation. Traditionally, these scales have been constructed such that they have a logical range between 0 and 100 and such that quantitative differences in scores have interval-level properties (e.g., a difference of 5 points is seen to convey the same meaning regardless of where in the distribution the two scores are located).

The question of whether a particular occupation scale is attractive or not is not at issue here (see Carlson 1992; Boyd and McRoberts 1982; Grusky and Van Rompaey 1992; Haug 1977; and Stevens and Cho 1985 for various points of view on this subject). The question we address is, when an interval scaling of occupation is accepted, what measures of intergroup inequality may then be considered and what are their strengths and weaknesses. At least two measures which have not already been discussed may be considered; the difference of median status and the difference of mean status.

The Difference of Median Status. The difference of median

status is a "point" measure of inequality. That is, it measures the difference in status between two groups at a particular "point" in their separate cumulative status distributions. While the median is a common choice because it represents the "center" or "typical" value in a distribution, other points such as the lower and upper quartiles might be considered based on theoretical reasons for focusing on lower- or higher-status segments of the occupation distribution.

The attractive quality of the difference of medians is that it is easy to interpret and is "resistant" to unusual distorting values in the occupation distribution should they be present. Furthermore, if occupation distributions are severely skewed, some might argue that the median is a better choice than the mean for representing the "center" of the distribution.

There are also several problems with the difference of medians (or differences at other "cut points" in the group distributions). One is that the measure does not conform to the principle of altered ranks, the principle of altered differences, or the principle of distribution dominance. The reason for this is readily apparent; the measure is wholly insensitive to the "shape" of each group's distribution above and below the "point of comparison" and will not register any changes in either group's distribution unless the change causes the group's median value to shift.

Another problem is that the theoretical rationale for adopting a particular point of comparison in each group's distribution may not be compelling and there is always the chance that other point's of comparison will yield different results. Criticism on this count may be avoided by using several different points of comparison, but this carries its own problems when the results vary for different points of comparison.

The difference of medians is most easily justified when the distribution of occupation scores has an unusual shape or contains outliers that render the mean a poor choice for a summary measure of central tendency. However, when this is the case, it might be argued that it is even better to adopt a measure of ordinal inequality such as ND because it summarizes comparisons across the full distributions for each group rather than the comparison at a single point.

The Difference of Mean Status. While sometimes mistakenly viewed as a "point-based" comparison, the difference of means is in fact a measure which reflects differences throughout the full range of each group's occupation distribution. This can be seen by examining the following equivalent expressions for the difference of means.

$$\begin{aligned} \text{DMS} &= MS_W - MS_B \\ &= \Sigma\, w_i S_i - \Sigma\, b_j S_j \\ &= \Sigma\, \Sigma\, (S_i - S_j) \cdot (w_i b_j) \end{aligned}$$

where MS indicates mean status and S_i indicates the status score assigned to occupation i.

The first expression requires no comment. The second expression shows the mean status for each group to be the result of the sum of status scores for occupations weighted by the proportion of the group's members in each occupation. The third expression shows the difference of mean status to be the weighted sum of all pairwise differences between Whites and Blacks. As such, it indicates the average status difference between randomly chosen Whites and Blacks.

The difference of means is simple to compute, easy to interpret, and readily amenable to hypothesis testing and the calculation of confidence intervals for point estimates of inequality. In addition, it meets all of the guidelines for measures of inequality we have suggested in this chapter. Unlike the difference of median status, it conforms to the principle of altered differences and thus will register any change in occupational status for members of either group. Similarly, it conforms to the principle of distribution dominance whereas the difference of medians does not.

On the whole, then, we argue that the difference of means is generally a more attractive measure of interval inequality than the difference of medians. The one characteristic of the difference of means that should be considered in any analysis is its lack of resistance to the potentially distorting impact of extreme values. However, practical experience suggests that distributions of occupational status scores are not commonly characterized by extreme outliers or unusual distributional forms that would render the mean a questionable measure of central tendency. In view of this, there is much to recommend the measure.

Concluding Remarks

Measures of ordinal and interval inequality between groups have been widely used by sociologists but their conceptual underpinnings have not been adequately developed or appreciated. Indeed, the most widely used measure, the index of dissimilarity, has few if any qualifications as a measure of intergroup inequality while other measures with more attractive qualities (e.g., the index of net difference) are often ignored.

Our discussion here advances a partial conceptualization of inequality measurement and outlines minimum criteria for measures of ordinal and interval inequality. In addition, we have reviewed popular measures and examined their strengths and weaknesses. Perhaps the most important contribution of our work in this chapter is that we are able to link Lieberson's index of net difference, an appealing measure of ordinal-level inequality, to several other well-known measures including the Gini index, the difference in mean percentile scores, and Somers' d_{yx}, a measure of ordinal association whose sampling distribution is well understood. Another contribution we have made here is to show that the simple and familiar (and perhaps for these reasons taken for granted) difference of mean status has much to recommend it as a measure of interval-level inequality.

Based on these conclusions, we rely primarily on two measures of inequality in this study — the White-Black difference in mean status and the index of net difference computed between the White and Black occupation distributions. The discussion in this chapter shows that both choices are well-justified on methodological grounds. The index of net difference is an attractive measure of ordinal inequality and the difference of mean status is an attractive measure of interval inequality.

Notes

This chapter was authored by Mark Fossett. We express thanks to Jeffrey A. Burr, Cynthia Cready, Omer R. Galle, and Stanley Lieberson for comments on earlier incarnations of this material. In addition to support from the Ford Foundation and the Aspen Institute's Rural Poverty Research Program, the preparation of the material presented in this chapter was also supported by NICHD Grant #HD 16837 and by the American Statistical Association/National Science Foundation's Census Research Program.

1. Previous studies of measures of *inter*group inequality include Gastwirth (1975), Dagum (1980), Lieberson (1975), Palmore and Whittington (1970), and Fossett and South (1983).

2. In some ways our efforts here are patterned after Fossett and South's (1983) study of measures of intergroup income inequality. One key

difference, however, is that, where Fossett and South examined measures of inequality in income — a variable measured on a ratio scale, we focus on inequality in occupation — a variable which has only ordinal and interval properties.

3. The interested reader may examine Fossett and South (1983) for a discussion of measures which summarize group comparisons on income and other ratio-level variables.

4. The ascending cumulative percentage distribution registers the percentage of the group that cumulates as one moves from the lowest rank position or value on the variable to the highest rank position or value. It begins at 0 and ascends toward 100 as successively higher ranks/values are considered.

5. The principle of altered ranks indicates that the inequality measure should be sensitive to the number of comparisons affected by the change in rank score. A similar requirement is subsumed in the requirement that measures of interval inequality respond to the size of the change in status score since, whether the change is large or small, it will affect all comparisons with members of the other group.

6. For example, it would be a simple matter to answer a question such as "Is the advantage women have relative to men in working conditions (presuming an ordinal measure of working conditions) comparable in magnitude to the disadvantage they have relative to men in income?"

7. The measure is an adaptation of the relative mean deviation which was proposed as a measure *intra*group income inequality as early as 1898 (Kakwani 1980). In this application, the measure indicates the proportion of total income which must be transferred from those who are above average on income to those who are below average on income so everyone in the population will have the mean income.

8. In many of these studies D was recognized as a measure of differentiation. However, results were invariably construed as having implications for descriptions and theories of inequality.

9. Winship (1977) provides formulas for the expected value of D under conditions of random distribution. However, the exact formulas are complex and he does not present a formula for computing confidence intervals around a sample estimate of D.

10. The data were aggregated over a random sample of 169 southern, nonmetropolitan counties previously studied by Fossett and Stafford (1990). Occupations are ranked from low to high based on Nam-Powers SES scores as follows: private household workers, farm laborers, nonfarm laborers, service workers (excluding private household workers), farmers and farm managers, transport operatives, nontransport operatives, clerical workers, crafts

workers, sales workers, managers and administrators, and professionals.

11. These results hold across a wide range of plausible alternative ranking schemes for the occupation categories. Thus, the example here does not depend on the ranking scheme used.

12. Percentile scores for each category are given by $T_i-(t_i/2)$ where T_i is the percentage of the combined population in categories ranked equal to or below category i and t_i is the proportion of the combined population in category i.

13. The theoretical range increases when more than two groups are represented in the combined status distribution. In this circumstance, the maximum difference in mean percentile status is $-Z$ to Z where $Z = 50 + 100-P_A-P_B$. The theoretical range thus approaches -100 to 100 when the two groups compared are concentrated at opposite extremes of the status hierarchy and their combined percentage representation in the overall distribution approaches 0.

14. This relationship holds only in the two-group situation, i.e., when the combined distribution used for computing percentiles consists of only members of the two groups being compared.

15. Lieberson (1975) alludes to the equivalence between the measures but does not discuss it explicitly.

16. This is stated as the negative form of the principle of distribution dominance because the cumulative percentage distributions are ascending rather than descending.

17. For example, two status distributions which follow a normal distributed and have identical means but have different standard deviations will have nonzero dissimilarity (D) scores but scores of zero on G and ND.

18. See Schwartz and Winship (1979) for a discussion of measures of *intra*group inequality which weight differences in the distribution differently depending on whether they are most pronounced at high or low values of the status distribution.

19. The White-Black difference on percent White collar would presumably be much smaller in 1890 than in 1990 because relatively few members of either group were in White-collar jobs in 1890. However, in light of changes in the occupational structure over time, few would accept this as evidence that inequality was more severe in 1990.

20. Some comparisons also involve ties on X (group membership). However, these pairing are not relevant to the computation of gamma or d_{yx}.

21. The number of relevant pairings includes only those pairings for which the hypothesis makes a definite prediction. Thus, for example, comparisons between members of the same group (i.e., ties on X) are ignored

because no predictions are made for these comparisons.

22. In the first scheme, occupations were ranked from low to high as follows: private household workers, farm laborers, nonfarm laborers, nondomestic service workers, farmers and farm managers, operatives, crafts workers, sales and clerical workers, and managers, administrators, and professionals. In the second scheme, operatives, service workers, farmers, and farm managers were grouped together, and nonfarm laborers, farm laborers, and private household workers were grouped together.

APPENDIX B

Measuring Inequality with Census Occupation Data

In this appendix chapter we discuss some of the problems associated with using census occupation data to measure racial inequality in occupational attainment. In particular, we examine five issues: (a) the limitations of using census occupation categories to capture differences in socioeconomic standing, (b) the impact of sampling on the reliability of census occupation tabulations, (c) the impact of undercount and allocation on racial comparisons, (d) the question of whether to use "fixed" or "decade-specific" status scores, and (e) the impact of using major rather than detailed occupation categories when measuring inequality. Ultimately we conclude that, despite their limitations, major category census occupation data have sufficient validity and reliability to sustain research investigating questions of how inequality varies over time and across areas.

Conceptual Limitations of Census Occupation Categories

Census occupation categories have evolved to meet many different needs. The "modern" census classification of occupations has its roots in work by Alba Edwards in the 1930s (Shryock and Siegel 1976:193) and was first applied in the 1940 census. Census occupation schemes have been subject to revision and modification in each successive census and an extensive reorganization of occupation titles was implemented in 1980. Despite these changes, however, census occupation titles have been fairly consistent with respect to certain underlying principles of classification.

A review of census documentation and technical papers going back to Edwards shows that census occupation categories reflect many different conceptual and practical concerns. For example, occupations are distinguished from each other based on: function performed; the education, training, and skill requirements of the occupation; the nature of the work and the working conditions; the authority and autonomy of the incumbent; economic rewards (not limited to income and earnings); and the status and prestige accruing to the incumbent.[1]

Other concerns not explicitly mentioned in census technical documentation also appear to have influenced census occupational classifications over the years. One unstated but apparent concern is that census categories should reflect certain important social distinctions among occupations such as the age, race, and sex composition of their incumbents. For example, barbers and hairdressers are identified as separate detailed occupations in 1960 though their functional roles and skill and training requirements are quite similar.

While many considerations have influenced the evolution of census occupation categories, none has totally dominated it and all have been partly frustrated. For example, census categories try to capture differences in functional specialization (a qualitative, dimension) and social and economic rewards associated with the occupation (a quantitative dimension). Yet even these basic goals have not been pursued uniformly. One area where this is obvious is in the lack of detail for agricultural occupations. This is a particular concern for us since a large fraction of the labor force in southern, nonmetropolitan counties was employed in agricultural occupations in 1940 and in 1950. We would have preferred that census data register distinctions between share croppers, tenant farmers, and owner-farmers and make further distinctions between farmers and farm managers based on farm size, asset value, gross receipts, and related concerns. Unfortunately, this was not the case.

We could discuss this concern at length. However, the point that we want to make is simply that the underlying logic of census occupational categories is complex and does not perfectly satisfy the requirements of any one conceptual goal. On the positive side this allows researchers to use census data to address many different questions. On the negative side it insures that census occupation categories will be at least partly flawed for most research questions.

Thus, while census occupation categories are strongly influenced by concerns about socioeconomic status, we recognize that they do not *perfectly* capture variation in socioeconomic status. Nevertheless, census categories *do* capture important variation in the socioeconomic rewards associated with different jobs. The validity and reliability of measures of status inequality developed from census data are located somewhere on a continuum between perfect and unacceptable. Our judgment is that they are well into the acceptable range and can readily sustain investigations of patterns of variation in racial inequality across areas and over time.

Sampling and Enumeration Methods

In the 1940 census, occupation was a "one-hundred percent" item (i.e., it was asked of everyone). In all subsequent censuses, occupation has only been asked of a subsample of respondents. However, published and unpublished census tabulations based on these sample data are multiplied to reflect population counts.[2] It is important for investigators to be mindful of this fact, especially when working with data for nonmetropolitan counties and small demographic subgroups. The reason for this is that the true sample size underlying reported census counts may only be a small fraction of the stated figures (e.g., in some decades it is sometimes less than 20 percent of the reported counts). Thus, for example a White-Black occupation comparison based on data reported for 250 Black men may in fact be based on a sample of fewer than 50 cases and thus be less reliable than might appear at first glance.

Another change in census methodology over the decades has been a shift from enumeration by a trained census employee to respondent self-enumeration via mail-back questionnaires. The move to self-enumeration may have reduced the accuracy of the occupation information obtained especially for groups with lesser educational attainments).

We know of no reason to believe that these changes in census methodology introduced any systematic distortion (i.e., bias) to occupation tabulations for Whites and Blacks. However, they may well have reduced the reliability of these tabulations over time. Reliability concerns may be especially great in studies like ours which focus on areas with small populations, make comparisons between subgroups in the population, and follow the comparisons over time. The potential problem is that increasing *random* error in occupation data may obscure underlying patterns, trends, and associations. On the one hand this means that findings established using these data are likely to be conservative in the sense that any patterns discovered would likely be even clearer and stronger if the data were more reliable. On the other hand, this means that some effects will be underestimated or might go undetected altogether.

Undercount, Substitution, and Allocation

In every census a portion of the population is not enumerated. This "undercount" is more pronounced for some socio-demographic groups than others (e.g., persons with lower socioeconomic status). Undercount is known to be disproportionately high for young Black men (Siegel 1974; Passel, Siegel, and Robinson 1982). Studies suggest that the completeness of the count has been improving in recent decades, but that it has been estimated to be as high as 15-20 percent for some demographic groups in some decades (Farley and Allen 1987: Table A.1).

Another problem is that no data or only partial data are obtained for many persons enumerated in the census. "Complete" records are constructed for these persons via substitution and allocation — processes whereby missing data is replaced with estimated data.[3] Substitution and allocation are more common for Blacks than Whites (Farley and Allen 1987: Table A.2). Allocation is more common for some variables than others. The allocation rate for occupation is particularly high and in some years allocation for occupation ranges from 6 to 9 percent.

Both undercount and allocation are thought to be less severe for nonmetropolitan populations, but they are nevertheless worrisome for the present study. Unfortunately, there are no definitive studies investigating the impact of undercount, substitution, and allocation on the measurement of group differentials in socioeconomic attainment. Such a study is beyond the scope of the present project, consequently, we can provide only informed speculation about the impact of these factors on descriptive and analytic results.

At a minimum, undercount, substitution, and allocation render measurements of status and inequality less *reliable* since they all reduce the "true" sample size available for performing analysis. In addition, substitution and allocation introduce random error into the measurement of socioeconomic status and hence intergroup inequality. A more serious question, however, is whether undercount, substitution, and allocation introduce systematic error which significantly *biases* the measurement of status and inequality.

Undercount is more common for persons of lower socioeconomic status than higher socioeconomic status. All else equal, undercount may well contribute to foster *upward* bias in measurements of socioeconomic status. Undercount is greater for Blacks than for Whites thus this effect should be more pronounced for Blacks than Whites. All else equal, then, undercount should tend to bias White-Black comparisons toward *lower* White advantage. Socioeconomic status would be *over*estimated for both groups, but moreso for Blacks than for Whites leading to *lower* White advantage.

Census substitution and allocation procedures are likely to have similar impacts on measured inequality. Substitution and allocation, like undercount, tend to be more common for Blacks than Whites and is probably more common for persons with lower socioeconomic status.[4] All else equal, it is thus probable that substitution and allocation tend to bias estimates of socioeconomic status upward and bias estimates of White-Black inequality downward.

In sum, we expect that undercount, substitution, and allocation tend to bias White and Black status levels upward and bias White-Black inequality downward. It is important to recognize this fact. However, it is equally important to recognize that *this bias does not necessarily distort either patterns of cross-sectional variation in inequality across areas or patterns of temporal variation in inequality for the same areas.* In fact, if the selection forces involved in undercount and allocation are similar across areas and over time, inequality comparisons will be biased in basically the same manner in all places and decades. Changes over time and variation from area to area would thus represent "true" variation in inequality.

We believe this assumption to be approximately correct. Farley and Allen (1987) present evidence suggesting that undercount has improved over time, especially for Black men but the over time changes are not so dramatic as to suggest that this would complicate the interpretation of inequality comparisons over time. If there were an effect, it would presumably be one of *increasing* the apparent advantage that Whites have over Blacks (since there is improvement over time in coverage of Blacks with lower socioeconomic status). At present, the literature provides no empirical or theoretical basis for assuming that this is in fact the case. We acknowledge, however, that this is an area where further methodological research is needed.

"Fixed" Versus "Decade-Specific" Status Scores

We use Nam-Powers socioeconomic status scores to measure the status of census occupations. These scores reflect the average of each occupation's percentile ranking on education and income relative to the education and income distributions of other occupations (Nam and Powers 1968). As such, they are relative, not absolute, status scores. That is, they measure the occupation's standing only in relation to other occupations. As a result, status scores for detailed occupations and broad occupation categories may change over time as the relative education and income comparisons among occupations change. The measures of inequality we use are based on "decade-specific" socioeconomic status scores (i.e., status scores computed for the decade in question). We also considered the possibility of computing inequality measures based on "fixed" status scores. Thus, we computed a separate set of group status means and inequality measures based on the status scores for the major occupation categories observed in 1960. This decade was chosen as the "benchmark" for fixed status scores because it is near the middle of our observation period. The status and inequality measures based on "fixed" status scores for occupations proved to be highly correlated with measures of status and inequality based on decade-specific status scores and analyses based on "fixed" status scores yielded results which were very similar to those obtained when we used "decade-specific" status scores.

Major Versus Detailed Categories

Prior to 1970 published and unpublished occupation tabulations for nonmetropolitan counties were limited to only about a dozen major categories. Consequently, investigators must necessarily work with major category data when undertaking longitudinal analyses of occupational inequality at the county level. The key question is whether the major categories are sufficiently detailed to capture occupational differentiation and inequality between groups and faithfully represent their variation across areas and over time.

One basis for concern on this point is that the major categories are aggregations of detailed categories which often vary significantly in socioeconomic status. For example, in 1970, the major category of "professional, technical, and kindred workers" includes both the high status occupations of physicians and lawyers and the middle status occupations of clergy and school teachers. What is the impact of using major category data to investigate occupation differences between Blacks and Whites or men and women when these kinds of occupations are lumped together in a single broad category?

We tried to answer this question by exploring data from the special EEOC data file from the 1980 Census (US Bureau of the Census 1982) which provides detailed occupation tabulations by race and sex for counties. For purposes of comparison, we aggregated the data in this file using an intermediate occupation scheme and two different major category schemes. These can be described as follows:

Detailed Occupations —the 503-category occupation scheme used in the 1980 census (i.e., the maximum detail that can be achieved using census occupation data).

Intermediate Occupations — a 37-category intermediate occupation scheme we created by aggregating the detailed occupation titles used in the 1980 census.

1980 Major Occupations — the 13-category major occupation scheme used in the 1980 census.

1970 Major Occupations — the 12-category major occupation scheme used in the 1970 census (obtained by mapping 1980 detailed titles to 1970 detailed titles and then aggregating).

We considered results based on the detailed occupational scheme from the 1980 census to be the benchmark against which results based on the other schemes should be evaluated.

The intermediate occupation scheme is one that we developed for use in this and other analyses of race and sex differences in occupation attainment (Fossett and Stafford 1992). Our goal was to reduce the number of categories to permit more parsimonious description yet do so with only minimal loss of the information regarding status contained in the detailed occupations.

We developed intermediate categories by grouping detailed occupations within each of the thirteen major categories used in the 1980 census into three groups of high, medium, and low status titles. We placed detailed occupations into these groupings based on Nam-Powers status scores for the 503 detailed occupational titles (Nam and Terrie 1988).[5] We did not subdivide the "Private Household" major category since the detailed titles within this category varied only minimally on the status dimension. Consequently, we obtained 37 categories instead of 39. The resulting categories are attractive because they are relatively homogeneous with respect to both type of occupation (e.g., professional and technical workers, operatives, laborers, etc.) and status.

The first broad category scheme is based on the thirteen major categories used in the 1980 census. These depart significantly from the broad categories used in earlier censuses. Because of this, we also developed a second broad category scheme based on the twelve major categories used in the 1970 census.[6] This was accomplished by mapping the detailed 1980 occupation titles onto detailed occupation titles for 1970 using a conversion table developed by the census (US Bureau of the Census 1989) and then aggregating to 1970 broad categories.

Measures Based on Different Occupation Schemes

The first question we investigated was whether the four occupation schemes produced differences in mean status for specific groups or differences in levels of inequality between groups. Data relevant to this question are presented in Table B.1 which gives the means (designated by "X") and standard deviations (designated by "s") for selected measures of socioeconomic status, status inequality, and occupational differentiation computed using the four different occupations schemes. Comparisons are between White men (non-Hispanic, Whites) and Black men, and between White men and White women. The measures presented include the mean socioeconomic status for each group based on Nam-Powers' SES scores, the mean SES difference between groups (also based on Nam-Powers' SES scores), and the index of dissimilarity.[7] The data are for our initial 300-county sample (described in Chapter 3).

Several findings emerge upon inspection of Table B.1. First, mean SES levels for White men tended to *increase* as the occupation categories became more detailed whereas mean SES scores for White women and Black men tended to *decline*. The changes in mean SES were greatest for White women. On average, they fell about 5.0 points from 48.22 when the 13 broad categories for 1980 were used to 43.28 when all 503 detailed categories for 1980 were used. The average mean SES score for White men increased by almost 2.5 points from 48.95 to when 13 categories were used to 51.58 when 503 categories were used. The average mean SES score for Black men declined by almost 2.0 points from 37.17 when 13 categories were used to 35.11 when 503 categories were used.

This pattern indicates that *inequality between White men and Black men and inequality between White men and White women is substantially underestimated when broad occupation categories are used*. On average, inequality measured by the difference in mean SES between White men and Black men was 11.78 points when the 13 broad categories for 1980 were used and 16.47 points when all 503 detailed categories for 1980 were used. Thus, the inequality measured using 1980 broad categories was 4.7 points lower on average than inequality measured using detailed categories and under estimated the "true" level of inequality by about 28 percent if inequality measured using the 1980 detailed categories is taken as the benchmark. The impact of using different occupation schemes was even more dramatic for measures of inequality between White men and White women. The average for the male-female difference in mean SES for Whites was only 0.73 points when the 1980 broad categories were used but it was 8.31 points when the 1980 detailed categories were used. The average level of male-female inequality for Whites was thus underestimated by 7.36 points or 86.3 percent.

Interestingly, the average levels of SES and inequality obtained using the 1970 broad categories came closer than those obtained

TABLE B.1 Descriptive Statistics for Selected Measures of Status, Inequality, and Differentiation Computed Using Different Occupation Schemes for 300 Southern Nonmetropolitan Counties in 1980[a]

	1970 Major		1980 Major		1980 Intermediate		1980 Detailed	
	X	s	X	s	X	s	X	s
Socioeconomic Status of White Men	48.94	2.69	48.95	2.76	51.50	3.24	51.58	3.28
Socioeconomic Status of White Women	47.83	2.56	48.22	2.79	43.49	3.46	43.28	3.58
Socioeconomic Status of Black Men	35.63	3.24	37.17	2.81	34.99	3.76	35.11	3.89
Status Difference Between White and Black Men	13.31	3.23	11.78	3.08	16.51	4.00	16.47	4.04
Status Difference Between White Men and Women	1.12	2.49	0.73	2.64	8.02	2.73	8.31	2.95
Index of Dissimilarity for White and Black Men[b]	37.23	6.67	34.47	6.75	44.08	7.03	—	—
Index of Dissimilarity for White Men and Women[b]	49.92	6.40	51.36	6.72	61.05	5.81	—	—

a 1970 Major denotes the 12 major categories used in the 1970 census; 1980 Major denotes the 13 major categories used in the 1980 census; 1980 Intermediate denotes 37 intermediate categories obtained by dividing the 13 major categories in 1980 into subcategories of high, medium, and low status; and 1980 Detailed denotes the 503 detailed categories used in the 1980 census.

b The index of dissimilarity was not computed using the 503 detailed occupation categories.

using the 1980 broad categories to approximating the benchmark scores obtained using the 1980 detailed categories. This was particularly true for the mean SES for Black males and for the inequality comparison between White men and Black men. This result suggests that *the broad category scheme adopted in the 1980 census does not group occupations on the basis of socioeconomic attainments as well as the broad category scheme used in earlier censuses.* However, this finding is secondary to the finding that inequality is significantly underestimated using either of these broad category schemes.

The explanation for why inequality is underestimated when broad categories are used is simple. Detailed titles within broad categories vary with respect to socioeconomic status and the inequality between groups in their distribution across detailed titles within the broad categories is an nontrivial part of total inequality.

We also found that *occupational differentiation was also underestimated when the major category schemes were used.* The mean values of the index of dissimilarity between the White male and Black male occupation distributions was 34.47 when the 1980 major category scheme was used and 44.08 when we used our 1980 intermediate category scheme (we did not compute dissimilarity using the 1980 detailed category scheme). For the comparisons between White men and White women the corresponding figures for average dissimilarity scores were 51.36 and 61.05, respectively. In both cases, occupational differentiation was underestimated by about 10 points on average. For the comparison between White and Black men, this represented an average underestimate of about 21.8 percent. For the comparison between White men and women this represented an average underestimate of 15.9 percent. Roughly similar underestimates were observed when we used the 1970 major categories.

While we did not compute comparisons based on the 1980 detailed occupation categories, it is reasonable to conclude that they would have revealed even greater average levels of differentiation than our intermediate occupation scheme. Thus, the level of downward bias documented here when dissimilarity is measured using 1980 major categories is probably a conservative estimate.

Correlations Among Measures Based on Different Schemes

It is not surprising that major category schemes produce downward bias in measures of inequality and differentiation. However, the question that is more central for our purposes is whether measures based on major category schemes can faithfully register variation in inequality. We investigated this question by examining the correlations among the different measures of status, inequality, and dissimilarity just examined. These are reported in Table B.2. The major finding to emerge from this analysis is that measures of status, inequality, and differentiation based on major categories have moderate to strong correlations correlations with the same measures based on detailed categories. For example, the correlations between mean SES computed using major categories (either 1970 or 1980 schemes) and mean SES computed using detailed categories range between 0.844 and 0.935 (squared correlations range between 0.712 and 0.874). These correlations indicate that, taking the scores based on more detailed categories as the benchmark, the measures based on the major categories had good but less than perfect reliability.[8] The correlations between mean SES computed using the intermediate categories and mean SES computed using detailed categories were much higher; the lowest correlation was 0.977 (with a squared correlation of 0.954). This indicates that very high reliability can be achieved without necessarily having to have fully detailed data.

The correlations between inequality measured using broad categories and inequality measured using detailed categories range between 0.851 and 0.870 (squared correlations range between 0.724 and 0.757). These correlations also indicate that measures based on the broad categories have good if less than perfect reliability. Again the intermediate categories offered much higher reliability. Correlations between the index of dissimilarity based on broad categories and based on intermediate categories also were only moderately strong. In the case of comparisons between White and Black men the correlations were 0.775 and 0.725 for the 1970 and 1980 broad categories, respectively (squared correlations were 0.601 and 0.526, respectively). In the case of the comparisons between White men and Women, the correlations were 0.858 and 0.907 for the 1970 and 1980 broad categories, respectively (squared correlations were 0.736 and 0.823, respectively). It is interesting to note that measures of status inequality based on broad categories are apparently more reliable than measures of occupational differentiation based on broad categories.

Correlations with Independent Variables

Another issue we examined was whether measures of inequality and differentiation based on different occupation schemes had similar correlations with independent variables. There can be no absolute and definitive answer to this question because differences between

TABLE B.2. Correlations of Selected Measures of Mean Status, Occupational Inequality, and Occupational Differentiation Computed Using Different Occupation Schemes for 300 Southern Nonmetropolitan Counties in 1980.[a]

Mean SES

White Men

	12	13	37
13	0.930		
37	0.912	0.927	
503	0.918	0.935	0.992

Black Men

	12	13	37
13	0.859		
37	0.812	0.887	
503	0.844	0.876	0.977

White Women

	12	13	37
13	0.971		
37	0.922	0.939	
503	0.925	0.935	0.994

Difference in Mean Status

White Men-Black Men

	12	13	37
13	0.843		
37	0.862	0.879	
503	0.870	0.858	0.983

White Men-White Women

	12	13	37
13	0.908		
37	0.855	0.864	
503	0.851	0.854	0.986

Dissimilarity

White Men - Black Men

	12	13
13	0.735	
37	0.775	0.725

White Men-White Women

	12	13
13	0.939	
37	0.958	0.907

[a] 12 denotes the 12 major categories used in the 1970 census; 13 denotes the 13 major categories used in the 1980 census; 37 denotes 37 intermediate categories obtained by dividing the 13 major categories in 1980; 503 denotes the detailed categories used in the 1980 census.

measures might be important in some circumstances and not in others. Still, we can gain insight into the issue by examining the bivariate correlations presented in Table B.3. The first panel of this table presents correlations between mean SES differences between White and Black men measured using different occupation schemes and four independent variables — percent Black in the county population, percentage of labor force employed in manufacturing, percentage of the labor force employed in white-collar occupations, and education requirements of the local occupation structure.[9] The second panel of this table presents a similar set of correlations, but for measures of inequality between White men and women. The third panel presents the correlations with the index of dissimilarity between White and Black men. The fourth panel presents correlations with the index of dissimilarity between White men and women.

Four patterns in the correlations merit comment. First, there *were* differences in the magnitudes of the correlations depending on whether the measures of inequality or differentiation were based on broad, intermediate, or detailed categories. In four of the 16 sets of correlations examined, the *sign* of the correlations varied depending on the number of categories used. However, the correlations in these circumstances were relatively small (the largest squared correlation in the sets where there was a sign difference was only 0.02) and thus the sign reversals should not be seen as substantively important.

The second notable pattern is that the range of the correlations in sets where the correlations were statistically significant tended to be limited. Thus, substantive implications and statistical significance tended to be similar whether measures were computed using broad, intermediate, or detailed categories.

The third important pattern was that the biggest differences were observed when correlations for measures based on major categories were compared with correlations for measures based on intermediate or detailed categories. This was not unexpected. However, the pattern of these differences was surprising. We had expected that correlations involving measures based on detailed occupation categories would be the strongest in each set. This was based on the assumption that measures based on broad categories were less reliable and that the lower reliability would tend to attenuate their correlations with the independent variables. However, correlations involving measures based on broad categories were often as large or larger than those involving measures based on detailed or intermediate categories.

This last finding may simply be peculiar to our sample but it deserves further investigation in future methodological studies. It

TABLE B.3. Correlations of Measures of Occupational Inequality and Differentiation Based on Different Occupational Schemes with Selected Independent Variables for 300 Southern Nonmetropolitan Counties in 1980.[a]

	Percent Black	Percent Manuf	Percent White Collar	Educ. Demand
Panel 1: SES Difference Between White and Black Men				
1970 Major Categories (12)	0.277	-0.116	0.151	0.038
1980 Major Categories (13)	0.195	0.024	0.268	0.228
1980 Intermediate Categories (37)	0.332	0.016	0.188	0.110
1980 Detailed Categories (503)	0.325	-0.015	0.185	0.096
Panel 2: SES Difference Between White Men and Women				
1970 Major Categories (12)	-0.279	0.353	0.251	0.344
1980 Major Categories (13)	-0.386	0.293	0.281	0.394
1980 Intermediate Categories (37)	-0.213	0.314	0.199	0.304
1980 Detailed Categories (503)	-0.228	0.351	0.165	0.282
Panel 3: Correlations with Dissimilarity Between White and Black Men				
1970 Major Categories (12)	0.194	-0.173	-0.039	-0.136
1980 Major Categories (13)	0.041	-0.095	0.142	0.118
1980 Intermediate Categories (37)	0.041	-0.294	0.011	-0.079
Panel 4: Correlations with Dissimilarity Between White Men and Women				
1970 Major Categories (12)	0.046	-0.488	-0.248	-0.342
1980 Major Categories (13)	0.058	-0.520	-0.260	-0.345
1980 Intermediate Categories (37)	0.175	-0.506	-0.210	-0.291

[a] Correlations with absolute values above 0.11 are significant at the 0.05 level.

raises the concern that measurement error introduced by using broad occupation categories is not random but is somehow systematically correlated with community characteristics. Previous theory and research provides no guidance in this area. The findings here suggest that if there is a problem it is more likely to affect analysis of inequality between men and women as correlations between measures of inequality between White men and women with the independent variables were consistently stronger when inequality was measured using broad occupation categories.

Finally, we were surprised to find that measures based on the 1970 major categories and measures based on the 1980 major categories occasionally had appreciably different correlations with the independent variables. The differences were less extreme when the correlations were statistically significant. Still, the differences were sufficiently large and frequent that we conclude that analyses of inequality over time should if possible use a consistent occupation scheme over time (as we do in this study) because changes in occupational classification at the broad category level may affect results in ways that are not yet well understood. Future methodological research should investigate this question more thoroughly to explain why the changes in broad category schemes affect correlations with independent variables, and to clarify the implications of shifting from one broad occupation scheme to another.

Correlations of Measures of Inequality and Differentiation

In Appendix A, we stressed that measures of inequality and differentiation are conceptually distinct. The key difference is that measures of differentiation such as the index of dissimilarity consider only whether occupation differences exist between two groups while measures of inequality consider whether differences between two groups reflect systematic advantage for one group or the other. Here we briefly consider the extent to which the two kinds of measures are empirically distinct in our sample. Evidence bearing on this is presented in Table B.4 which gives correlations between the mean status difference between groups and the index of dissimilarity using different occupation schemes. Correlations for comparison between White and Black men are presented in Panel 1 and correlations for comparisons between White men and women are presented in Panel 2.

The most important pattern can be briefly summarized. Measures of dissimilarity and status difference are not necessarily highly correlated as is often implicitly assumed in the literature. The conceptual differences between inequality and differentiation allow the possibility of weak correlations among measures and this possibility was realized in our sample. For the comparisons of White and Black men, the measures of inequality and differentiation were positively correlated, but the correlations were surprisingly weak considering the index of dissimilarity has often been used in the past to measure inequality. The strongest correlation was 0.692 (with a squared

TABLE B.4 Correlations Among Measures of Inequality and Differentiation Based on Different Occupational Schemes for 300 Southern Nonmetropolitan Counties in 1980.[a]

SES Difference Based on	Index of Dissimilarity Based on		
	1970 Major	1980 Major	1980 Intermed.
Panel 1: Comparisons Between White Males and Black Males			
1970 Major Categories (12)	0.692	0.514	0.469
1980 Major Categories (13)	0.475	0.570	0.311
1980 Intermediate Categories (37)	0.528	0.460	0.396
1980 Detailed Categories (503)	0.546	0.470	0.418
Panel 2: Comparisons Between White Males and White Females			
1970 Major Categories (12)	-0.530	-0.600	-0.546
1980 Major Categories (13)	-0.528	-0.539	-0.535
1980 Intermediate Categories (37)	-0.424	-0.448	-0.334
1980 Detailed Categories (503)	-0.421	-0.450	-0.335

[a] 1970 Major refers to the 12 major categories used in the 1970 census; 1980 Major refers to the 13 major categories used in the 1980 census; 1980 intermediate refers to 37 intermediate categories obtained by subdividing the 13 major categories in 1980 into groups of high, medium, and low status; 1980 Detailed refers to the 503 detailed categories used in the 1980 census.

correlation of 0.479) and the median correlation was 0.472 (with a squared correlation of 0.223).[10] Clearly, measures of differentiation cannot be substituted for measures of inequality without risking considerable measurement error and distortion of results.

The findings were even more dramatic for the comparisons of White men and women. For these comparisons the correlations were not only weak, they were *negative* rather than positive. The median correlation was -0.489 (the squared correlation was 0.239). This indicated that inequality and differentiation were weakly correlated at best and that inequality actually tended to be lower in areas where dissimilarity was high.[11] In this case, then, substituting one type of measure for the other not only risks considerable measurement error; it risks systematically *biased* results.

Implications and Discussion

The analyses reported in this chapter make clear that investigators should be careful in conceptualizing and operationalizing their dependent variables so as to distinguish between inequality and differentiation. We have shown that measures of inequality and differentiation are empirically as well as conceptually distinct. Thus, one is not only *not* a reliable surrogate for the other, but also may be an *invalid* surrogate in some circumstances. Unfortunately, it was common in past research for investigators to infer inequality from differentiation. Our results show this practice is unacceptable and should be avoided in future studies.

The arguments and analyses reported here also make clear that census occupation data have many important limitations. Changes in enumeration techniques and sampling over the decades may have resulted in decreasing reliability of the data for nonmetropolitan areas over time. However, this conclusion is speculative as we could find no documentation of this effect in the literature.

Undercount and nonresponse are also potentially significant problems, but their precise impacts on inequality and differentiation are yet to be firmly established. We speculate that they might lead to *underestimates* of the magnitude of race inequality since lower SES Blacks are likely to be disproportionately underrepresented in the data. However, this bias should be relatively consistent across areas and over time and thus should not distort the results of analyses of variation in inequality across areas and over time.

Problems associated with using data for broad occupation category categories are better understood. Inequality and differentiation are *underestimated* when broad categories are used. In the case of comparisons between White and Black men, inequality appears to be underestimated by as much as one-quarter to one-third and differentiation by about one-fifth. The downward bias in the measures of inequality and differentiation based on broad category data suggests that the findings regarding the *levels* of racial inequality and differentiation in our descriptive analyses should be interpreted as being conservative.

The use of major categories also introduces a measurement error into the dependent variables in our analyses. This was reflected in the fact that the correlations between measures based on detailed and major categories, while strong to moderate, were less than perfect. Assuming the error introduced is random (after taking into account the downward bias), the likely consequence of this measurement error is to make the measures more difficult to "explain." For example, the effects of the independent variables in regression models predicting measures of inequality should be attenuated. Likewise, the explained variance for the equations should be attenuated and the standard deviation of the residuals is likely to be inflated. In light of this, findings of structural effects on inequality and differentiation in our analyses should be seen as conservative. The effects we find might well be stronger if we were able to develop measures for all decades based on detailed occupational data.

Finally, while we have noted certain problems associated with measuring inequality with census data, we nevertheless stress that we believe *the measures used in this study are very useful for testing hypotheses about the structural determinants of racial inequality.* One reason for this conclusion is that, while perfect validity and reliability are goals to strive for in research, they can never be completely achieved. Valuable work can still be conducted, however, when we understand the nature and consequences of the limitations of our measures. A second and equally important reason for concluding that the measures reviewed here can be useful is that the "signal-to-noise" ratio in the data is high; the measures vary substantially over time and across areas and the differences observed are too large and too systematic to attribute to measurement problems. Furthermore, since the errors in the measures are likely to be somewhat uniform across areas and over time, the observed *patterns* of variation in inequality and differentiation across time and areas is meaningful even though the precise value of inequality estimated for a given locality in a given decade may be questioned. Ultimately, measures should be evaluated in relation to the potential knowledge to be gained by using them. In this case, it is a great deal indeed.

Notes

1. Conspicuously absent is any concern for notions of class categories.

2. Yet a further complication is that the final totals in some decades are based on multi-stage ratio estimation – a method wherein sample cases are weighted differentially based on the estimated representation of certain household types and age-race-sex groups in the total population.

3. Substitution occurs when a person or household is known to be present but no other information is available. Under certain criteria, the information for a previously processed person or household is duplicated and substituted for the missing information. Allocation occurs when missing information is only partial. In this case, omitted or unacceptable entries on census questionnaires are replaced with entries that are consistent with observed entries for persons with similar demographic characteristics. These

procedures for dealing with missing data preserve both the central tendency and the variance in the variables.

4. Census allocation procedures substitute information on occupation taken from a respondent who is similar on other demographic characteristics (e.g., age, race, sex, and area of residence). The allocated occupation will be tend to be biased upward on socioeconomic status if, among persons with a given demographic profile, individuals with lower socioeconomic status have higher nonresponse rates on occupation.

5. For further details, see Stafford and Fossett (1991).

6. This is similar to the broad-category schemes used 1940-1960.

7. The status scores for detailed categories were taken from Nam and Terrie (1988). Status scores for intermediate and major categories were obtained by taking the weighted average of the SES scores for the detailed occupations in each major category with weights reflecting the total number of persons employed in the detailed occupation at the national level.

8. The squared correlation between the measure computed using broad categories and the measure computed using detailed categories is an optimistic estimate of the reliability of the measure since it assumes the measure based on detailed categories has perfect reliability.

9. These measures are explained in more detail in Appendix C.

10. In analyses not reported here we found similar results when inequality was measured using Lieberson's index of net difference.

11. We do not have a definitive explanation for this negative correlation but in this sample it is partly associated with variation in the representation of agricultural jobs in the occupational structure. Occupational differentiation between men and women tended to be greatest when agricultural occupations were prevalent and inequality between men and women tended to be lower in these areas (due to the disproportionate concentration of men in low status farm occupations). However, the negative correlation between differentiation and inequality persisted net of controls for percent of labor force in farm occupations.

APPENDIX C

Measures

This appendix chapter reviews the strategies we used to measure key variables in our analysis . It supplements Chapter 3 by discussing variables and issues not mentioned in Chapter 3 and by providing more detailed information about points which were addressed only briefly in Chapter 3.

Dependent Variables

We used one measure of occupational differentiation and two measures of occupational inequality as dependent variables in this project. The measure of occupational differentiation is the index of dissimilarity (D) which measures the overall degree of difference between two percentage distributions (Duncan and Duncan 1955). The first measure of inequality is Lieberson's (1976) index of net difference (ND) which measures ordinal inequality between group occupation distributions. The second is the mean status difference between whites and blacks (SD) which measures interval-level status differences between groups. The two measures of inequality meet all of the relevant criteria for measures of ordinal and interval inequality, respectively, set forth in Appendix A. The computing formulas for these measures are also set forth in Appendix A.

Socioeconomic Status Scores

It is necessary to rank order occupations on some criterion in order to compute the index of net difference for occupational inequality. Similarly, it is necessary to score occupations an interval-level status scale to compute the mean status difference between groups.

We elected to use Nam-Powers socioeconomic status (SES) scores for both purposes.

Many aspects of occupations (e.g., income, benefits, prestige, authority, autonomy, qualifications, job security, quality of working conditions, and mobility prospects) might be used as a basis for assigning status scores to occupations and establishing a rank-ordering of occupations. The Nam-Powers scores emphasize objective economic aspects of occupational standing based on education-skill requirements and income rewards (Haug 1977). Unlike prestige scores, the Nam-Powers scores do not incorporate a subjective or evaluative dimension. We prefer the status scores over prestige scores because we believe they more closely track life chances flowing from income, fringe benefits, job stability, and quality of working conditions.[1] However, we note that status scores and prestige scores tend to be closely correlated, and that we may well have obtained similar results if we had used prestige scores. Whether this speculation is in fact true is a question for future research.

Nam-Powers status scores for occupations reflect the average of the occupation's percentile standing on income and education relative to other occupations. We obtained scores for the major occupation categories used in census tabulations in each decade by computing the weighted average of the status scores for the detailed occupations within the major categories.[2] The results are reported in Table C.1.

Obtaining Appropriate SES Scores

Nam-Powers status scores for detailed occupations based on the total civilian labor force were already available for 1970, 1980, and 1990. The scores for 1970 were previously published in Powers and Holmberg (1978) and we used these without modification. Scores based on the total civilian labor force were available for 1980 (Nam and Terrie 1988), but differed slightly from scores prepared for earlier years (described below) so we computed an alternative set of scores for 1980 as a precaution. We ultimately found that the scores we prepared for 1980 performed almost identically to the scores available in Nam and Terrie (1988). Thus, we used scores for 1990 prepared by Nam and Terrie (1994) and did not prepare our own scores for 1990.

Scores based on data for the total civilian labor force were not available for 1940, 1950, and 1960 so we applied the Nam-Powers methodology to compute the required scores for each of these decades. The status scores for each decade from 1940 to 1980 are presented in the appendix tables of a more detailed paper (Stafford and Fossett 1991).[3] This paper also references data sources used to compute

TABLE C.1 Socioeconomic Status Scores for Major Occupation Categories
Computed from Data for the Total Labor Force, 1940-1990.

Occupational Category	1940	1950	1960	1970	1980	1990
Professionals	—	83.9	83.7	80.5	80.0	82.3
Professionals	86.0	—	—	—	—	—
Semi-Professionals	82.0	—	—	—	—	—
Managers	81.0	79.1	82.8	80.0	78.0	77.5
Clerical and Sales Workers	66.0	—	—	—	—	—
Clerical Workers	—	64.1	57.0	46.0	46.0	45.4
Sales Workers	—	60.1	50.8	56.0	55.0	57.7
Crafts Workers	65.5	60.7	59.0	55.0	54.0	49.7
Operatives	49.0	43.3	40.3	—	34.0	32.6
Nontransport Operatives	—	—	—	32.0	—	—
Transport Operatives	—	—	—	40.0	—	—
Service Workers	40.0	33.5	27.3	24.0	24.0	25.9
Laborers	30.0	23.5	18.2	22.0	22.0	19.9
Farmers	23.0	16.0	14.8	31.0	41.0	38.5
Farm Laborers	—	—	5.4	6.0	8.0	8.7
Farm Laborers - Unpaid	16.0	6.8	—	—	—	—
Farm Laborers - Wage	10.0	6.1	—	—	—	—
Domestic Workers	9.0	7.0	6.0	3.0	2.0	7.5

Source: Stafford and Fossett (1991).

the scores and discusses technical issues involved in computing Nam-Powers-Terrie scores for earlier census years.

Computation of Nam-Powers SES scores is straightforward. The score for a given detailed occupation category represents the arithmetic average of its percentile score on education and its percentile score on income. Percentile scores for each detailed occupation were computed for education based on the occupation's ranking on median education and the number of persons in the occupation as follows. First, we obtained the median years of school completed for incumbents of each occupation category. Second, we sorted the occupation categories from low to high on median education.[4] Then we assigned each occupation a percentile score based on the percentage of persons in occupations ranking lower on education plus one half the percentage of persons in the occupation in question. We computed percentile scores for income in a like manner. We then averaged the two separate scores to obtain the SES score for the detailed occupation.

We were able to implement this procedure as described for 1950, 1960, and 1980 with few complications.[5] However, scores for 1940 could not be computed in this manner because appropriate tables cross-tabulating detailed occupation categories by education and income were not available.[6] To overcome this problem we adopted a compromise methodology wherein we matched 1940 detailed occupation categories to 1950 detailed occupations categories and assigned median education and median income scores based on those reported for 1950. This was accomplished using a special tabulation of the 1950 census which provided detailed occupation distributions for 1940 and 1950 using a common occupation scheme.[7] The match between titles for 1940 and 1950 was reasonably good; approximately 70 percent of the 1940 titles had an exact match in 1950. The remaining 1940 titles usually mapped onto 1950 titles with relatively little difficulty even though some matches were not exact.[8]

We then implemented the procedures described above with the modification that the 1940 categories are ranked on the basis of the median education and median income of matched occupations in 1950. The percentile scores on education and income were then computed using the marginal distributions for occupations in 1940. The result is an approximate status score for 1940 which is accurate to the extent that the rankings of occupations on median education and median income were stable over time.

We investigated the assumption of stability of the education and income rankings of occupations between 1940 and 1950 by comparing the percentile scores on education for men in 1940 computed first using median education scores from 1940 and then using median education scores from 1950.[9] In both cases the occupation marginals were from 1940. We limited our focus to education because occupation data cross-tabulated by income were not available for 1940. We limited the comparison to men because comparable data for women were not available for detailed occupation categories in 1940. The correlation between the 1940 and 1950 education percentile scores was 0.94, which indicates a high degree of consistency in the percentile ranking of occupations on education between 1940 and 1950.[10]

The stability of education rankings between 1940 and 1950 is not surprising since previous research has indicated there is a "high degree of overall stability in the status patterns of occupations" (Nam and Powers 1968:165). For example, the correlation of Nam-Powers scores for matched occupations for 1950 and 1960 is 0.96 (Nam and Powers 1968) and the similar correlation for 1960 and 1970 scores is 0.97 (Nam, LaRocque, Powers, and Holmberg 1975:571). Thus, available data suggests that the education and income standings of detailed occupations are somewhat stable over time and that changes in Nam-Powers SES scores for detailed occupations tend to reflect changes in the marginal distributions of persons across occupations (i.e., the growth and decline of occupations at higher and lower standings on education and income). This is reassuring and suggests that the scores we developed for 1940 are reasonable and useful, especially in view of the absence of alternative scores.

Previous studies publishing Nam-Powers status scores for 1950, 1960, and 1970 presented separate status scores for industry groups or class of worker groups within selected occupations. Computing scores separately for these subgroupings is desirable because it follows the Census Bureau's practice of subdividing selected occupation categories in published tabulations. Additionally, the subdivided categories tend to be large (i.e., contain many people) and are characterized by substantial heterogeneity in status levels. Thus, subdividing is desirable because it creates smaller categories (i.e., fewer people) which are more homogenous with respect to status.

"Total" Status Scores

In detailed analyses (not reported here) we also computed status scores by decade using data for males only. We then compared estimates of occupational inequality based on "total" scores (i.e., scores computed using data for the total civilian labor force) and estimates based on "male" scores (i.e., scores computed using data for the male civilian labor force only) for 1940 and 1950. The results indicated that inequality measured using "male" scores consistently and substantially underestimated inequality between men and women when compared against inequality measured using "total" scores (Stafford and Fossett 1991). For example, at the national level, the mean status difference between men and women was at least 7 points higher in 1940 and 1950 when it was computed using total scores rather than male scores. This contradicts the assumption that the use of "male" scores in 1940 and 1950 may be less likely to distort estimates of occupational sex inequality since women comprised a relatively small portion of the labor force in these decades (Powers and Holmberg 1978; Nam et al. 1975).

The choice between total scores and male scores has important implications for measuring sex inequality even though the two sets of scores are closely correlated (e.g., using occupations as units of analysis, the correlation between total and male scores is 0.96).[11] The reason for this is that, while the scores are correlated, the differences between them are systematic rather than random; total scores are consistently lower for occupations that are disproportionately female and higher for occupations that are disproportionately male (Stafford and Fossett 1991). Detailed inspection of the data reveals that negative differences are large for clerical occupations where female workers are highly concentrated and positive differences are large for crafts and operatives occupations which are disproportionately male. The consequences are nontrivial. For example, we find, as did Powers and Holmberg (1978), that the clerical major category ranks above the crafts major category when male status scores are used but falls below crafts when total status scores are used. Thus, status scores based on data for the male civilian labor force tend to underestimate men's status and overestimate women's status and the combination leads to underestimation of occupational sex inequality.

We should note that male-female inequality is examined only in the descriptive analyses we present in Chapter 4. Using "total" scores rather than "male-only" scores has a less dramatic, but nontrivial, impact on measures inequality between White and Black men. Thus, it is important to use status scores computed using a consistent methodology and for our purposes they should be based data for the total labor force.

Concluding Remarks on SES Scores

We use Nam-Powers status scores to develop our measures of occupational inequality. However, we want to stress that the ranking of major occupations yielded by these scores is hardly controversial. Under almost any defensible scaling system, professionals and managers will consistently rank higher than clerical and sales workers, crafts workers, and operatives who in turn will rank higher than service workers and laborers who will in turn rank higher than farm laborers and domestic workers. Thus, we wish to set aside any notion that our inequality measures and the results of our analyses are fundamentally dependent on our use of status scores generated by the Nam-Powers methodology.

We believe Nam-Powers scores are attractive on conceptual and practical grounds. However, we also believe that we could have used other defensible schemes for ranking occupations without fundamentally changing the basic patterns we observe in our data. Our finding that Whites have large occupational advantages over Blacks is not an artifact of this methodological choice nor are our findings regarding trends in inequality over time or variation in inequality across areas. Thus, while reasonable people can discuss the relative merits of Nam-Powers status scores, it is important to remember that the issues raised in this debate are not likely to have important practical relevance for analyses of racial occupational inequality.

Independent Variables

Relative Minority Size. We measure relative minority size by percent Black in the total population (PB) given by

$$PB = 100 \cdot B/T$$

where B is the number of Blacks in the county population (Nonwhites in some decades) and T is the total number of persons in the county population. We considered computing this measure for adults only (on the presumption that it might better reflect White-Black labor force competition), but these alternative measures were highly correlated with the measure described here. In regression analyses, percent Black is subjected to a square root transformation because this scaling better captures the relationship between relative minority size and inequality.

Female Labor Force Share. Female labor force share (FLFS) is measured by the percentage female for the total civilian labor force given by

$$FLFS = 100 \cdot FLF/TLF$$

where FLF is the number of women in the civilian labor force and TLF is the total number of persons in the civilian labor force. This measure was computed for all women in the labor force. We considered computing it separately for White women and Black women, but this provided no advantage because the two were very highly correlated (especially when percent Black in the labor force was controlled).

Expected Female Labor Force Share. We measured the "expected" sex composition of the labor force by the method of indirect standardization based on the national sex-occupation distribution. Specifically, we applied the female percentages in each occupation observed in the national sex-occupation distribution to the local occupation distribution. The result was the female labor force share that would have been expected if occupations were strongly "sex-typed" and created specific demands for female or male labor. This expected female labor fore share (EFLFS) was given by:

$$EFLFS = 100 \cdot \Sigma(p_i t_i/T)$$

where p_i is the proportion female in occupation i at the national level,

t_i is the total number of persons employed in occupation i in the local area, and T is the total number of persons employed the local labor force.

Measures of Industry/Occupation Mix. To measure the industry and occupation mix in each county we computed the percentage of the labor force employed in selected occupations and industries. The form for all of these measures was $100 \cdot N/T$ where N represents the total number of persons employed in the relevant occupation or industry group and T represents the total number of employed persons in the county.

We aggregated major occupation categories to obtain summary percentages for the white collar, blue collar, and farm occupations. White collar consists of professional, managerial, sales, and clerical occupations.[12] Blue collar consists of crafts, operatives, service, and nonfarm laborer occupations. Farm occupations consist of farmers, farm managers, and farm laborers and farm foremen.

We separated industry into manufacturing, trade, service, and agricultural categories. We also considered other categories (e.g., government, extraction, education, health, etc.) but did not report them here as they proved either unimportant or redundant. We separated manufacturing concentration into durable- and nondurable-goods categories but dropped this distinction as it also proved unimportant.

Labor Force and Population Size. We measured labor force size by the natural log of the total number of persons in the civilian labor force. Similarly, we measured population size by the natural log of the total population for the county. As noted in the text, we used the natural log transformations for two reasons. First, labor force and population size are highly skewed in their original metrics. Second, most theories linking size to inequality or status emphasize proportional changes and/or differences in size. The natural log versions of the measures are thus appropriate and imply that differences in size of a fixed amount (e.g., 100 persons) have a lesser impact on the natural log of size when size is initially large.

Labor Force Growth. We measure growth in the labor force by the change in the natural log of labor force size. This measure is preferable to percentage change measures which are asymmetrical.[13] The change in the natural log of labor force size is symmetrical in construction and less subject to skew than measures of percentage change. Changes in the natural log of labor force size and percentage change in labor force size are highly correlated when the percentage changes in population is modest (i.e., less than 20 percent in either direction). However, many counties in our sample experience large percentage increases in labor force size in some decades and under these circumstances the change in the natural log of labor force size is a more attractive measure of growth.

Economic Growth. We measured economic growth in two ways. Long-term economic growth was measured by labor force growth as given by change in the natural logarithm of total labor force size just described. Short-term economic growth was measured by percent employed for the total civilian labor force. We explored alternative measures of long-term economic growth based on income growth but these proved unworkable due to insufficient data for earlier time periods.

Status Diversity. We used two measures of status diversity. One was a measure of occupational diversification (OD) given by one minus the gini index of concentration applied to the occupational distribution. In this context, the gini index registers the extent to which the labor force is concentrated in only a few of the broad occupational categories. It ranges from a minimum of 0 which indicates even distribution of the labor force across all categories to a maximum of 1 which indicates the labor force is concentrated in only one category. One minus the gini index thus indicates the extent of occupational diversification. The measure is given by

$$OD = 1 - Gini = 1 - (\Sigma p_i X_{i+1}) - (\Sigma p_{i+1} X_i)$$

where occupation categories are ranked from high to low based on the total employed in each category, p_i is the cumulative proportion of the labor force employed in the first i occupations, and X_{i+1} is the cumulative proportion of the labor force in the first $_{i+1}$ occupations.

The second measure we used was the mean absolute deviation in socioeconomic status for the labor force (MADSES). This was computed from occupation data where each occupation category was assigned a Nam-Powers SES score. The measure was computed according to:

$$MADSES = \Sigma p_i |SES_i - MSES|$$

where p_i indicates the proportion of the total labor force in occupation category i, SES_i indicates the status score for category i, and MSES indicates the mean status score for the total labor force (given by $\Sigma p_i SES_i$).

Urbanization. The extent of urbanization was measured by the percentage of the county population living in urban areas as specified in the census. Comparisons between 1940 and earlier to 1950 and later were complicated by a significant revision of the census definition of urban areas in 1950. Fortunately, a special table in the 1950 census provided urban-rural breakdowns for the 1950 population according to both the 1940 and 1950 definitions. We used these special tabulations to identify counties where the change in procedures affected the measured level of urbanization and projected appropriate adjustments backwards to 1930 to obtain a consistent measurement of urbanization from 1930 to 1990.

Indigenous Labor Supply. We measured indigenous labor supply based on the difference between the size of age cohorts poised to enter and exit the labor force. We expressed this difference relative to the size of population in the prime years of labor force participation. The final version of the variable was thus given by

$$ILS = 100 \cdot (P_{10\text{-}19} - P_{55\text{-}64}) \, / \, P_{20\text{-}64}$$

where P denotes an age cohort and the subscripts indicate the age range for the cohort (adapted from Poston and White 1978). We computed the measure using data for the total population. Alternative versions based on the male population only were highly correlated with the measure we used and yielded similar results. The same was also true for alternative versions based on 5-year entry and exit age cohorts.

Demand for Education. We measured demand for educated labor implied by the occupational structure in two ways. One was the expected demand for high school graduates (HSG*). The other was the expected demand for mean years of completed schooling (Ed*). Both were obtained by the method of indirect standardization wherein we applied the national education distributions for occupations to the occupation distributions for each county as follows.

$$HSG^* = \Sigma \, p_i PHSG_i$$

$$Ed^* = \Sigma \, p_i X_i$$

where p_i indicates the proportion of the county's total labor force employed in occupation category i, $PHSG_i$ indicates the national percentage of high school graduates in occupation category i in 1960, and X_i indicates the national mean years of schooling completed for occupation i in 1960. The resulting scores indicate the extent to which the local occupation mix is dominated by occupations with high demands for education.

We used the 1960 national occupation-education distribution as the "standard" for the computations to eliminate the impact of "grade inflation" over time. We chose 1960 as the standard decade because it was near the mid-point of our observation period. This choice is not particularly important as the results were similar when other decades were adopted as the standard.

Notes

1. They do not directly incorporate fringe benefits, job security, or quality of working conditions, but these aspects of occupations correlate closely with income and education (Jencks, Perman, and Rainwater 1988).

2. For example, the mean status score for the broad category "crafts workers" was based on the average of the separate status scores for all detailed occupations within this broad category weighted to reflect their proportionate share of the total number of persons employed in the crafts category.

3. The earlier and more detailed version of this paper appendix tables is available from the University of Texas Population Research Center Working Paper Series for a nominal fee and includes a machine-readable version of the appendix tables on computer diskette (in IBM-PC format). Address inquiries to Population Research Center, 1800 Main Building, The University of Texas at Austin, Austin, Texas, 78712 or phone (512) 471-5514.

4. We also considered ranking occupations on the basis of mean years of schooling completed, percentages of high school graduates, percentages of college graduates, and distributional comparisons against the educational distribution for the employed labor force using Lieberson's index of net difference (Lieberson 1975). We found the resulting rankings to be quite similar and decided to rank on the basis of median education to maintain comparability with prior research. We also conducted similar experiments with alternative methods of ranking occupations on income with obtained similar results.

5. Education and income data used to compute the scores for 1950 were taken from Tables 10 and 19 of the 1950 census subject report on occupational characteristics (US Bureau of the Census 1956). The separate tabulations for men and women were combined to yield education and income distributions for the total civilian labor force. Education and income data used to compute the scores for 1960 were taken from Tables 9 and 25 of the 1960 census report on occupational characteristics (US Bureau of the Census 1963). As with data for 1950, education and income distributions for the total civilian labor force were obtained by combining the separate distributions for men and women. Education and income data used to compute the scores for 1980 were taken from tabulations created using the Public Use Micro Samples of the 1980 Census (US Bureau of the Census 1983).

6. We explored the possibility of using the 1940 PUMS files to prepare the necessary tabulations, but found this was not possible due to severe problems with the measurement of income in 1940.

7. Occupations were matched based on Table 125 of the 1950 Census of

Population, Volume II Characteristics of the Population, Part I, United States Summary (US Bureau of the Census 1953)

8. In a small number of cases, the mapping of the 1940 detailed occupations onto a detailed occupation in 1950 was unclear. We resolved these ambiguities by drawing on the Alphabetical Indexes of Occupations and Industries for 1940 and 1950 to make the most reasonable assignments possible (US Bureau of the Census 1940; 1950). Fortunately, the number of occupations involved was small and they contained relatively few people.

9. Data for 1940 were taken from Table 3 of the 1940 subject report on occupational characteristics (US Bureau of the Census 1943) which provides data for 181 occupation categories cross-tabulated by education. Data for 1950 were taken from the previously noted source. Occupation categories in 1950 were more detailed and were aggregated to 1940 groupings using the mapping scheme described above.

10. The correlation reported used occupations as units of analysis. The weighted correlation of the 1940 and 1950 Nam-Powers scores for education from the point of view of individuals is 0.96. The weights used to obtain this correlation were obtained by averaging the total in each occupation in 1940 and 1950.

11. The correlation using individuals as the units of analysis was 0.97.

12. The major occupation groupings were revised in 1980. From 1940 to 1970 white-collar occupations included the major categories of professionals, managers, sales workers, and clerical workers. For 1980 and 1990, white-collar occupations included the major categories of managerial and professional specialists and technical, sales, and administrative support workers.

13. That is, percentage declines are logically restricted to 0-100 percent while percentage increases are logically unbounded and range from 0 to positive infinity.

References

Abrahamson, Mark, and Lee Sigelman. 1987. "Occupational sex segregation in metropolitan areas." *American Sociological Review* 52:588-597.

Abrahamson, Mark, and Valerie J. Carter. 1986. "Tolerance, urbanism, and region." *American Sociological Review* 51:287-294.

Allen, Walter R. 1995. "African American education since An American Dilemma." *Deadalus* 124:77-100.

Allison, Paul D. 1978. "Measures of inequality." *American Sociological Review* 43:865-880.

Allport, Gordon W. 1954. *The Nature of Prejudice*. Boston, MA: Beacon Press.

Alt, James E. 1995. "Race and voter registration in the South." pages 313-332 in Paul E. Peterson (ed.) *Classifying by Race*. Princeton, NJ: Princeton University Press.

Ashenfelter, Orley. 1972. "Racial discrimination." *Journal of Political Economy* 80:435-464.

_____. 1973. "Discrimination and trade unions," in O. Ashenfelter, A. Rees (eds.) *Discrimination in Labor Markets*. Princeton: Princeton University Press.

Atkinson, Anthony B. 1970. "On the measurement of inequality." *Journal of Economic Theory* 2:244-263.

Bahr, Howard M., and Jack P. Gibbs. 1967. "Racial differentiation in American metropolitan areas." *Social Forces* 45:521-532.

Baron, James N., and William T. Bielby. 1984. A woman's place is with other women: Sex segregation within organizations." in Barbara F. Reskin (ed.) *Sex Segregation in the Workplace*. Washington, D.C.: National Academy Press.

Beck, E. M. 1980. "Labor unionism and racial income inequality: A time series analysis of the Post-World War II period." *American Journal of Sociology* 85:791-814.

Becker, Gary S. 1957. *The Economics of Discrimination*. Chicago, IL: University of Chicago Press.

Bentler, Peter M. 1989. EQS Structural Equations Manual. Los Angeles, CA: BMDP Statistical Software.

Blalock, Hubert M. 1956. "Economic discrimination and Negro increase." *American Sociological Review* 21:584-588.

_____. 1957. "Percent Nonwhite and discrimination in the South." *American Sociological Review* 22:677-682.

_____. 1959. "Urbanization and discrimination in the South." *Social Problems* 7:146-152.

_____. 1967. *Toward A General Theory of Minority Group Relations.* New York, NY: Wiley.

Blau, Peter M. 1977. *Inequality and Heterogeneity.* New York, NY: The Free Press.

Blau, Peter M., and Otis Dudley Duncan. 1967. *The American Occupational Structure.* New York: John Wiley.

Blumer, Herbert. 1965. "Industrialization and race relations." in Guy Hunter (ed.) *Industrialization and Race Relations.* New York, NY: Oxford University Press.

_____. 1990. *Industrialization as an Agent of Social Change: A Critical Analysis.* (Edited by David R. Maines and Thomas J. Morrione.) New York, NY: Aldine de Gruyter.

Bohrnstedt, George W., and David Knoke. 1982. *Statistics for Social Data Analysis.* Itasca, IL: F.E. Peacock Publishers, Inc.

Bollen, Kenneth A. 1989. *Structural Equations with Latent Variables.* New York, NY: Wiley.

Bonacich, Edna. 1980. "Class approaches to ethnicity and race." *Insurgent Sociologist* 10:9-23.

Boyd, Monica and Hugh A. McRoberts. 1982. "Women, men, and socioeconomic indices: An assessment," Pages 129-159 in Mary G. Powers (ed.) *Measures of Socioeconomic Status: Current Issues.* Boulder: Westview Press.

Breton, Raymond. 1964. "Institutional completeness of ethnic communities and personal relations to immigrants." *American Journal of Sociology* 70:193-205.

Brown, David L., and Glenn V. Fuguitt. 1972. "Percent Nonwhite and racial disparity in nonmetropolitan cities in the South." *Social Science Quarterly* 53:573-582.

Burr, Jeffrey A., Mark A. Fossett, and Omer R. Galle. 1991. "Racial occupational inequality in southern metropolitan areas 1940-1980: Revisiting the visibility-discrimination hypothesis. *Social Forces.* 27:519-564.

Burr, Jeffrey A., Omer R. Galle, and Mark A. Fossett. 1990. "The retrospective construction of metropolitan areas for longitudinal analysis: An application to racial occupational inequality." *Social Science Research.* 19:250-265.

Burr, Jeffrey A., Lloyd B. Potter, Omer R. Galle, and Mark A. Fossett. 1992. "Migration and metropolitan opportunity structures: A demographic response to racial inequality." *Social Science Research* 21:380-405.

Burstein, Paul (ed.). 1994. *Equal Employment Opportunity: Labor Market Discrimination and Public Policy.* New York, NY: Aldine de Gruyter 1994.

Carlson, S. M. 1992. "Trends in race/sex occupational inequality: Conceptual and measurement issues." *Social Problems* 39:268-290.

Colclough, Glenna. 1988. "Uneven development and racial composition in the deep South." *Rural Sociology* 53:73-86.

_____. 1989. "Industrialization, labor markets, and income inequality amoung Georgia counties: 1970-1980." pages 207-222 in William W. Falk and Thomas A. Lyson (eds.), *Research in Rural Sociology and Development, Volume 4.* Greenwich, CN: JAI Press.

Coleman, James S. 1971. *Resources for Change: Race in the United States.* New York, NY: Wiley.

Cotton, Jerimiah. 1989. "Opening the gap: The decline of Black economic indicators in the 1980s." *Social Science Quarterly* 70:803-819.

Cox, Oliver C. 1948. *Caste, Class, and Race: A Study in Social Dynamics.* New York: Doubleday and Company.

Dagum, Camilo. 1980. "Inequality measures between income distributions with applications." *Econometrica* 48:1791-1803.

Dalton, H. 1920. "The measurement of inequality of incomes." *Economic Journal* 30:348-361.

Daymont, Thomas N. 1980. "Racial Equity or Racial Equality." *Demography* 17:379-393.

Dollard, John. 1937. *Caste and Class in a Southern Town.* New Haven, CT: Yale University Press.

Duncan, Beverly, and Otis D. Duncan. 1968. "Minorities and the process of stratification." *American Sociological Review* 33:356-364.

Duncan, Otis D., and Beverly Duncan. 1955. "A methodological analysis of segregation indexes." *American Sociological Review* 20:210-217.

Elgie, Robert A. 1980. "Industrialization and racial inequality within the American South, 1950-1970." *Social Science Quarterly* 61:458-472.

Engstrom, Richard L., and Michael D. McDonald. 1981. "The election of Blacks to city councils: Clarifying the impact of electoral arrangements on the seats/population relationship." American Political Science Review 75:344-354.

Falk, William W., and Thomas A. Lyson (eds.). 1989. *Research in Rural Sociology and Development, Volume 4.* Greenwich, CN: JAI Press.

Falk, William W., and Thomas A. Lyson. 1988. *High Tech, Low Tech, No Tech: Recent Industrial and Occupational Change in the South.* Albany, NY: State University of New York Press.

Farley, Reynolds (ed.). 1995. *State of the Union, America in the 1990s, Volume One: Economic Trends.* New York, NY: Russell Sage Foundation.

_____ (ed.). 1995. *State of the Union, America in the 1990s, Volume Two: social Trends.* New York, NY: Russell Sage Foundation.

Farley, Reynolds, and Walter R. Allen. 1986. *The Color Line and the Quality of Life in America.* New York: Russell Sage.

Farley, Reynolds, and Albert Hermalin. 1972. "The 1960s: A decade of progress for Blacks?" *Demography* 9:353-369.

Featherman, David L. 1980. "Retrospective Longitudinal Research: Methodological Considerations." *Journal of Economics and Business* 32:152-168.

Featherman, David L., and Robert M. Hauser. 1976. "Changes in the socioeconomic stratification of the races, 1962-1976." *American Journal of Sociology* 82:621-651.

_____. *Opportunity and Change.* New York: Academic Press.

Finkel, Steven E. 1995. *Causal Analysis with Panel Data.* Thousand Oaks, CA: Sage.

Fligstien, Neil. 1981. *Going North: Migration of Blacks and Whites from the South 1900-1950.* New York: Academic Press.

264

Ford, K., and J. Gehret. no date. "Occupational status scores from the 1980 Census Public Use Samples." Unpublished manuscript.

Ford, Thomas R. 1977. Contemporary rural America: Persistence and change," in Thomas R. Ford (ed.) *Rural U.S.A.: Persistence and Change.* Ames, IA: University Press.

Fossett, Mark A. 1983. *Racial Income Inequality and Market Discrimination in Metropolitan Areas of the United States in 1970.* Dissertation. The University of Texas at Austin. Austin, Texas.

_____. 1984 "City differences in racial occupational differentiation: A note on the use of odds ratios." *Demography* 21:655-666.

_____. 1988. "Ecological analyses of racial economic differentials: A cautionary note." *Sociological Methods and Research.* 16:454-491.

_____. 1991. "Measures of intergroup occupational inequality." Texas Population Research Center Papers, No. 10.06. Austin, TX: University of Texas.

Fossett, Mark A., and C. Gray Swicegood. 1982. "Rediscovering city differences in racial occupational inequality." *American Sociological Review* 47:681-689.

Fossett, Mark A., and K. Jill Kiecolt. 1989. "The relative size of minority populations and white racial attitudes." Social Science Quarterly 70:820-835.

Fossett, Mark A., and M. Therese Stafford. 1990. "Racial occupational inequality in southern nonmetropolitan Areas, 1940-1980." Paper presented at the Annual Meetings of the Rural Sociological Society, August, Norfolk, Virginia.

_____. 1992. "Structural determinants of race-based occupational inequality in southern nonmetropolitan areas, 1940-1980." Report to the Aspen Institute and Ford Foundation.

Fossett, Mark A., and Scott J. South. 1983. "The measurement of intergroup income inequality: A conceptual review." *Social Forces.* 61:855-871.

Fossett, Mark A., Omer R. Galle, and Jeffrey A. Burr. 1989. "Racial occupational inequality, 1940-1980: A research note on the impact of changing regional distribution of the Black population." *Social Forces* 68:415-427.

Fossett, Mark A., Omer R. Galle, and William R. Kelly. 1986. "Racial occupational inequality, 1940-1980: National and regional trends." *American Sociological Review* 51:421-430.

Fox, William S., and John R. Faine. 1973. "Trends in White-Nonwhite income inequality." *Sociology and Social Research* 57:288-299.

Franklin, R. S. 1968. "A framework for the analysis of interurban Negro-White economic differentials." *Industrial and Labor Relations Review* 21:367-374.

Freund, John E., 1962. *Mathematical Statistics.* Englewood Cliffs, NJ: Prentice-Hall.

Frisbie, W. Parker, and Lisa J. Neidert. 1977. "Inequality and the relative size of minority populations: A comparative analysis." *American Journal of Sociology* 82:1007-1030.

Gastwirth, J. L. 1975. "Statistical measures of earnings differentials." *The American Statistician* 29:32-35.

265

Glaser, James M. 1994. "Back to the Black Belt: Racial environment and White racial attitudes in the South." *Journal of Politics* 56:21-41.

Glenn, Norval D. 1963. "Occupational benefits to Whites from the subordination of Negroes." *American Sociological Review* 28:443-448.

_____. 1964. "The relative size of the Negro population and Negro occupational status." *Social Forces* 43:42-49.

_____. 1966. "White gains from Negro subordination." *Social Problems* 14:159-178.

Goodman, Leo, and William Kruskall. 1954. "Measures of association for cross classifications I." *Journal of the American Statistical Association* 49:732-764.

Gordon, Robert. 1968. "Issues in mutiple regression." *American Journal of Sociology* 73:592-616.

Grusky, D. B., and S. E. Van Rompaey. 1992. "The vertical scaling of occupations: Some cautionary comments and reflections." *American Journal of Sociology* 97:1712-1728.

Gwartney, James. 1970. "Changes in the Nonwhite/White income ratio - 1939-1967." *American Economic Review* 60:872-883.

Hamilton, Lawrence. 1992. *Regression with Graphics: A Second Course in Applied Statistics*. Pacific Grove, CA: Brooks/Cole.

Hanushek, Eric A., and John E. Jackson. 1977. *Statistical Methods for Social Scientists*. New York, NY: Academic Press.

Hare, Nathan. 1965. "Recent trends in the occupational mobility of Negroes 1930-1960." *Social Forces* 44:166-173.

Hathaway, D. E., J. A. Beegle, and W. K. Bryant 1968. *People of Rural America*. (1960 Census Monograph) Washington, DC: U.S. Government Printing Office.

Haug, Marie R. 1977. "Measurement in social stratification." *Annual Review of Sociology* 3:51-77.

Hawley, Amos H. 1944. "Dispersion versus segregation: Apropos of a solution of race problems." Papers of the Michigan Academy of Science, Arts, and Letters 30:667-674.

_____. 1971. *Urban Society*. New York, NY: Ronald Press.

Hayduk, Leslie A. 1987. *Structural Equation Modeling with LISREL*. Baltimore: Johns Hopkins University Press.

Heistand, D. L. 1964. *Economic Growth and Employment Opportunities for Minorities*. New York: Columbia University Press.

Hill, Richard C. 1974. "Unionization and racial income inequality in the metropolis." *American Sociological Review* 39:507-522.

Horowitz, Donald L. 1985. *Ethnic Groups in Conflict*. Berkeley, CA: University of California Press.

Hwang, Sean-Shong, and Steve H. Murdock. 1988. "Population size and residential segregation." *Social Science Quarterly* 69:818-834.

Jencks, Christopher. 1977. *Who Gets Ahead? The Determinants of Economic Success in America*. New York: Basic Books.

Jencks, Christopher, L. Perman, and L. Rainwater. 1988. "What is a good job?" A new measure of labor market success." *Amerian Journal of Sociology* 93:1322-1357.

Jiobu, Robert, and Harvey H. Marshall. 1971. "Urban structure and the differentiation between Blacks and Whites." *American Sociological Review* 36:638-649.

Johnson, Michael. P., and Ralph. Sell. 1976. "The cost of being Black: A 1970 update." *American Journal of Sociology* 82:183-190.

Jöreskog, K. G., and D. Sörbom. 1993. LISREL 8 Users Reference Guide. Chicago, IL: Scientific Software International.

Kakwani, Nanak C. 1980. *Income Inequality and Poverty: Methods of Estimation and Policy Implications*. London: Oxford University Press.

Karnig, Albert K., and Susan Welch. 1980. *Black Representation and Urban Policy*. Chicago, IL: University of Chicago Press.

Kessler, Ronald C., and David F. Greenberg. 1981. *Linear Panel Analysis*. New York: Academic Press.

Kluegel, James R. 1990. "Trends in White's explanations of the Black-White gap in socioeconomic status, 1977-1989." *American Sociological Review* 5:512-589.

Kluegel, James R., and Eliot R. Smith. 1986. *Beliefs About Inequality: American Views of What Is and What Ought to Be*. Hawthorne, New York: Aldine de Gruyter.

Kolm, S. C. 1976a. "Unequal inequalities, I." *Journal of Economic Theory* 12:416-442.

_____. 1976b. "Unequal inequalities, II." *Journal of Economic Theory*. 13:82-111.

Kubitschek, Warren N., 1986. "On recoding the 1980 detailed occupation codes to 1970 major occupation categories." Center for Demography and Ecology Working Paper 86-6. University of Wisconsin.

Kuznets, Simon. 1955. "Economic growth and income inequality." *American Economic Review* 65:1-28.

Kuznets, Simon. 1963. "Quantitative aspects of economic growth of nations: Distribution of income by size." *Economic Development and Cultural Change* 11:1-80.

Lagory, Mark, and Robert J. Magnani. 1979. "Structural correlates of Black-White occupational differentiation: Will U.S. regional differences remain?" *Social Problems* 27:157-169.

Lenski, Gerhard. 1966. *Power and Privilege: a Theory of Social Stratification*. New York: McGraw-Hill.

Leonard, J. S. 1985. "The effect of unions on the employment of Blacks, Hispanics, and women." *Industrial and Labor Relations Review* 39:115-132.

Levy, Frank. 1987. *Dollars and Dreams: The Changing American Income Distribution*. New York: Russell Sage.

_____. 1995. "Incomes and income inequality." in Reynolds Farley (ed.) *State of the Union: America in the 1990s*. Volume I. New York: Russell Sage.

Lieberson, Stanley. 1975. "Rank-sum comparisons between groups." pages 276-291 in David Heise (ed.), *Sociological Methodology 1976*. San Francisco, CA: Jossey-Bass.

_____. 1980. *A Piece of the Pie: Blacks and American Immigrants Since 1980*. Berkeley, CA: Univeristy of California Press.

_____. 1985. *Making it Count: The Improvement of Social Research and Theory*. Berkeley, CA: University of California Press.

Lieberson, Stanley, and Glenn V. Fuguitt. 1967. "Negro-White occupational differences in the absence of discrimination." *American Journal of Sociology* 73:188-200.

Light, Ivan. 1972. *Ethnic Enterprise in America: Business and Welfare among Chinese, Japanese, and Blacks*. Berkeley, CA: University of Calfornia Press.

Lyson, Thomas A. 1985. "Race and sex segregation in the occupational structures of southern employers." *Social Science Quarterly* 66:281-295.

Mare, Robert D. 1995. "Changes in educational attainment and school enrollment." Pages 155-214 in Reynolds Farley (ed.) *State of the Union, America in the 1990s, Volume One: Economic Trends*. New York, NY: Russell Sage Foundation.

Marshall, Susan E. 1986. "In defense of separate spheres: Class and status politics in the antisuffrage movement." *Social Forces* 65:327-351.

Martin, Walter T., and Dudley L. Poston, Jr. 1972. "The occupational composition of White females." *Social Forces* 50:349-355.

_____. 1976. "Industrialization and occupational differentiation." *Pacific Sociological Review* 19:82-97.

Massey, Douglas S. and Nancy A. Denton. 1993. *American Apartheid: Segregation and the Making of the Underclass*. Cambridge, MA: Harvard University Press.

McGruder, Patria Hollis. 1995. *The Effect of Incarceration Rates on Mate Availability and its Effect on the Formation and Structure of the African American Family: A Theoretical and Empirical Analysis*. Masters Thesis. Texas A&M University. College Station, Texas.

McKinney, J. and L. B. Bourque. 1971. "The changing South: National incorporation of a region." *American Sociological Review* 36:399-411.

Mueller, Ralph O. 1996. *Basic Principles of Structural Equation Modeling: An Introduction to LISREL and EQS*. New York: Springer-Verlag New York.

Myrdal, Gunnar. 1965 [1944]. *An American Dilemma*. New York: Harper and Row.

Nam, Charles B., and Mary G. Powers. 1968. "Changes in the relative status level of workers in the United States, 1950-1960." *Social Forces* 47:158-177.

Nam, Charles B., and Mary G. Powers. 1983. *The Socioeconomic Approach to Status Measurement*. Houston, TX: Cap and Gown Press.

Nam, Charles B., and Walter E. Terrie. 1988. "1980-based Nam-Powers occupational status scores." Working Paper Series #88-48. Center for the Study of Population. Tallahassee, FL: Florida State University.

Nam, Charles B., John LaRocque, Mary G. Powers, and Joan Holmberg. 1975. "Occupational status scores: Stability and change." *Proceedings of the American Statistical Association: Social Statistics Section*, Pp. 570-575.

National Research Council. 1989. *A Common Destiny: Blacks and American Society*. Washington, D.C.: National Academy Press.

Neidert, Lisa J. 1980. *Industrial Diversification, Industrial Composition, and Majority-Minority Income Inequality: Anglos, Blacks, and Mexican*

Americans in the Southwest, 1970. Dissertation. The University of Texas at Austin. Austin, Texas.

Neidert, Lisa J. and Reynolds Farley. 1985. "Assimilation in the United States: an analysis of ethnic and generation differences in status and achievement." *American Sociologial Review* 50:840-850.

O'Hare, William. 1986. "Racial composition of jurisdictions and the election of Black candidates." *Population Today* 14:6-8.

Olzak, Susan, and Joane Nagle. 1986. *Competitive Ethnic Relations.* New York, NY: Academic Press.

Oster, S. 1975. "Industry differences in the level of discrimination against women." *Quarterly Journal of Economics* 89(2)215-229.

Palmore, Erdman, and Frank J. Whittington. 1970. "Differential trends toward equality between Whites and Nonwhites." *Social Forces* 49:108-117.

Park, Robert Ezra. 1950. *Race and Culture.* Glencoe, IL: Free Press.

Passel, Jeffrey S., Jacob S. Siegel, and J. Gregory Robinson. 1982. "Coverage of the national population in the 1980 Census, by age, sex, and race: preliminary estimates by demographic analysis. Current Population Reports P-23, No. 115.

Piore, Michael J. 1975. "Notes for a theory of labor market stratification." in Richard C. Edwards, Michael Reich, and David M. Gordon (eds.) *Labor Market Segmentation.* Lexington, MA: D.C. Heath.

Portes, Alejandro, and Leif Jensen. 1989. "The enclave and the entrants." *American Sociological Review* 54:929-949.

Portes, Alejandro, and Robert D. Manning. 1986. "The immigrant enclave: Theory and empirical examples." In Susan Olzak and Joane Nagle (eds.) *Competitive Ethnic Relations.* New York, NY: Academic Press.

Poston, Dudley L. Jr., and Ralph White. 1978. "Indigenous labor supply, sustenance organization , and population redistribution in nonmetropolitan America: An extension of the ecological theory of migration." *Demograpy* 15:637-641.

Powers, Mary G., and Joan J. Holmberg. 1978. "Occupational status scores: Changes introduced by the inclusion of women." *Demography* 15:183-204.

Reich, Michael. 1981. *Racial Inequality: A Political Economic Analysis.* Princeton, NJ: Princeton University Press.

Reiss, Albert, Otis D. Duncan, Paul K. Hatt, and C. C. North. 1961. *Occupations and Social Status.* Glencoe, IL: Free Press.

Riedesel, P. L. 1979. "Racial discrimination and White economic benefits." *Social Science Quarterly* 60:120-143.

Roof, Wade Clark. 1972. "Residential segregation of Blacks and racial inequality in southern cities: Toward a causal model." *Social Forces* 51:87-91.

Reskin, Barbara F., and Patrical Roos. 1990. *Job Queues and Gender Queues: Explaining Women's Inroads into Male Occupations.* Philadelphia, PA: Temple University Press.

Roos, Patricia, and Barbara F. Reskin. 1984. "Institutional factors contributing to sex segregation in the workplace." in Barbara F. Reskin (ed.) *Sex Segregation in the Workplace.* Washington, D.C.: National Academy Press.

Rose, David L. 1989. "Twenty-five years later: Where do we stand on equal employment opportunity law enforcement?" *Vanderbilt Law Review* 42:1121-1181. [Reprinted in Paul Burstein (ed.) *Equal Employment Opportunity: Labor Market Discrimination and Public Policy*. New York, NY: Aldine de Gruyter 1994.]

Schuman, Howard, Charlotte Steeh, and Lawrence Bobo. 1985. *Racial Attitutudes in America: Trends and Interpretations*. Cambridge, MA: Harvard University Press.

Schwartz, J., and Christopher Winship. 1979. "The welfare approach to measuring inequality." in K.F. Schuessler (ed.), *Sociological Methodology 1980*. San Francisco, CA: Jossey-Bass.

Semyonov, Moshe and Richard Ira Scott. 1983. "Percent Black, community characteristics and race linked occupational differentiation in the rural South." *Rural Sociology* 48:240-252.

Semyonov, Moshe. 1983. "Community characteristics, female employment, and occupational segregation." *Rural Sociology* 48:104-119.

Semyonov, Moshe, D. R. Hoyt, and Richard Ira Scott. 1984. "Place, race, and differential occupational opportunities." *Demography* 21:259-270.

Shryock, Henry S., and Jacob S. Siegel. 1976. *The Methods and Materials of Demography*. New York, NY: Academic Press.

Siegel, Jacob S. 1974. "Estimates of coverage of the population by sex, race, and age in the 1970 Census." *Demography* 11: 1-23.

Siegel, Paul. 1965. "On the cost of being a Negro." *Sociological Inquiry* 35:41-57.

Smith, James P., and Finis R. Welch. 1986. *Closing the Gap: Forty Years of Economic Progress for Blacks*. Santa Monica, CA: Rand.

_____. 1989. "Black economic progress after Myrdal." *Journal of Economic Literature* 27:519-564.

Solon, Gary. 1992. "Intergenerational income mobility in the United States." *American Economic Review* 82:393-408.

Somers, Robert H. 1962. "A new asymmetric measure of association." *American Sociological Review* 27:799-811.

_____. 1980. "Simple approximations to null sampling variances: Goodman and Kruskall's gamma, Kendall's tau, and Somers' dyx." *Sociological Methods and Research* 9:115-126.

Spilerman, Seymour and R. E. Miller. 1976. "Community and industry determinants of the occupational status of Black males. Discussion Paper #330. Madison, Wisconsin: Univerisity of Wisconsin, Madison, Institute for Poverty Research.

Stafford, M. Therese, and Mark A. Fossett. 1989. "Occupational sex inequality in the nonmetropolitan South, 1960-1980." *Rural Sociology* 54:169-194.

_____. 1991. "Measuring occupational sex inequality over time using Nam-Powers SES scores." Texas Population Research Center Working Paper Series No. 12.1, University of Texas, Austin, Texas.

_____. 1992. "Structural determinants of sex-based occupational inequality in southern nonmetropolitan areas, 1940-1980." Report to the Aspen Institute and Ford Foundation.

Stevens, Gillian, andd J. H. Cho. 1985. "Socioeconomic indexes and the new 1980 census occupational classification scheme." *Social Science Research* 14:142-168.

Stinner, William R., and Gordon F. DeJong. 1969. "Southern Negro migration: Social and economic components of an ecological model." *Demography* 6:455-473.

Stokes, Randall, and Anthony Harris. 1978. "South African development and the paradox of racial particularism: Toward a theory of modernization from the center." *Economic Development and Cultural Change* 26:245-269.

Stolzenberg, Ross M., and R. D. D'Amico. 1977. "City differences and nondifferences in the effect of race and sex on occupational distribution." *American Sociological Review* 42:937-950.

Street, James, Raymond J. Carrol, and David Rupert. 1988. "A note on computing robust regression estimates via iteratively reweighted least squares." *The American Statistician* 42:152-154.

Summers, Gene F. 1986. "Rural community development." *Annual Review of Sociology.* 12:347-371.

Summers, Gene F., S. D. Evans, F. Clemente, E. M. Beck, and J. Minkoff. 1976. *Industrial Invasion of Nonmetropolitan America.* New York, NY: Praeger.

Szymanski, Albert. 1977. "Racism and sexism as functional substitutes in the labor market." *The Sociological Quarterly* 17:65-73.

Terrie, Walter E., and Charles B. Nam. 1994. "1990 and 1980 Nam-Powers-Terrie occupational status scores." Working Paper Series #94-118. Center for the Study of Population. Tallahasee, FL: Florida State University.

Tienda, Marta., and Ding-Tzann Lii. 1987. "Minority concentration and earnings inequality: Blacks, Hispanics, and Asians compared." *American Journal of Sociology* 93:141-65.

Thurow, Lester C. 1969. *Poverty and Discrimination.* Washington, D.C.: Brookings Institution.

Tickamyer, Ann R., and Cynthia M. Duncan. 1990. "Poverty and opportunity structure in rural America." *Annual Review of Sociology.*16:67-86.

Treiman, Donald J. 1970. "Industrialization and social stratification," in Edward O. Lauman (ed.) *Social Stratification Research.* Bobbs-Merrill.

_____. 1975. *Occupational Prestige in Comparative Perspective.* New York: Academic Press.

Tuma, Nancy B., and Michael T. Hannan. 1984. *Social Dynamics: Models and Methods.* Orlando, FL: Academic Press.

Turner, Ralph H. 1951. "The relative position of the Negro Male in the labor force of large American cities." *American Sociological Review* 16:524-529.

U.S. Bureau of the Census. 1923. *Census of Population: 1920, Characteristics of the Population.* Washington, D.C.: U.S. Government Printing Office.

_____. 1933. *Census of Population: 1930, Characteristics of the Population.* Washington, D.C.: U.S. Government Printing Office.

_____. 1943. *Census of Population: 1940, Characteristics of the Population.* Washington, D.C.: U.S. Government Printing Office.

_____. 1943. *Census of Population: 1940, The Labor Force.* Washington, D.C.: U.S. Government Printing Office.

_____. 1943. *Census of Population: 1940. Alphabetical Index of Occupations and Industries.* Washington, D.C.: U.S. Government Printing Office.

_____. 1952. *Census of Population: 1950, General Population Characteristics.* Washington, D.C.: U.S. Government Printing Office.

_____. 1952. *Census of Population: 1950, General Social and Economic Characteristics.* Washington, D.C.: U.S. Government Printing Office.

_____. 1952. *Census of Population: 1950. Alphabetical Index of Occupations and Industries.* Washington, D.C.: U.S. Government Printing Office.

_____. 1956. *Census of Population: 1950. Vol. IV, Special Reports, Part 1, Chapter B, Occupational Characteristics.* Washington D.C.: U.S. Government Printing Office.

_____. 1962. *Census of Population: 1960, General Population Characteristics.* Washington, D.C.: U.S. Government Printing Office.

_____. 1962. *Census of Population: 1960, General Social and Economic Characteristics.* Washington, D.C.: U.S. Government Printing Office.

_____. 1963. *Census of Population: 1960. Subject Reports. Occupation by Earnings and Education.* Final Report PC(2)-7B. Washington, D.C.: U.S. Government Printing Office.

_____. 1970. "Measurement of overlap of income distribution of White and Negro families in the United States." *Current Population Reports.* Technical Papers No. 22 . Washington D.C.: U.S. Government Printing Office.

_____. 1972. *Census of Population: 1970, General Population Characteristics.* Washington, D.C.: U.S. Government Printing Office.

_____. 1972. *Census of Population: 1970, General Social and Economic Characteristics.* Washington, D.C.: U.S. Government Printing Office.

_____. 1977. *County and City Data Book, 1977.* Washington, D.C.: U.S. Government Printing Office.

_____. 1982. *Census of the Population: 1980 Equal Employment Opportunity Special File.* Washington, D.C.: U.S. Government Printing Office.

_____. 1983. *Census of Population and Housing, 1980: Public-Use Microdata Samples.* Washington, D.C.: U.S. Government Printing Office.

_____. 1983. *Census of Population: 1980, General Population Characteristics.* Washington, D.C.: U.S. Government Printing Office.

_____. 1983. *Census of Population: 1980, General Social and Economic Characteristics.* Washington, D.C.: U.S. Government Printing Office.

_____. 1984. *U.S. Census of Population: 1980, Volume 1: Characteristics of the Population, Chapter D: Detailed Population Characteristics, Part1: United States Summary.* Washington D.C.: U.S. Government Printing Office.

_____. 1989. "The Relationship Between 1970 and 1980 Industry and Occupation Classification Systems." Technical Paper 59. Washington, D.C.: U.S. Government Printing Office.

272

_____. 1993. *Census of the Population: 1990 Equal Employment Opportunity Special File*. Washington, D.C.: U.S. Government Printing Office.

_____. 1993. *Census of the Population: 1990 Summary Tape File 1C*. Washington, D.C.: U.S. Government Printing Office.

_____. 1993. *Census of the Population: 1990 Summary Tape File 3C*. Washington, D.C.: U.S. Government Printing Office.

_____. 1993. *Census of Population: 1990, General Population Characteristics*. Washington, D.C.: U.S. Government Printing Office.

_____. 1993. *Census of Population: 1990, General Social and Economic Characteristics*. Washington, D.C.: U.S. Government Printing Office.

U.S. Commission on Civil Rights. 1978. *Social Indicators of Equality for Minorities and Women*. Washington, D.C.: U.S. Government Printing Office.

Villemez, Wayne J. 1977. "The functional substitutability of Blacks and females in the labor market: A closer look." *Sociological Quarterly* 18:548-563.

_____. 1978. "Black Subordination and White Economic Well-Being: Comment on Szymanski." *American Sociological Review* 16:772-776.

Waite, Linda. 1981. "U.S. women at work." *Population Bulletin* 36 (2). Washington D.C.: Population Reference Bureau.

Welch, Finish. 1967. "Labor-market discrimination: An interpretation of income differences in the rural South." *The Journal of Political Economy* 75:225-240.

Wilcox, Jerry and Wade Clark Roof. 1978. "Percent Black and Black-White status inequality: Southern versus nonsouthern patterns." *Social Science Quarterly* 59:421-434.

Williams, Robin. 1947. "The reduction of intergroup tensions." Chapter 3 in Social Science Research Bulletin, No. 57.

Willits, Fern K., Robert C. Bealer, and Donald M. Crider 1982. "Persistance of rural/urban differences," in Don A. Dillman and Daryl J. Hobbs (eds.) *Rural Society in the United States*. Boulder CO: Westview Press.

Wilson, Kenneth L., and W. Allen Martin. 1982. "Ethnic enclaves: A comparison of the Cuban and Black economies in Miami." *American Journal of Sociology* 88:135-160.

Wilson, Thomas P. 1974. "Measures of association for bivariate ordinal hypotheses." pages 327-342 in H.M. Blalock (ed.), *Measurement in the Social Sciences: Theories and Strategies*. Chicago, IL: Aldine.

Wilson, Thomas C. 1986. "Urbanism and tolerance." *American Sociological Review* 50:117-123.

Wilson, William Julius. 1987. *The Truly Disadvantaged: The Inner City, the Underclass and Public Policy*. Chicago, IL: University of Chicago Press.

Winship, Christopher. 1977. "A reevaluation of indices of residential segregation." *Social Forces* 55:1058-1066.

Wirth, Louis. 1938. "Urbanism as a way of life." *American Journal of Sociology* 44:1-24.

Zimmerman, David J. 1992. "Regression toward mediocrity in economic stature." *American Economic Review* 82:409-429.

Index

ability, 4, 50, 60, 88, 137, 246, 259
Abrahamson, M., 66, 202
affirmative action, 17, 155
  enactment of policies, 1
  support by Whites, 5
  unintended consequences of, 6
agricultural employment, 122
  see also industry mix and farm
  employment
Allen, W. R., 7-8, 17, 217, 232, 233
Allison, P. D., 196
allocation, 54, 60, 127, 142, 229,
  232-233, 247
Allport, G. W., 24
Alt, J. E., 26
ascriptive stratification, 19, 52-55,
  59, 60, 65
Ashenfelter, O., 51
Asian minority groups, 40, 50, 84,
  90
assimilation, 3, 7
Atkinson, A. B., 196
autocorrelation, 165, 170, 176

backlash
  by working class whites, 4
Bahr, H. M., 14, 202
Baron, J. N., 48
Bealer, R. C., 65
Beck, E. M., 51, 60, 61, 64, 202
Becker, G. S., 60, 63
Beegle, J. A., 65
Bentler, P. M., 180
Bielby, W. T., 48
Black Power, 4
Blalock, H. M., 11, 14, 18, 19, 21-
  25, 27, 50, 64, 65, 71, 188
Blau, P. M., 55, 67, 196
blue-collar occupations/workers
  trends over time, 120-122
  see also occupational mix

Blumer, H., 52, 55, 65
Bobo, L., 1, 17
Bohrnstedt, G. W., 218
Bollen, K. A., 180
Bonacich, E., 45
bounded influence, robust
  regression, 157
Bourque, L. B., 105
Boyd, M., 221
Breton, R., 45, 66
Brown, D. L., 19, 21-23, 136, 214
Bryant, W. K., 65
Burr, J. A., 9-11, 14, 17, 162, 206,
  224
Burstein, P., 1

Carlson, S. M., 221
Carrol, R. J., 157
Carter, V. J., 66
causal inference, 14, 188
census procedures, 84, 97, 132
  undercount, substitution, and
  allocation, 232-233
  chi square test of model fit, 179-
  181
Cho, J. H., 221
civil disturbances, 4
Civil Rights, 1-3, 6, 17, 25, 26, 61,
  192
  support by Whites for Civil
  Rights, 2, 3
Civil Rights movement, 2, 25, 47
  goals of equality of opportunity
  and inclusion, 3
  endorsement of pluralistic and
  nationalistic goals, 4
  legitimation in terms of values
  shared by Whites, 3
  goals of equality of outcomes, 4
Colclough, G., 51
Coleman, J. S., 60, 63

About the Book and Authors

The authors investigate trends in racial inequality in the occupational attainment in rural areas of the South since 1940. Drawing on data from the six censuses spanning the last five decades, they examine how inequality varies across local areas and how it has changed over time in different local areas. While modest reductions in inequality have been observed in recent decades, the authors document that racial inequality in rural areas of the South persists at very high levels to the present day.

Guided by structural-demographic theory, the authors investigate the connections between inequality and important changes taking place in the economic and social structures of rural communities of the South. They concluce that inequality is linked, sometimes in enexpected ways, with economic growth, urbanization and the decline of agricultural employment, the movement of women into the labor force, increasing minority educational attainment, and changes in racial demography.

Mark A. Fossett is associate professor of sociology at Texas A&M University. M. Therese Seibert is assistant professor of sociology at the University of Virginia.

WITHDRAWN